LATINOS IN HIGHER EDUCATION

DIVERSITY IN HIGHER EDUCATION

Series Editor: Henry T. Frierson, Jr.

LATINOS IN HIGHER EDUCATION

EDITED BY

DAVID J. LEÓN

California State University, Sacramento, USA

2003

JAI

An Imprint of Elsevier Science

Amsterdam – Boston – London – New York – Oxford – Paris
San Diego – San Francisco – Singapore – Sydney – Tokyo

ELSEVIER SCIENCE Ltd
The Boulevard, Langford Lane
Kidlington, Oxford OX5 1GB, UK

First edition 2003

Library of Congress Cataloging in Publication Data
A catalog record from the Library of Congress has been applied for.

British Library Cataloguing in Publication Data
A catalogue record from the British Library has been applied for.

ISBN: 0-7623-0980-6

♾ The paper used in this publication meets the requirements of ANSI/NISO Z39.48-1992 (Permanence of Paper).
Printed in The Netherlands.

CONTENTS

LIST OF CONTRIBUTORS

Adalberto Aguirre, Jr.   Department of Sociology,
                                University of California,
                                Riverside, USA

Maria D. Avalos   Department of Educational Psychology
                                College of Education, University of Texas,
                                Austin, USA

Anthony P. Carnevale   Educational Testing Service,
                                Washington, D.C., USA

Jose D. Colchado   Northern Arizona University, USA

Helen Contreras   Department of Educational Psychology
                                College of Education, University of Texas,
                                Austin, USA

Toni Falbo   Department of Educational Psychology,
                                College of Education, University of
                                Texas, Austin, USA

Patricia Gándara   School of Education, U.C. Davis, USA

Eugene Garcia   College of Education,
                                Arizona State University, USA

Reynold Gonzalez   Psychology Department,
                                U.C. Santa Cruz, USA

Roberto Haro   Professor Emeritus,
                                College of Ethnic Studies,
                                San Francisco State University, USA

Aída Hurtado   Psychology Department and University
                                 of California, Santa Cruz, USA

Romero Jalomo, Jr.   Hartnell College, Salinas, USA

David J. León   Ethnic Studies Department and
                                 Chicano Studies Program, California
                                 State University, Sacramento, USA

Rubén O. Martinez   Sociology Department and
                                 Hispanic Research Center,
                                 University of Texas, San Antonio, USA

Harriett Romo   Social and Policy Studies,
                                 University of Texas, San Antonio, USA

Joanne Salas   Texas School Performance Review,
                                 Austin, USA

Luis A. Vega   Sociology Psychology Department,
                                 California State University-Bakersfield,
                                 USA

FOREWORD

This book comes at a critical point in time. The nation has changed dramatically since 1986 when the groundbreaking volume, Latino College Students, edited by Michael Olivas, was published. The data presented in that volume reflected what was known about the Hispanic population up to the beginning of that decade, and it arrived in the midst of what Time magazine had touted as the "Decade of the Hispanic" Growth of the Hispanic population had outpaced all earlier projections, and the day when Hispanics would be the nation's largest minority was on the horizon. There was a mood of anticipation about the status of Latinos in all aspects of the society, including higher education, based in good part on the significant gains that Latinos had made during the 1970s in the wake of the Civil Rights movement. The 1970s, we would come to see, were the glory days for minorities in higher education. Most of the progress in access to higher education during the second half of the 20th century was made in that decade. While Olivas' book took aim at policies and practices that had unfairly disadvantaged Latinos in education, there was nonetheless an air of expectation that once the inequities were pointed out, they could be addressed. At the beginning of the 1980s, there was reason to be hopeful.

But, the decade of the 1980s turned out to be a major disappointment for minorities seeking access to higher education. In fact, the data suggest that the 1980s were a period of decline in college-going rates for underrepresented students. Only in the 1990s did colleges and universities regain the ground lost during that decade. For example, it was not until 1997 that Hispanics had finally returned to a level of college enrollment equivalent to the all time high posted in 1976. (In 1976, 35.8% of 18–24 year old Hispanics were enrolled in some kind of college university versus 36% in 1997). But, the Hispanic population had increased by more than 200% over that period, meaning that the gains had fallen far short of real progress. Today, fewer than 10% of Latinos in the 25–29 year old cohort hold a B.A. degree compared to almost 54% of Asians, 34% of Whites, and almost 18% of Black students. There is much work to be done to close this enormous education gap.

Just as Latinos, and other minorities, began to gain new educational momentum in the mid-1990s, an anti-affirmative action campaign began to sweep the country. In 1995, the regents of the University of California passed a resolution that prohibited the use of race, ethnicity, or gender as a consideration in university admissions. California voters followed suit in 1996 by passing Proposition 209, which placed the ban on affirmative action in state statute. The following year, 1997, the Fifth Circuit Court of Appeals ruled in favor of Cheryl Hopwood in a case against the University of Texas law school. Hopwood had been denied admission to the law school, while a small number of minority applicants with lower test scores and grades had been admitted. The court agreed with Hopwood that her constitutional right to equal protection had been violated and held that the University of Texas could not consider race or ethnicity in selecting its entering class. First the voters, and then the courts had decided that campus diversity was not a sufficiently critical goal to warrant consideration of students' ethnicity in admissions. It was inevitable that these decisions, and others that have followed, would have a major impact on Hispanic participation in higher education. But, even some of the most pessimistic prognosticators fell short of the mark in predicting the extent of that impact.

In 1998, the year after Proposition 209 took effect, 53% fewer Latinos were admitted to UC Berkeley, and 33% fewer were admitted to UCLA. In the years since, the university has rebounded to now having a freshman class that approximates the diversity that existed prior to Proposition 209. But, the Latino population has continued to grow in the interim, and to lose ground with respect to the proportion of Latino students who are accommodated by the University of California system. Likewise, the Fall 1997 entering freshman class at the University of Texas had about 10% fewer Hispanic students than the year prior. The University of Texas has also rebounded, but the gains have only returned the system to pre-Hopwood levels, and these were already devastatingly low.

We now find ourselves at the beginning of a new century with a grave dilemma: how to provide equal access to higher education for Latino and other underrepresented students in the face of multiple barriers and few political tools. The dilemma extends as well to the need to educate the whole population about the important role of a diverse student body and faculty in preparing the next generation of leaders to function in a multi-ethnic global society. Moreover, a number of recent studies have demonstrated that without a dramatic increase in the education levels of Hispanic students, the economies of states with very large Latino populations, such as California and Texas, cannot be sustained. It is in everybody's interest to solve this dilemma and it will require everybody's participation. Simply exhorting Latino students and their parents to "do better" will not meet the challenge. Because the parents of Latino students have the lowest educational level of all groups, and because they are more likely than white and Asian students to grow up in neighborhoods with few resources and to attend inferior schools, it is hardly surprising that they have difficulty competing on a par with their more economically and educationally advantaged white and Asian schoolmates. A history of educational neglect is not wiped out simply by wishing it so, and it does not happen overnight, or even in one generation.

Nationwide, Latinos have the highest school drop out rates of any ethnic group, and they are the least likely to attend college, even when grades are held constant. That is, among all students with the same grade point average, Latinos are least likely to opt for a college education. Latinos tend to take themselves out of the race for higher education even before others close the starting gates. When they do go to college, Latinos are more likely than any other group to attend (affordable and local) two-year colleges where their chances of transferring to a four-year institution and earning a degree are exceptionally low. While more than half of all Latino college students are found in community colleges, it is estimated that no more than 5% of these students will actually go on to complete a B.A. As Carnevale points out in this volume, this is not because Latino parents do not value education for their children or support them in this endeavor; rather, it is related to lack of experience with American schools, lack of information about what is needed to succeed in school, and lack of educational opportunity in the form of rigorous academic preparation. It also appears to be related to lower expectations for these students on the part of many teachers. And, these low expectations appear to become internalized by the students themselves. A number of studies have shown that Latinos have the lowest aspirations to attend college of all ethnic groups.

Research that we have conducted at the University of California suggests that the dilemma of access will have to be addressed at several levels. We cannot wait for schools to improve and public attitudes to change in order to increase the numbers of Latino students going on to complete higher education degrees, but this must be one prong of a multi-pronged effort. At the same time, we must support and encourage those students who have the skills and abilities to enter college, recognizing that many of these students remain at risk for not going to college in spite of good grades and test scores. I am always reminded of Alex, a 4.0 student who excelled in math and science and had dreams of going to college, but couldn't leave his mother behind with three children to support on her own. He went to work instead. There were other options for Alex and his family, but no one viewed him as an "at risk" student and so he fell through the cracks. We also need to learn much more about the kinds of interventions that can attract and retain Latino males to a college pathway. Most educational gains in the last two decades have been for Latinas. Gender disparities are becoming as alarming as ethnic disparities in educational attainment for Latino students.

The insights captured in the chapters of this book hold promise for a better understanding of the problem of access to higher education for Latinos at the beginning of this new century. This is a place to begin. But the political will must be found to address the hard questions: How do we increase ethnic diversity in our colleges and universities without considering ethnicity in the process? How do we increase the proportion of Latinos who go to college in a period of increasing demand for a limited resource? How do we increase the educational level of a whole population group without committing massive resources to the task? The answers to these questions will require not just creativity but a keen appreciation for the high stakes that are involved. As the nation's largest minority group in the 21st century, postponing a response to the challenge of improving the education of Latino students is no longer an option. Latinos in Higher Education is a fine opening to a long delayed, and increasingly urgent, conversation.

Patricia Gándara

INTRODUCTION

David J. León

Latinos are the most overlooked group in the United States. Today their numbers almost equal the population of Argentina, and they have become the largest ethnic minority group in the country. And much of their growth has been recent. In the 10 years between 1990 and 2000, their ranks increased from 22.4 to 32.8 million, a rise of 47%. The U.S. has yet to fully absorb these facts, but they will affect the whole texture of national life. So will another fact: Latinos are scarce in higher education. For instance, in 1998 among first-time full-time students in public universities, only 1.7% were Latino, compared to 82.6% Caucasian, 7.3% Asian, 7.2% African American, and 1.8% American Indian. Yet Hispanics represent about 12% of the U.S. population, and the Latino presence in the K-12 student population is growing rapidly (see Romo & Salas, this volume).

What does it mean for America's colleges and universities? Because Latinos are on average younger than the general population, they will make up a greater and greater percentage of the applicants to higher education. Will postsecondary institutions be ready for this coming surge? Can the community college accommodate it, and if not, what steps should four-year institutions take? And how can Latinos themselves increase their presence in higher education? Ultimately, it's not enough for Latinos to attend colleges. They must also become part of the colleges. Will distance learning boost their enrollment in graduate programs? How can they increase their numbers among the faculty and administrators?

Drawing from the works of Latino and non-Latino scholars, this volume sheds light on these questions. It has three main sections: Demographics and Demand, The Crossover to College, and Rising in Academia. The first analyzes the figures behind the looming Latino demand for higher education. The second examines

Latinos in Higher Education, Volume 3, pages 1–6.
Copyright © 2003 by Elsevier Science Ltd.
All rights of reproduction in any form reserved.
ISBN: 0-7623-0980-6

the best means of crossing the crucial high school-college boundary. And the third reveals potential routes to positions as faculty and administrators. The problem overall has many facets, and each article illuminates a different one.

Demographics and Demand. By the middle of the 21st century, people from minority groups will be the majority of America's population. So we begin with Anthony Carnevale's "Seize the Moment: A Unique Window of Opportunity," which discusses the huge impact the growing Latino population can have on America's postsecondary institutions and society overall.

Though Hispanics will become a larger share of the traditional college-age cohort (18 to 24), Carnevale does not predict that a larger share of Hispanics will go to college. Why not? They have the highest high school dropout rate and take a less rigorous academic curriculum in the high schools, and they will remain trapped in the lowest tier of higher education. He points out that Hispanics rely heavily on two-year community colleges and Hispanic Serving Institutions (HSIs). Community colleges lose 54% of their freshmen class, and only 27% of their Hispanics transfer to four-year institutions. HSIs will have an important role to play, and aggressive recruitment and retention efforts in HSIs can have a tremendous positive impact on Hispanics in higher education.

The author notes that America is a "new knowledge economy," and the fact has enormous implications. It means, first, that America has become a nation of college-haves and college-have-nots, with a wide economic divide between the two groups. On the other hand, if Latinos had the same educational attainment as non-Latino Whites and received equivalent pay, they would add billions to America's economy. The "infusion of new, more highly educated human capital would increase U.S. income by $118 billion every year, adding $41 billion in annual tax revenues to the national coffers. The income gains in California and Texas alone would total $80 billion."

In the next article, "Resource Shares and Educational Achievement: The U.S. Latino Population in the Twenty-First Century," Adalberto Aguirre and Rubén Martinez analyze Latino higher education in terms of distribution of total resources. Latinos have not progressed as far as Blacks. For instance, more Latinos than Blacks have remained in poverty, working at blue-collar jobs. And while the gap in education narrowed between Whites and Blacks from 1971 to 2000, it widened between Blacks and Latinos. Latinos are victims of racism in education despite advances made during the Civil Rights era, the authors note. There is no pipeline of Latinos into the universities. There are serious cultural and social gaps between Latinos and postsecondary institutions. And academic and financial support programs for Latinos in colleges and universities are limited or nonexistent. In each of these areas the authors provide specific recommendations.

The Crossover to College. The second section focuses on the importance of building a pipeline between K-12 and higher education, and specifically on moving easily from high school into college. This channel is critical to increasing the number of Latinos in higher education.

Latinos are less likely to earn a bachelor's degree than any other ethnic group. But why? Toni Falbo, Helen Contreras, and Maria Avalos confront that question in "Transition Points from High School to College." They outline three transition points that send Latinos toward or away from college: full participation in high school, college preparation coursework, and college decision-making. Another challenge that Latinos face is the Scholastic Aptitude Test (SAT). Since their scores are generally lower than other groups, it discourages some from continuing on. However, Latinos do attend college and succeed. Many of them receive verbal support and encouragement from home, and possess the instilled values of hard work and persistence. Latino college graduates also indicate that teachers, counselors, and older siblings play important roles as well. The authors offer specific recommendations to increase the transition of Latinos from high schools to colleges and universities.

Academic achievement is clearly vital for Latinos to enter college. Does a strong sense of Latino identity harm it? In "Social Identification and the Academic Achievement of Chicano Students," Aida Hurtado, Eugene Garcia, Luis Vega, and Reynold Gonzalez examine that question. They first note that the effects of social identity on academic achievement among minority students seem mixed. Some argue the impact is negative, others that it is positive, and still others that it is nonexistent. The authors say these contradictory assessments stem from "different conceptualizations of social identity." To test the idea, they use results from a survey of Chicano college students in a South Texas public university. They find that social identification based on ethnicity does not adversely affect scholastic attainment. At the same time, they also note that "it is not easy to be head of household and academically successful." The authors suggest that providing childcare for heads of households would reduce the stresses of family, work, and school.

Community colleges are central to the Latino experience in higher education. Over 60% of Latinos in postsecondary education during 1999–2000 were in two-year colleges – the largest percentage of any ethnic group. Romero Jalomo's " 'Being There For Us': Latino Students and Their First Year Experiences in Urban Community Colleges" gives us an excellent ethnographic picture of how new Latino students view these institutions. Jalomo contends that we need to understand the community college experience if we want to improve Latino educational achievement. He reports on focus group interviews with 44 Latino first-year students attending community colleges in California, Texas, and New

York. Among other findings: The respondents dichotomized their "first-year experience as either 'easy' (academically unchallenging) or 'hard' (academically challenging)." Parents played a key role in making a smooth transition from high school to college. Families assisted with tuition and related expenses, childcare, household responsibilities, and even academic tutoring. Jalomo also wanted to know how the college experience affected students' relationships with family members. He discovered that it "most often improved family relations, although it limited the amount of time students could spend with family members." The students "beamed with pride" as they recounted numerous occasions where family members "bragged about them" to friends and family. The students had mostly positive experiences during their first-year, and in fact they saw the community colleges as "being there for us."

Next, Harriett Romo and Joanne Salas examine key issues affecting transition in "Successful Transitions of Latino Students from High School to College." The authors discuss poor high school preparation and parents' lack of education as two major hurdles Latinos must overcome. They point out that Latinos must attend high quality colleges and universities to realize true equity in higher education, but emphasize that these institutions must be affordable and programs must be in place to help Latinos make timely progress toward their degrees. The authors suggest that successful institutional strategies for Latinos should include freshmen seminars, learning communities, and 2 + 2 collaborations between community colleges and four-year institutions.

Rising in Academia. While obviously more Latinos must attend college, earn degrees, and go out into the world, they must also enter the fabric of the colleges themselves. This section treats the inner workings of that process. Contributors examine graduate school education for Latinos, the rocky path for new faculty members to gain tenure, the dearth of Latino college and university presidents, and finally, the effect of higher education leadership institutes on Latinos.

What impact will distance learning have on Latinos in graduate school? Jose Cochado examines the intriguing experience of Northern Arizona University (NAU) in "Distance Site Programs – A New Way for Hispanics to Enter the Graduate Program Pipeline." When NAU developed its Statewide Campus to provide distance learning, it found an unexpected consequence: a dramatic increase in Latino graduate students. Cochado describes the snowballing growth of the program, from faculty visits to rural locales, to instructional offerings on a network of interactive TV cameras, to the assignment of faculty to distant sites on a full-time basis. Currently the program has 5,469 statewide students, or 38% of the 14,495 total student body. The vast majority of the statewide students, 4,155 of them, were enrolled in graduate programs in 2000. The program is clearly creating a viable means for Hispanics to enter the upper echelons of the educational process. Cochado conducted a survey to gauge the statewide students' opinions about the program, and they offered a variety of suggestions for improvement. He concludes by noting that "when the conditions that have kept Hispanics from enrolling in graduate programs are addressed, they will enroll and complete graduate programs."

The educational pipeline does not end with graduate school. It continues with the hiring of more Latino faculty and the development of programs to help insure their success. In my "Faculty Mentoring Programs: Pass the Torch, Please," I report results from a nationwide survey I conducted to identify programs that help new faculty make the transition from graduate school to becoming tenured professors. I found that few programs existed, though one in particular offers a model that colleges and universities may wish to emulate. It is located at Miami University and directed by Professor Milton Cox. I include a description of this program as well as others of interest.

At the pinnacle of higher education are college and university presidents. In "Latino and Academic Leadership in American Higher Education," Roberto Haro confronts a disturbing fact that few like to acknowledge: the dearth of Latinos in these positions. Data on presidential attainment between 1995 to 2000 indicate that "no Latinos were hired as presidents at private, selective four-year liberal arts colleges, and with one exception, no Latinos were hired as presidents or academic vice presidents at major research universities." The road to a presidency often involves service as an academic dean and academic vice president, and Haro observes that few Latinos occupy these positions. This situation becomes acute when one considers the faculty positions Latinos hold. Since there are few Latino men and women in senior faculty ranks at four-year colleges and universities, there are even fewer who can become department chairs and academic deans.

Haro interviewed 117 people, including ten Latino administrators. His in-depth interviews with Latino leaders explored three critical topics: "what factors or strategies were most significant in their appointment; what major challenges had they faced during the first two years; and what groups or individuals were most critical of their leadership." Certain interviewees noted that they had received their positions because of an ongoing court case against the university, or in response to pressure from a coalition of Latino businessmen. Regarding the challenges Latino administrators faced in their first two years, Haro noted problems with the governing board, white faculty, and in one case, Chicano students themselves. The author concludes with specific recommendations aimed at executive search firms and higher education associations, including the Hispanic Association of Colleges and Universities.

What can be done about the absence of Latinos in top-level positions? In my "Building a LEAP for Latinos in Higher Education," I outline one solution: a Latino-oriented leadership institute. Leadership institutes can give participants an advantage in the jockeying for highly-coveted positions, and I first look at the four major leadership programs in higher education: (1) the Fellows Program; (2) the Harvard Institutes for Higher Education; (3) the Millennium Leadership Initiative; and (4) the Summer Institute for Women in Higher Education. Few Latinos apply to or attend any of them. A fifth is LEAP, the Leadership and Education for Asian Pacifics summer institute, which I attended in 2001. To increase the numbers of Latinos, I discuss two strategies. The first is the establishment of a Latino Institute based on LEAP. The second involves recommendations to the other leadership programs to improve their poor track record of Latino attendees.

As more and more Latinos seek entry into higher education, the questions posed in this book and the solutions offered will become increasingly urgent. The earlier we address them, the easier the societal transition will be. For at some point we will have to address them.

DEMOGRAPHICS AND DEMAND

SEIZE THE MOMENT

Anthony P. Carnevale

INTRODUCTION

A Unique Window of Opportunity

Access to college is the keystone in a fully integrated strategy for Hispanic[1] inclusion. College is the culminating educational experience in the transition from youthful dependency to adult autonomy. It also is the starting point and intellectual foundation for lifelong learning. We already know from the evidence of the past few decades that people aren't going anywhere in the new knowledge economy unless they go to college first. Jobs that require at least some college have increased from 19% of all jobs in 1959 to 56% of all jobs in 1997. Those with at least some college are one-and-a-half times as likely to get training from their employer and have much greater access to technology on the job. The growing income disparity between those with college and those without college has already turned us into a nation of college-haves and college-have-nots. Access to college has become the new threshold for realizing our individual hopes and aspirations as well as the ante for earning a family wage.

Looking into the future, there is every reason to believe that the economic demand for college-educated workers will only grow. According to employment projections from the Bureau of Labor Statistics, between now and 2010, jobs that require college degrees or postsecondary awards will grow twice as fast as jobs that do not require college degrees. Moreover, as the oversized generation of baby boomers begins to retire, they will take their experience and college credentials with them, creating a growing need for college-educated youth.

Latinos in Higher Education, Volume 3, pages 9–35.
Copyright © 2003 by Elsevier Science Ltd.
All rights of reproduction in any form reserved.
ISBN: 0-7623-0980-6

The first 15 years of the twenty-first century present a unique window of opportunity for improving Hispanic access to college and to the growing share of good jobs that require college-level attainment. Three powerful forces contribute to this unprecedented opportunity. The Hispanic community's unparalleled aspirations to higher education, the momentum from the slow but steady improvement in academic readiness for college among Hispanics over the past decades, and the demographic surge in the number of college-age Hispanic youth. Our ability to take advantage of this unprecedented opportunity is of critical importance to both Hispanic families and the nation.

Polling data show that Hispanics value college as a means to social and economic mobility more than any other group in American society. The momentum from Hispanic educational aspirations, in combination with the growing number of Hispanic youth and their steady educational progress, should increase the number of Hispanics on college campuses and the Hispanic share of college enrollments substantially by 2015. In the first decade and a half of this century, the population of Hispanics, especially among 18–24-year-olds, will increase more than that of any other race/ethnic group, substantially increasing the share of Hispanics in the traditional college-going age population.[2]

Data from the National Assessment of Educational Progress (NAEP) suggest that this growing cohort of college-age Hispanic youth has performed as well and even a little better than previous cohorts in their elementary and secondary educational preparation for college. Even at current rates of college enrollment, the increasing size of the 18–24-year-old Hispanic population through 2015 will result in both an increase in the number of Hispanic students qualified for college and an increase in the share of Hispanics as a share of all qualified college students.

This rosy scenario for Hispanic college participation requires important caveats. While the prospects for an increasing number of Hispanic youth qualified for college are good, we cannot assume that they all will be able to attend. A larger 18–24-year-old cohort will raise financial barriers that could reduce access, especially for low-income Hispanic families.

In addition, we need to be careful not to mistake the effects of demographic momentum for deeper social progress. The likely increase in Hispanics qualified for college results principally from the growing number of Hispanic students in the 18–24-year-old population, not from an increase in the share of Hispanic youth going on to college. Because the pool of Hispanic 18–24-year-olds will grow so rapidly through 2015, the number and share of Hispanic students on campus will grow even if the share of Hispanics going to college stays the same or declines somewhat. But the share of Hispanic youth going to college would not improve. Moreover, because colleges will be picking from a much larger pool of Hispanic youth, they will be able to admit more highly qualified Hispanic freshmen, whose subsequent grades and graduation rates will rise relative to previous freshman cohorts of Hispanic students. As a result, demographic momentum could overstate both educational attainment and achievement among Hispanics, reducing pressures for greater inclusion.

Improving access to college among Hispanic youth requires both short-term and long-term policies. Improvements in elementary and secondary preparation for college remains the principle long-term barrier to increasing Hispanic access to college – especially among Hispanics from low-income families with low levels of parental education. At the same time, however, improvements in access to college need not await long-term reforms in elementary and secondary education. Significant and more immediate improvements in access can be made by focusing policies on Hispanic families with children who are prepared for college. Even now, many 18–24-year-old Hispanics who are ready for college do not attend. In addition, the increasing size of the Hispanic 18–24-year-old population ensures that there will be many more college-qualified Hispanics in the first 15 years of the twenty-first century.

HISPANIC FAMILIES AND HIGHER EDUCATION: UNPARALLELED ASPIRATIONS

The gap in college preparation between Hispanic youth and their non-Hispanic peers persists, but the steady progress in educational attainment and college enrollment among Hispanic youth clearly shows that the education gap is not a value's gap. In fact, a survey by Public Agenda, a nonprofit public opinion research and citizen education organization based in New York City, revealed that Hispanic parents lead the nation in the priority they place on education (Public Agenda, 2000). When asked what factor is the most important for success, 65% of Hispanic parents identified a college education – a far stronger and more consistent response than that of the general public (see Fig. 1).

Hispanic parents clearly understand that education is what will ultimately level the playing field for their children. But they value more than just the degree and its ensuing economic benefits. Like other parents, Hispanic parents are concerned with the intangible benefits of a higher education. Nearly three-quarters of the Hispanic parents cited in the Public Agenda survey believe that college should teach students "a sense of maturity and how to manage on their own." Almost 70% of both Hispanic and non-Hispanic parents want colleges to foster in their children "an ability to get along with people different from themselves." Half of the Hispanic parents – compared with 40% of all parents – believe college should teach students how to execute their rights and

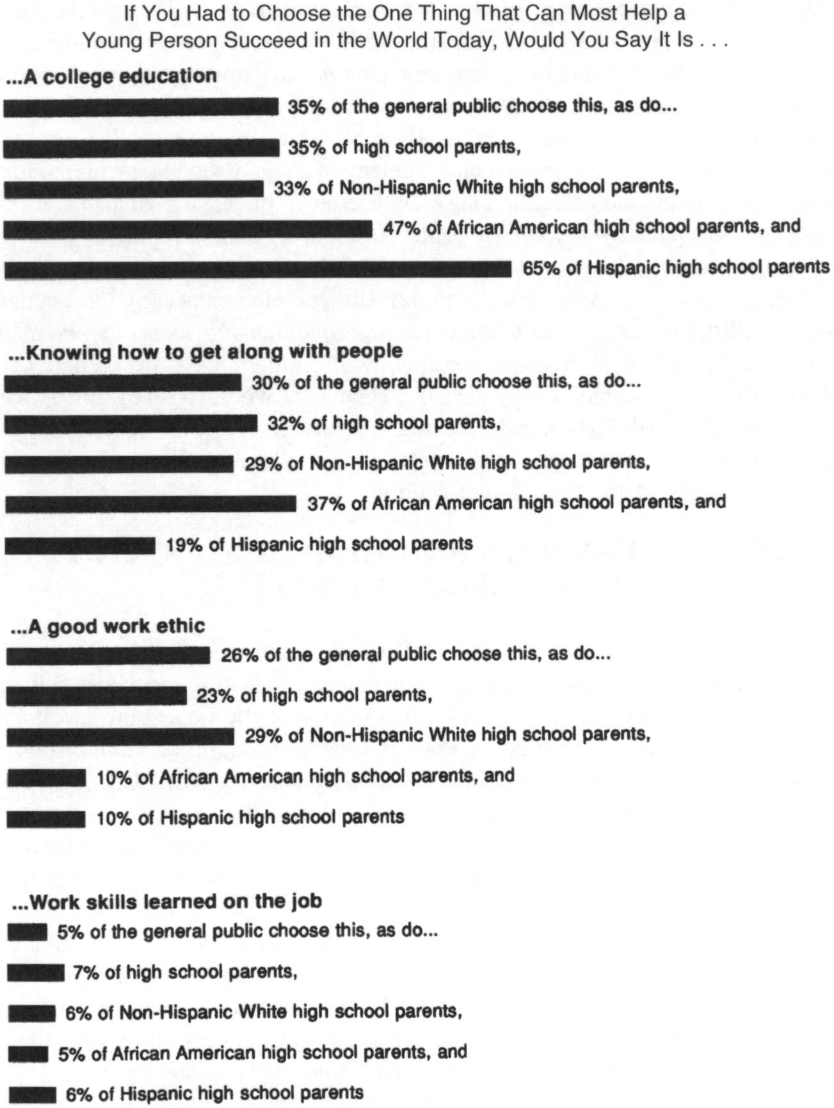

If You Had to Choose the One Thing That Can Most Help a
Young Person Succeed in the World Today, Would You Say It Is . . .

...A college education

35% of the general public choose this, as do...

35% of high school parents,

33% of Non-Hispanic White high school parents,

47% of African American high school parents, and

65% of Hispanic high school parents

...Knowing how to get along with people

30% of the general public choose this, as do...

32% of high school parents,

29% of Non-Hispanic White high school parents,

37% of African American high school parents, and

19% of Hispanic high school parents

...A good work ethic

26% of the general public choose this, as do...

23% of high school parents,

29% of Non-Hispanic White high school parents,

10% of African American high school parents, and

10% of Hispanic high school parents

...Work skills learned on the job

5% of the general public choose this, as do...

7% of high school parents,

6% of Non-Hispanic White high school parents,

5% of African American high school parents, and

6% of Hispanic high school parents

Fig. 1.

Source: Public Agenda (May 2000).

responsibilities as conscientious citizens, such as "voting and volunteering" (Public Agenda, 2000).

THE HISPANIC EDUCATION MOMENTUM: MAJOR STRIDES, MAJOR CHALLENGES

It is commonly known that Hispanic children lag their non-Hispanic White peers in elementary and secondary educational progress and completion. Significant gaps appear before the first grade and persist through high school graduation. In assessing Hispanic educational progress, it is important to remember that a variety of distinctions apply among subgroups in the overall Hispanic population. First, women have made more progress than men. Second, wide differences exist among Hispanic nationalities. And third, in general, U.S.-born Hispanics tend to be better educated than foreign-born Hispanics. For instance, 78% of U.S.-born Hispanic adults finished high school, compared with 47% of foreign-born Hispanics (Carnevale, 1999). Nevertheless, overall education growth lags consistently.

Some Striking Successes . . .

A leap in college enrollments. Between 1976 and 1998, the number of Hispanic 18- to 24-year-olds enrolled in college increased astronomically – by 165%, compared with 20% for Whites and 49% for African Americans. In fact, Hispanic enrollment in postsecondary education increased close to 100% in just eight years – from about 435,000 in 1990 to about 0.8 million in 1998.

A doubling of college degrees. Hispanics also doubled their undergraduate and graduate degree attainment from 1975–1976 to 1995–1996. In 1996, Hispanic students earned 7% of all associate degrees, 5 percent of all bachelor's degrees, about 4% of all master's degrees, and 3% of all doctoral degrees awarded (NCES, 1997).

. . . But Many Challenges Remain

Hispanics have made great strides in educational attainment,[3] but, on the whole, they remain consistently concentrated at the lower track of the education hierarchy. For example:

- In 1998, only 36% of Hispanic three- and four-year-olds were in nursery school programs, compared with 53% of non-Hispanic White children (U.S. Bureau of the Census, 1999).

- Hispanic students made slightly less formal progress through elementary and secondary education. At age 15, 700,000 non-Hispanic White students (28%) out of 2.5 million students enrolled are enrolled below the 10th grade (the modal grade). Out of 517,000 Hispanic students at age 15 enrolled in school, 177,000 (34%) are enrolled below 10th grade (U.S. Bureau of the Census, 1999).
- Hispanic youth are more likely to drop out of high school. In 1996, the high school dropout rate (defined as the proportion of youth who are not enrolled in school and do not have a high school diploma) for non-Hispanic White 16–24-year-olds was 7%, compared to 18% for native-born Hispanic 16–24-year-olds (NCES, 1998).
- White high school graduates tend to complete a more rigorous academic curriculum than do their Hispanic peers. For example, 45% of White high school graduates completed an advanced academic-level mathematics curriculum (which includes courses such as trigonometry and calculus) in 1998, compared to 26% of Hispanic high school graduates (NCES, 2000).

Running Faster Just to Keep Up

While educational attainment has improved among Hispanics, other groups have achieved similar or even greater gains. For instance, as Fig. 2 shows, the decline in the dropout rates for Hispanics and non-Hispanic Whites are similar. At the same time, while Hispanic bachelor's and advanced degree attainment has increased by 7 percentage points, bachelor's and advanced degree attainment has increased by 14 percentage points among non-Hispanic Whites. As a result, the Hispanic population – on average – still has fewer years of schooling than non-Hispanic Whites, African Americans, and the population as a whole.

Improvements in the number of Hispanic students in higher education need to be viewed in context. Recent reports applaud the growth in the number of Hispanics on campus. But some of these increases simply reflect continuing growth in the size of the Hispanic population rather than growth in the share of Hispanics enrolled in college. The ultimate goal is parity: Hispanics should have at least the same share of college seats as their share of the population. In that light, while there has been improvement, we are still a long way from achieving the goal.

At current participation rates in higher education, the increasing number of Hispanics who are college age – 18 years old and older – will likely increase the number of Hispanics on campus by more than one million new students, compared with the number of Hispanics in college in 1995. This increase also will raise the Hispanic share of all undergraduate students from 11% in 1995 to 15% in 2015. At the same time, however, there still will be a large gap

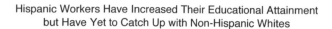

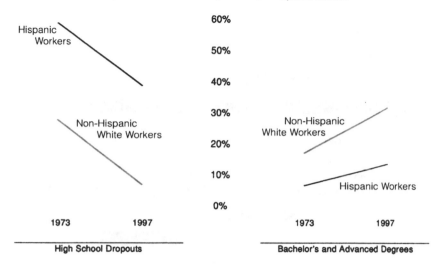

Fig. 2. Share of Prime-Age Workers Who Were High School Dropouts, Or Who Had Earned Bachelor's and Advanced Degrees.

Auhtors' analysis of Current Population Study (March 1974; March 1998).

between the share of Hispanics in college relative to their share of the 18 and older college-age population (see Fig. 3).

A gap between college qualification and college enrollment remains. Across all races and ethnic groups, there are a sizable number of students who appear qualified to go to a four-year college but who don't enroll. Sixty-five percent of all high school graduates are "college-qualified" – that is, they meet the minimum academic requirement for admission to a four-year college. But only 45% of high school graduates actually enroll in four-year colleges. This gap is especially prominent among Hispanic high school graduates. Fifty-three percent of Hispanic high school graduates are academically ready to go to four-year colleges; only 31% do (NCES, 1997).

Hispanic Pathways in Higher Education

Maintaining and improving Hispanic participation in higher education will depend on our ability to improve access to the unique pathways that Hispanics

Because of Their Growing Numbers, the Hispanic Share of
Undergraduates Will Increase More Than Any Other Group . . .

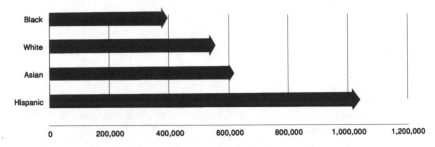

. . . But the Gap Between Hispanic Share of the College-Age Population and
the Number of Hispanics on Campus Will Still Be More Than 500,000 Students

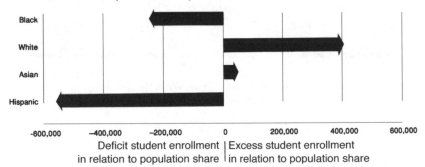

Fig. 3.   Increase in Number of Undergraduates.

Authors' analysis of U.S. Census Bureau data and population projections.

have already created in blazing the trail from high school to college. Hispanics
are unique in their reliance on two-year colleges and their concentration in
Hispanic Serving Institutions (HSIs).[4]

Community colleges especially appeal to Hispanic students for many reasons.
Thanks to their open admission policies and flexible educational environments,
community colleges are the gateway to college for at least half of all Hispanic
students. For some Hispanic students – including many who are older and already
in the workforce – community colleges are particularly attractive options. The
community colleges link to local communities and foster an environment that is
more responsive to Hispanic students' histories, backgrounds, and cultural needs.

For example, because the college is part of the community, the student may feel less pressed to adopt the majority culture found in most institutions. Likewise, this proximity may even eliminate some of the negative effects associated with separation. These are key elements in the successful recruitment and retention programs for Hispanic students, especially those who are the first of their immediate families to attend college (Rendon, 1992; Rendon et al., 1999; Rodriguez, 1974–1975).

Community colleges also have smaller class sizes, which allow more individual attention. They also are affordable and tend to cooperate with community businesses to offer programs that facilitate lifelong learning or retraining of the local workforce.

In some ways, however, the disproportionate share of Hispanics who enroll in two-year colleges poses a problem. As with many other first-generation college attendees and nontraditional students, Hispanics are concentrated on the lower rungs of the higher education ladder. Only 27% of Hispanic students jump from two-year colleges to four-year institutions (Ganderton and Santos, 1995). While the two-year colleges offer many attractions, they may not provide the same opportunities that are available in the more prestigious four-year colleges.

Many Hispanic students are older than the typical undergraduate, are parents, or are working. These facts underlie many of the other issues affecting Hispanic higher education. More than half of the Hispanics in college are over the age of 25 (Carnevale & Fry, 2000) and are more likely to enroll in nearby community colleges and to attend part-time, since parenting and employment obligations tend to make relocation and full-time study difficult. Both of these factors affect how likely students are to complete their studies. Two-year colleges lose 54% of their freshmen, compared to only 29% for four-year colleges (Tinto, 1993). And part-time attendance extends the period of study, which further reduces the chance that students will complete their higher education.

Hispanic undergraduates are concentrated in a relatively small number of two-year and four-year colleges, especially HSIs. Close to half of all HSIs have 50% or more undergraduate Hispanic student enrollment. In 1997–1998, 195 institutions qualified as HSIs and served 40% of all Hispanic undergraduate students (IPEDS, 1997–1998).

All of the colleges that qualified as HSIs in 1997–1998 are located in 12 predominately southwestern states and Puerto Rico. Nearly 70% of these colleges, enrolling over 1.1 million students, are in just three locations – California (58 colleges), Puerto Rico (43 colleges), and Texas (30 colleges). At least one-third of all HSIs are located in large cities; another one-third are in midsize cities or on the urban fringe of large cities (IPEDS, 1997–1998).

The location of these HSIs – which conferred about 42% of all degrees earned by Hispanics in 1996–1997 – mirrors the distribution of Hispanics in the country and suggests that many Hispanics are enrolling in colleges close to home.

The nature of the HSIs relates to other characteristics of Hispanic participation in higher education. Many of these institutions do not award higher-level degrees. Just over half (52%) offer an associate degree as their highest degree. Another 15% offer bachelor's degrees, and about 20% offer master's degrees. Only 11% provide educational offerings all the way through doctoral degrees. Close to 70% of associate degrees and 50% of bachelor's degrees awarded by HSIs were in the social sciences or business (IPEDS, 1997–1998).

DEMOGRAPHIC MOMENTUM: THE NEXT 15 YEARS

Will Hispanic Participation Rates Hold?

Demographics will shape the future of Hispanics in higher education. The youngest of the traditional college-age population who will turn 18 in 2015 were born in 1998. There will be 31 million students in the traditional college-age population by 2015, an increase of 4.3 million, compared with the year 2000. If current participation rates do not decline (and the analysis shows that to be unlikely), the number of 18–24-year-old postsecondary students ready and willing to enroll in college directly after high school could grow by as much as 1.6 million students by 2015.

In 1998, Hispanics comprised 16% – 4.0 million – of the traditional college-age population and 800,000 of the country's 18–24-year-old students. By the year 2015, Hispanics will comprise 19% of the traditional college-age population. And if current participation rates in college among Hispanics do not decline, we project that Hispanics will account for 1.2 million of the nation's 18–24-year-old undergraduate students (Carnevale & Fry, 2000).

Will the New Hispanic Students be Prepared?

Many are surprised by the increases in overall enrollments as well as the dramatic increases in Hispanic enrollments projected through 2015 and question whether the new cohort of 18–24-year-olds will be prepared for college in 2015. The estimates, however, are plausible for a variety of reasons. First of all, the assumptions about the overall participation rates in both the overall 18–24-year-old cohort and among Hispanic 18–24-year-olds are conservative. Projections of overall enrollments, including Hispanic enrollments, presume participation rates derived on a group-by-group basis from the 1998 Current

Population Survey (CPS) by the U.S. Bureau of the Census. The analysis assumes that overall participation rates in higher education will not increase between 1998 and 2015. In fact, participation rates in higher education have increased steadily throughout the past century, especially after 1940. Hispanic participation in higher education has followed a similar pattern. Between 1990 and 1998, for instance, overall participation rates among 18–24-year-olds in higher education increased from 16 to 20%. Participation rates among Hispanic men increased from 15 to 16% and participation by Hispanic females increased from 16 to 25%.

This analysis assumes that the share of Hispanics who want to enroll in college is unlikely to dip below the 1998 levels. It also assumes that the unequaled college ambitions that Hispanic parents have for their children will not wane, that the steady increase in Hispanic educational attainment (years of schooling) in the pre-K-12 higher education pipeline will not decline below 1998 levels, or that the economic pull of better jobs at better earnings for college-educated workers will not reverse itself in the new knowledge economy.

The projections also assume that educational achievement overall and among Hispanics will not decline. This assumption is based on an analysis of the NAEP, which begins testing students in the fourth grade. So far, NAEP scores suggest that the new youth cohort will be at least as qualified as current high school graduates when they were in the fourth grade (Carnevale & Fry, 2000). Early test results from NAEP and other sources also suggest that the current share of Hispanic students ready for college will stay the same or grow slightly if current trends continue.[5]

How Will Immigration Effect Readiness?

There is an often-stated belief that new immigration will affect Hispanic readiness for college. It is true that the nine-year-old cohort of Hispanics tested in NAEP will not be the same group of individuals when the cohort reaches college age. Some students will drop out. Some will leave the United States and others will immigrate into the U.S. But an analysis of the available data suggests that these factors are unlikely to affect the projections.

Emigration out of the U.S. has little effect on the size or make-up of the 18–24-year-old Hispanic population. The dropout rate among Hispanics is declining, suggesting that future cohorts will be better prepared for college. Immigration clearly has a large impact on the Hispanic population. But currently more than half of college-age (18–24-year-old) Hispanic youth were born in the U.S. and most foreign-born 18–24-year-olds have been through the U.S. K-12 college pipeline.

Although four in ten college-age Hispanic youth between the ages of 18 and 24 were born outside the United States, a substantial proportion of these 1.5 million young adults were educated in the United States. Fewer than one million of the 1.5 million Hispanic immigrant 18–24-year-olds arrived in the U.S. after age 15. Nearly 600,000 foreign-born Hispanic young adults arrived before 1990, and thus they clearly arrived in the United States during adolescence or early childhood and participated in the U.S. elementary or secondary education system.

The proportion of foreign-born 18–24-year-olds that has recently arrived in the United States appears to have fallen since 1990. In 1990, for instance, according to the CPS March surveys, 31% of Hispanic 18–24-year-olds had arrived within the past three years, compared with 24% in 1999.In sum, there is nothing in the data on dropouts, emigration, or immigration that suggests future cohorts of 18–24-year-old Hispanics will be less prepared for college than current cohorts. If anything, the decline in dropouts, the improving NAEP performance of Hispanic elementary school students, and the decline in immigration among 18–24-year-old Hispanics suggest an increasingly qualified pool of Hispanics in the early decades of this century.

HISPANICS AND THE WORKFORCE: THE STATISTICS

The Stakes Are High

The good news is that, as a result of educational improvements, Hispanics are getting better jobs at better wages. The bad news is that, despite these gains, they still trail non-Hispanic Whites, African Americans, and the population in general in access to good jobs.

Access to postsecondary education or training has become an increasingly important threshold for economic success in the new economy. This was not always so. In 1959, 29% of the workers in the top two-thirds of the earnings distribution had some college, compared to 69% in 1998. Until the early 1980s, good jobs were available for high school graduates and even high school dropouts, especially for men in blue-collar jobs.

From the 1950s through the 1970s, the earnings advantages of workers with at least some college,[6] relative to the earnings of workers with only high school, actually declined to 43% as the glut of highly educated baby boomers entered the workforce. As would be expected, an increasing supply of college-educated workers reduced the earnings advantages between workers with college and high school graduates.

Remarkably, however, since the 1980s the supply of college-educated workers has continued to grow but the wage advantages of college-educated workers have continued to increase as well. Even though the share of college-educated workers in the labor force has increased from 37% in the 1980s to almost 60% in the late 1990s, the wage premium for those with at least some college over those with high school or less has jumped from 43% to a whopping 73% over the same time period.

The share of college-educated workers has grown across a broad spectrum of occupational categories. In 1973, for example, 59% of managers and professionals had at least some college and 33% only had high school diplomas. By 1998, more than 80% had at least some college and 18% only had high school diplomas.

High-technology jobs follow a similar pattern. In 1973, roughly 60% of high-technology workers had at least some college; that number grew to 85% in 1998.

Education and health care workers have always been highly educated but, even among them, the proportion with at least some college has risen from 83% in 1973 to 95% in 1998.

The proportion of skilled blue-collar workers with at least some college has increased from 17 to 28% since 1973, and the share of clerical workers with at least some college has more than doubled, from 25 to 54%.

The Earnings Gap

Given the rapidly growing requirement for college degrees and the college education gap that already exists between Hispanic workers and non-Hispanic White workers, the corresponding earnings gap should come as no surprise. On average, non-Hispanic White men earn $17,000 more a year than Hispanic men, and non-Hispanic White women earn $6,700 a year more than Hispanic women (Carnevale, 1999).

The continuing education gap for Hispanics translates directly into an earnings gap. The rising demand for educational credentials among prime-age (30 to 59 years of age) workers puts many of the highest-paying jobs out of reach for Hispanics with no postsecondary education. In 1997, prime-age Hispanic males had an average income of $26,900, compared to $43,900 for non-Hispanic White males. Hispanic women earned $18,300, while non-Hispanic White women earned $24,900 (Carnevale, 1999). Hispanic women still earn less than Hispanic men over time, increasing educational requirements as well as the shift from factory jobs to education, health care, and office work has created new opportunities and higher earnings for Hispanic women, even while it resulted in a decline in earnings for Hispanic males.

The education, earnings, and occupational hierarchy in the United States divides roughly into three major segments:

Elite managerial and professional jobs. These are the highest-paid jobs, and they primarily go to people with bachelor's degrees. Thirty million of all prime-age workers are in these jobs. More than 60% of them have bachelor's degrees; another 23% have some college. On average, these jobs pay $63,000 for men and $38,000 for women.[7]

In 1998, 16% of prime-age Hispanic and 23% of prime-age African American workers were in elite managerial and professional jobs, compared with 39% of non-Hispanic Whites. These statistics did reflect *some* progress. The overall share of Hispanics in elite jobs grew 4% between 1973 and 1998. But that growth was due mainly to an increasing share of Hispanic females in elite jobs (see Fig. 4). In fact, by 1998 a higher proportion of Hispanic women than men had elite jobs, due largely to unequal participation in the education and health care fields. Equal proportions of Hispanic men and women had managerial and professional jobs in business, but the percentage of Hispanic women who held managerial and professional jobs in education and health care was *triple* that of Hispanic men (Carnevale, 1999).

Good jobs held by crafts workers, technicians, clericals, and others. These are well-paid jobs, averaging $38,000 for men and $23,000 for women (Carnevale, 1999). People who have some college but no bachelor's degree made up about 36% of this group. Workers with bachelor's degrees constituted only about 17%.

Compared to elite jobs, "good" jobs are distributed more equally among non-Hispanic Whites, African Americans, and Hispanics. Between 1973 and 1998, the share of Hispanics with good jobs increased by about 5 percentage points, divided equally between Hispanic men and women (Carnevale, 1999) (see Fig. 5).

Less-skilled jobs in retail, personal services, and other minimally skilled occupations. These are the low-wage jobs, paying an average of $25,000 for men and $14,000 for women. The category includes machine operators, sales-clerks, janitors, and hotel workers. Only 7% of these workers had at least some college; 21% had some college but no bachelor's degree. A substantial proportion of these workers were under the age of 30 and were in transition to more skilled jobs or were combining work and schooling (Carnevale, 1999).

A much higher proportion of Hispanics and African Americans were in these less-skilled jobs than were non-Hispanic Whites. Fifty-one percent of prime-age Hispanic workers between the ages of 30 and 59 held these lowest-paid jobs, compared with 23% of non-Hispanic Whites in 1998 (Carnevale, 1999).

But there is progress. The share of prime-age Hispanic workers in less-skilled jobs declined from 63 to 51% between 1973 and 1998. This movement out of

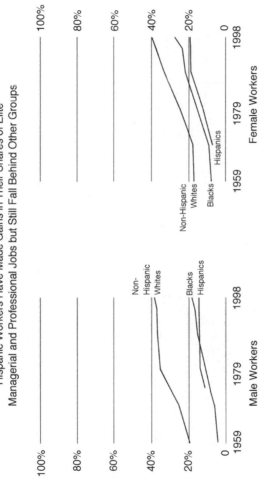

Hispanic Workers Have Made Gains in Their Shares of Elite
Managerial and Professional Jobs but Still Fall Behind Other Groups

Fig. 4. Percentage of Prime-Age Workers (30–59 Years Old).

Authors' analysis of Current Population Survey (March 1974; 1980 & 1999) and Public Use Microdata Sample, 1960 Census (CPS data for Hispanics were unavailable prior to 1973).

Fig. 5. Percentage of Prime-Age Workers (30–59 Years Old).

Authors' analysis of Current Population Survey (March 1974; 1980 & 1999) and Public Use Microdata Sample, 1960 Census (CPS data for Hispanics were unavailable prior to 1973).

the bottom tier of the job market was greater for Hispanic women than men, largely because Hispanic women started out farther behind. The share of Hispanic men in these jobs declined from 60% in 1973 to 51% in 1998. Over the same period, the share of Hispanic women in these jobs declined from 68 to 51% (Carnevale, 1999) (see Fig. 6).

The General Economic Benefits of Inclusion

The value of increasing the share of Hispanics on college campuses translates directly into economic value both for Hispanics and the broader population. If Hispanic workers had the same educational attainment as non-Hispanic White workers, and if they were paid equally for their given level of education, the infusion of new more highly educated human capital would increase U.S. income by $118 billion every year, adding $41 billion in annual tax revenues to the national coffers. The income gains in California and Texas alone would total $80 billion (Carnevale & Fry, 2000) (see Fig. 7). In addition, the proportions of Hispanic families with officially "inadequate incomes"[8] would be reduced by 50%, from 41 to 21%, moving us closer to realizing our egalitarian goals (Carnevale & Fry, 2000).

Moreover, diversity on college campuses adds diversity on the job, which has its own economic value. In a global economy, the ability to work and communicate effectively with diverse populations, both at home and abroad, is an important asset. In addition, research on group interactions shows that the presence of diverse perspectives in groups discourages "groupthink" and encourages learning, creativity, and flexibility, which are, in themselves, increasingly important competitive assets (McLeod & Lobel, 1996; Rhodes, 1992). Other important competitive skills in the new economy include leadership, problem solving, communication, self-management, negotiations, teamwork, and interpersonal competencies. Research indicates that both majority and minority students who study in diverse groups tend to demonstrate these skills to a greater degree than do students from more homogeneous schools (Chang, 1996; Hurtado et al., 1999; Watson et al., 1993).

LOOKING AHEAD: THE NEXT FIFTEEN YEARS

So what does all this mean? The American population clearly recognizes that, today, college graduation is critical to lifetime success. College enrollments have increased by almost 20% since the 1980s. And there is no segment of the

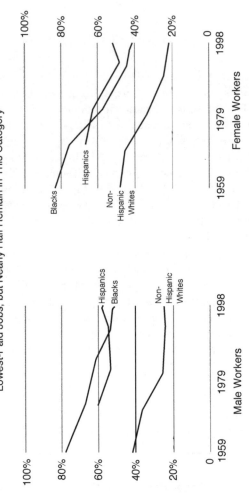

Hispanic Workers Have Reduced Their Share in the Least-Skilled and
Lowest-Paid Jobs, but Nearly Half Remain in This Category

Fig. 6. Percentage of Prime-Age Workers (30–59 Years Old).

Authors' analysis of Current Population Survey (March 1974; 1980 & 1999) and Public Use Microdata Sample, 1960 Census (CPS data for Hispanics were unavailable prior to 1973).

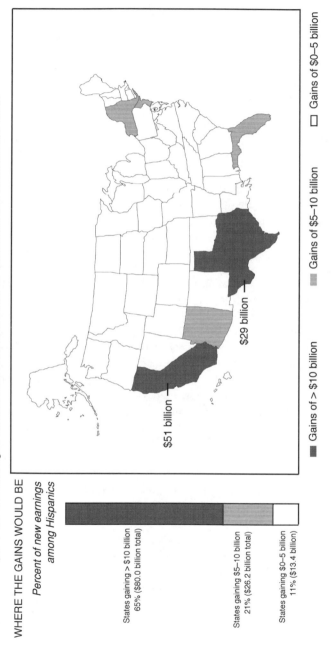

Hispanic Gains in Earnings from Additional Education Would Be Concentrated in California and Texas

WHERE THE GAINS WOULD BE

Percent of new earnings among Hispanics

States gaining > $10 billion
65% ($80.0 billion total)

States gaining $5–10 billion
21% ($26.2 billion total)

States gaining $0–5 billion
11% ($13.4 billion)

$51 billion

$29 billion

Gains of > $10 billion

Gains of $5–10 billion

Gains of $0–5 billion

Fig. 7.

Authors' analysis of U.S. Current Population Surveys.

population that has grasped the relationship more clearly than Hispanics. However, Hispanics are not yet where they need to be.

While the prospects for Hispanic access to postsecondary education are optimistic, it is too soon to celebrate. Even if our projections come true, education and consequent job opportunity gaps will remain. There will be more Hispanics ready to go to college by 2015. However, the Hispanic share of college seats will not be proportional to their share of the population. We need to be careful that the growing numbers of Hispanic students who are likely to go to college do not give us a false sense that we have achieved our diversity goals.

Despite steady improvements, gaps remain not only in Hispanic educational attainment but in job opportunities. As a result of educational improvements, Hispanics are getting better jobs at better wages. Yet, despite these gains, Hispanic earnings and access to high-wage, high-skilled jobs still trail those of non-Hispanic Whites, African Americans, and the population in general. Not only are non-Hispanic Whites increasing their educational attainment as fast or faster than Hispanics, but the economy also is boosting educational requirements. Hence, Hispanics are in an education race for the best jobs not only with other groups of workers but also with the growing demands of the economy.

Many Hispanic college students may be bumped to less selective institutions or crowded out altogether. Unless the number of seats in postsecondary education increases to accommodate the rush of new students, Hispanic students may remain concentrated on the lower rungs of postsecondary education selectivity-in two-year colleges and the less selective four-year colleges. As the size of the 18–24-year-old cohort increases, competition for seats could start a process of bumping some Hispanic students down and in some cases off the postsecondary education and training ladder. Some students who would have gone to more selective four-year colleges would be bumped to less selective four-year colleges. Other Hispanic students, who would have gone directly to four-year colleges if there had been enough room on campus, would be bumped down to two-year degree programs. In addition, the demographic surge in available freshmen would probably make four-year colleges less interested in accepting transfers from two-year schools. Some students who would normally be in two-year degree programs by present standards would be bumped to certificates and short-term training, and some prospective students would be bumped out of the postsecondary education system altogether.

Finally, the surge in 18–24-year-old students also raises the possibility that adults and other nontraditional students will be crowded out, especially those who have special requirements as they attempt to balance their education with work and family commitments. Traditional college-age students are the preferred customers in higher education. They tend to enroll in full-time coursework more than older students. As a result, they not only pay more, they qualify themselves and colleges for more state and federal aid. They are more amenable to a standardized curriculum and scheduling than older students or students with work and family responsibilities. Hispanics are more highly concentrated among nontraditional students than any other group. For instance, more than one-half of Hispanic undergraduates are over the age of twenty-five (Carnevale & Fry, 2000).

Who will pay for all these new students? Resource constraints that result from the surge in college-age students may inhibit our ability to capitalize on the demographic momentum among 18–24-year-olds from Hispanic families who make up the largest share of new college-ready students. Given current spending patterns and participation rates, new postsecondary education costs could exceed $19 billion.

Cost pressures will extend beyond the higher education sector (Carnevale, 1999; Carnevale & Fry, 2001). Higher education is only one of the competing demands for greater investments in human capital necessary to integrate fully the growing Hispanic community into the knowledge economy and culture of the twenty-first century. The new higher education funds will be hard to find, especially given the complementary resource demands for new funds to establish a universal preschool system, the need to meet standards in elementary and secondary education, and the growing demands for lifelong learning among adults. In addition, these combined fiscal pressures will tend to be concentrated in the same states that will experience the most substantial growth in the nation's burgeoning youth population, especially among Hispanics (Hossler et al., 1999).

It is unlikely that a "reengineering" of higher education that will allow us to serve more students at lower cost will come in time to serve the flood of new students that began arriving on college campuses in 1997. Nor is it likely that technology will provide the necessary access by creating "virtual universities" for new students. In general, our experience with technology in other service industries shows that technology adds value in the form of educational quality, variety, customization, and convenience more than reducing costs (Carnevale & Rose, 1998; Ehrenberg, 2000).

Students from low-income families, where Hispanics are more highly concentrated than any other race/ethnic group, would be the most adversely affected by increasing college costs, especially in light of the current shift from need-based aid to middle-income assistance in both federal and state policies. While 65% of Hispanic parents believe that a college education is a prerequisite for success, due to financial restraints, only 43% believe that their children will actually go to a postsecondary institution (Public Agenda, 2000).

We need to intensify capacity along the distinctive trails to higher education that Hispanic families have already blazed. Many Hispanic students pursue postsecondary education through the nation's 195 HSIs. These institutions represent 5% of degree-granting institutions but serve more than 40% of Hispanic college students. HSIs, especially two-year institutions, are more accessible to Hispanic students because they are located near large concentrations of Hispanic families, are more supportive of the Hispanic community and its culture, and are less expensive. Flexible scheduling allows Hispanics to tend to family obligations while going to college (Kane 1995; Rendon, 1992, 1994; Terenzini et al., 1994; Turner, 1998). HSIs will need increased capacity if they are to accommodate the increasing number of students. At current participation rates, the number of Hispanic students at HSIs alone could increase by 400,000 by 2015.

Establishing or creating new pathways into higher education for Hispanics is a prerequisite to access. The current pathways into postsecondary education that are most accessible to Hispanics should not become ruts that track Hispanics away from four-year and graduate degrees or the more selective colleges and universities. Already, more than half of Hispanic high school graduates are capable of going to a four-year college but only 31% actually attend (NCES, 1997). Among those who do go on to college, 67% are concentrated in two-year colleges and the least selective four-year institutions (Carnevale, 1999; Nettles et al., 1997; Phillippe, 1997). Graduation rates for Hispanic students at two-year colleges are lower than any other race/ethnic group. Graduation rates among those who attend four-year colleges are less than half those of non-Hispanic Whites. Hispanics represent 5% of the postgraduate population and comprise 5% of four-year college graduates.

If Hispanics are to attain leadership roles in the broad range of professions and institutions, they will need more direct access to selective four-year colleges and a higher rate of transfer between community colleges and four-year institutions. A first step would be to increase the share of Hispanics enrolled in four-year programs by focusing on those Hispanic high school graduates who are qualified for four-year college programs but do not attend.

We can make real progress in the short term with financial aid and social support, even though real parity will require long-term solutions. Clearly, the data on college preparation and college going among Hispanic high school graduates indicate that many more well-prepared Hispanic youth could go to college or to the more selective four-year colleges than actually do. These qualified students are the low-hanging fruit in any strategy to increase Hispanic enrollments. They need more robust financial aid as well as better information and more social support.

Achieving true parity in the share of Hispanics who go to college will require longer term strategies.

- *Pre-K-12 education must improve so that more Hispanic students are ready for college*. The gap in readiness between Hispanic and non-Hispanic White students is closing but still wide, even among native-born Hispanic students or those immigrant children who started out in American elementary schools. Hispanic children lag their non-Hispanic White peers in elementary and secondary educational progress and completion.
- *Adults need access to postsecondary education and training to catch up or keep up with changing skill requirements on the job*. Many adults, especially immigrants who arrive with little formal education, need a second chance to get the educational preparation they missed in their childhood and adolescent years. This is especially true for Hispanics. Only one-quarter of Hispanic adults have the college-level skills that have become the threshold for jobs that pay a family wage.

Hispanic adults' lack of educational attainment can be a vicious cycle that not only affects their earning potential, but their ability to provide their children with supportive educational strategies (Rendon, 1992; Rodriguez, 1974–1975). Parents need literacy skills and experience to understand the educational system well enough to help their children navigate through the system successfully (Pascarella & Terenzini, 1991). They also need good jobs that only postsecondary education or training can guarantee in order to afford college costs for their children.

Ensuring that Hispanics achieve educational excellence is in the interest of all Americans. Increasing access to education is beneficial both to national competitiveness and national income. But education is not just about dollars and cents. Improvements to education for Hispanics would bring critical societal benefits. Hispanic college graduates serve as role models for other Hispanics as they succeed in professions ranging from medicine to law to education and as they become political and economic leaders. As Hispanics forge ahead to shape policy from the schoolhouse to the White House, these leaders serve as inspirations to subsequent generations. And we need more of them to reinvigorate our society and its institutions with their fresh, diverse talents and perspectives.

These educational benefits cannot be completely realized until Hispanics participate fully in the education system. Our efforts in the next 15 years are key. The aspirations of Hispanic Americans ride on their hopes of educating the next generation. And to the degree they succeed, we all gain.

NOTES

1. The term "Hispanic" masks the enormous diversity among Americans from Mexico, Spain, Central or South America, and the Spanish-speaking Caribbean nations. Although there are inherent and significant limitations in grouping the educational and economic characteristics of such a diverse population, analysis of the aggregate data still offers a useful starting point for public dialogue. Use of the term "Hispanic" dates back to official government statistics of the early 1970s. The term "Latino" has since emerged as a grassroots alternative to the governmentally imposed designation. "Hispanic" is used throughout this chapter for the sake of consistency with the official statistics.

2. The traditional college-age population includes all individuals who are between the ages of 18 and 24.

3. Nearly all racial/ethnic groups have made tremendous strides in educational attainment over the twentieth century, including native-born Hispanics. About 40% of Whites born in 1900 finished high school, rising to about 85% for Whites born in the late 1960s. Native-born Hispanics have dramatically cut the gap. Less than 20% of native Hispanics born in 1900 completed high school. Among those born in the late 1960s, about 75% of native Hispanics finished high school (Mare, 1995).

4. Higher education institutions officially designated by the U.S. Department of Education as Hispanic Serving Institutions because their undergraduate enrollments are at least 25% Hispanic.

5. It is not known with any certainty how well prepared the current cohort of Hispanic children will be until they reach college-going age. However, today's Hispanic children at nine years of age appear to be at least as well prepared as nine-year-old children in earlier generations. The NAEP average scale scores for Hispanic nine-year-olds in 1999 on the mathematics and reading assessments were 213 and 193 (on a scale of 0 to 500), respectively. These averages are significantly above the average scale score of Hispanic nine-year-olds in 1973 in mathematics and 1975 in reading (NCES, 2000a).

6. We cannot be absolutely sure that children in this cohort will continue to be well prepared when they reach age 17. However, the history of "cohort growth" evident in the NAEP does not show that we should expect significant deterioration in average Hispanic performance as the nine-year-olds mature (Barton & Coley, 1998). Hispanic nine-year-olds in 1978 scored 203 on average on the mathematics assessment. Eight years later, this same cohort (at age 17) scored 283 on the mathematics assessment, for a cohort growth of 80 points in the average scale score. A later cohort, nine-year-olds in 1986, scored 205 on average in math (not significantly different than the 203 average earlier). Eight years later, at age 17, this cohort scored 291 in 1994, for a cohort growth of 86 points in the mathematics average scale score. The 1986 cohort performed the same as the 1978 cohort at age nine, but by the age of 17, the 1986 cohort performed significantly better than the 1978 cohort did at the same age. So the history of NAEP does not provide any evidence that today's nine-year-olds should be expected to perform less well than earlier cohorts when they reach age 17.

7. The phrase "at least some college" as well as the term "college-educated" includes all those who have had coursework that leads to two-year or four-year degrees, including both those who attain a degree as well as those who pursue college coursework but do not attain a degree.

8. The differences between men and women's pay are due in part to unequal pay for the same work, but primarily to the concentration of women in lower-paying industries (e.g. not-for-profits, education, health care).

9. What does it take for a family to live minimally well but adequately? In the 1970s, the U.S. Department of Labor estimated that a family could maintain a "minimum but adequate" life style if its income was about 75% more than the poverty line, which differs for families of different sizes. The government's mechanism for defining living standards for households of different sizes is based on the principle that there are economies of scale when people share expenses. Using this approach, in 1997, for instance, $28,000 represented a "minimum but adequate" income level for a family of four.

REFERENCES

Barton, P., & Cole, R. (1998). *Growth in School: Achievement Gains from the Fourth to the Eighth Grade*. Princeton, NJ: Educational Testing Service.

Carnevale, A. (1999). *Education = Success: Empowering Hispanic Youth and Adults*. Princeton, NJ: Educational Testing Service.

Carnevale, A., & Rose, S. (1998). *Education for What? The New Office Economy*. Princeton, NJ: Educational Testing Service.

Carnevale, A., & Fry, R. (2000). *Crossing the Great Divide: Can We Achieve Equity When Generation Y Goes to College?* Princeton, NJ: Educational Testing Service.

Carnevale, A., & Fry, R. (2001). Economics, Demography and the Future of Higher Education Policy. In: *Higher Expectations: Essays on the Future of Postsecondary Education*. These essays are part of the Postsecondary Education Initiative of the National Governors Association Influencing the Future of Higher Education. Washington, D.C.: NGA Center for Best Practices.

Chang, M. (1996). Racial diversity in higher education: Does a racially mixed student population affect educational outcomes? Unpublished doctoral dissertation. Ann Arbor, MI: UMI Dissertation Services.

Ehrenberg, R. (2000). *Tuition rising: Why college costs so much*. Cambridge, MA: Harvard University Press.

Ganderton, P., & Santos, R. (1995). Hispanic College Attendance and Completion: Evidence from the High School and Beyond Surveys. *Economics of Education Review, 14*(1).

Hossler, D., Schmit, J., & Vesper, N. (1999). *Going to college: How social, economic, and educational factors influence the decisions students make*. Baltimore, MD: The Johns Hopkins University Press.

Hurtado, S., Clayton-Pedersen, A., Milem, J., & Allen, W. (1999). Enacting Diverse Learning Environments: Improving the Climate for Racial/Ethnic Diversity in Higher Education. *ASHE-ERIC Higher Education Report 26, No. 8*. Washington, D.C.: The George Washington University, Graduate School of Education and Human Development.

Integrated Postsecondary Education Data Systems (IPEDS) (1997–1998). U.S. Department of Education. National Center for Education Statistics. *Fall Enrollment Survey*. Washington, D.C.: U.S. Government Printing Office.

Kane, T. (1995). *Rising public college tuition and college entry: How well do public subsidies promote access to college?* NBER Working Paper 5164. Cambridge, MA: National Bureau of Economic Research.

Mare, R. (1995). Changes in Educational Attainment and School Enrollment. In: R. Farley (Ed.), *State of the Union: America in the 1990s* (1st ed., Vol. I: Economic Trends). New York: Russell Sage.

McLeod, P., & Lobel, S. (1996). Ethnic Diversity and Creativity in Small Groups. *Small Group Research, 27*, Issue 2 (May), 248.

National Center for Education Statistics. U.S. Department of Education (1997). *Access to Postsecondary Education for the 1992 High School Graduates*. NCES 98–105 by Lutz Berkner & Lisa Chavez (MPR Associates, Inc.). Washington, D.C.: U.S. Government Printing Office.

National Center for Education Statistics. U.S. Department of Education (1998). *Digest of Education Statistics* (Table 207). Washington, D.C.: U.S. Government Printing Office.

National Center for Education Statistics. U.S. Department of Education (2000). *Digest of Education Statistics*. NCES 2000–031. Washington, D.C.: U.S. Government Printing Office.

National Center for Education Statistics. U.S. Department of Education (2000a). *NAEP 1999 Trends in Aademic Progress: Three Decades of Student Performance*. NCES 2000–469 by J. Campbell, C. Hombo & J. Mazzeo. Washington, D.C.: U.S. Government Printing Office.

Nettles, M., Perna, L., & Edelin, K. (1997). Based on Educational Testing Service SDQ Database 1997. *The Role of Affirmative Action in Expanding Student Access at Selective Colleges and Universities*. Washington, D.C.: The Frederick D. Patterson Research Institute of UNCF.

Pascarella, E., & Terenzini, P. (1991). *How college affects students: Findings and insights from twenty years of research*. San Francisco, Jossey-Bass.

Phillippe, K. (1997). *National Profile of Community Colleges: Trends & Statistics 1997–1998*. Washington, D.C.: Community College Press.

Public Agenda, National Center for Public Policy and Higher Education, Consortium for Policy Research in Education, and National Center for Postsecondary Improvement (2000). *Great Expectations: How the Public and Parents – White, African American, and Hispanic – View Higher Education*. A report by public agenda (May).

Rendon, L. (1992). From the Barrio to the Academy: Revelations of a Mexican-American Scholarship Girl. In: L. S. Zwerling & H. B. London (Eds), *First-Generation Students: Confronting the Cultural Issues* (pp. 55–64). New Directions for Community Colleges (No. 80). San Francisco: Jossey-Bass.

Rendon, L. (1994). Validating Culturally Diverse Students: Toward a New Model of Learning and Student Development. In: *Innovative Higher Education* (Vol. 19, No. 1).

Rendon, L., Jalomo, R., & Nora, A. (1999). Theoretical Considerations in the Study of Minority Student Retention in Higher Education. In: J. Braxton (Ed.), *Rethinking the Departure Puzzle: New Theory and Research on College Student Retention*. Knoxville, TN: Vanderbilt University Press.

Rhodes, N. (1992). Introduction. In: S. Worchel, W. Wood & J. Simpson (Eds), *Group Process and Productivity* (pp. 95–111). Newbury Park, CA: Sage.

Rodriguez, R. (1974–1975). Going Home Again: The New American Scholarship Boy. *The American Scholar, 44*, 15–28.

Terenzini, P., Rendon, L., Upcraft, M., Miller, S., Allison, K., Gregg, P., & Jalomo, R. (1994). The Transition to College: Diverse Students, Diverse Stories. *Research in Higher Education, 35*(1).

Tinto, V. (1993). *Leaving college: Rethinking the causes and cures of student attrition* (2nd ed.). Chicago: University of Chicago Press.

Turner, S. (1998). *Does federal aid affect the price students pay for college?* Evidence from the Pell Program. (November). Mimeo.

U.S. Bureau of the Census. Current Population Reports (1999). *School enrollment – Social and economic characteristics of students* (September), 20–521. Detailed Tables. Washington, D.C.: U.S. Government Printing Office.

Watson, W., Kumar, R., & Michaelsen, L. (1993). Cultural Diversity's Impact on Interaction Process and Performance: Comparing Homogeneous and Diverse Task Groups. *Academy of Management Journal, 36*, 590–602.

RESOURCE SHARES AND EDUCATIONAL ATTAINMENT: THE U.S. LATINO POPULATION IN THE TWENTY-FIRST CENTURY

Rubén O. Martinez and Adalberto Aguirre, Jr.

INTRODUCTION

The last decade has witnessed a tremendous increase in the numbers of Latino persons in the U.S. population. Between 1990 and 2000 the Latino population increased from 22.4 million persons to 32.8 million persons, an increase of 47% (U.S. Bureau of the Census, 2001a, 1991). American society has been slow in opening its eyes to see Latinos as participants in its social fabric. During the 1990s Latinos became visibly noticeable in places from which they had been relatively absent, or at least from places where one would not expect to find them in sizable numbers. Latinos became noticeable in the 1990s in cities such as Memphis, Tennessee, Bentonville, Arkansas, and Raleigh, North Carolina (Tobar, 2001). Cook County in Illinois, that includes the city of Chicago, is home to over one million Latinos (Branch-Brioso, 2001). If Cook county is grouped with the counties of Los Angeles, Miami-Dade, and Harris (TX), then all four counties would account for 22% of the Latinos living in the United States. The 1990s was thus a decade that not only witnessed the Latino population's growth in the U.S., it also witnessed the emerging reshaping of U.S. society by Latinos (Bustos & Mathis, 2000; Tobar, 1999).

Latinos in Higher Education, Volume 3, pages 37–55.
Copyright © 2003 by Elsevier Science Ltd.
All rights of reproduction in any form reserved.
ISBN: 0-7623-0980-6

Despite the Latino population's growth in the United States, the population continues to face obstacles to its participation in U.S. society. Latinos are the victims of language and racial discrimination (Bender, 1996; Cornell & Bratton, 1999; Soto, 1997). Latino workers, especially women, are sexually harassed in the workplace by Anglo workers (Greenhouse, 2000). Latinos are rejected more often than similar white applicants for conventional mortgage loans or home refinancing loans (Feigenbaum, 1999; Grillo, 2000). Mexican immigrants are the targets of white vigilante groups and recent immigration policies (DePalma, 2000; Doyle, 1997; Gearty, 2000). As a result, despite increasing their numbers, Latinos continue to be in a precarious position in U.S. society.

We have set two tasks for ourselves in this essay. Our first task is to discuss the Latino population's share of valued resources in U.S. society. Implicit in our discussion is the argument that a minority population's share of valued resources determines its vulnerability to prejudice and discrimination. For example, a low share of valued resources, such as income or education, increases a minority population's exposure to prejudicial attitudes and institutional discriminatory practices that exploit and oppress the population. To this end, we focus on key indicators that characterize the resource shares of Latinos in the United States.

By examining the resource shares of Latinos we can address the second task of this essay: to contextualize the educational condition of Latinos in the United States. In contextualizing the Latino educational condition we demonstrate the operation of social forces, such as racial stratification, in the structuring of educational outcomes. In contextualizing the Latino educational condition we argue for the need to challenge educational institutions in meeting their responsibility to educating a growing population of Latino students.

RESOURCE SHARES OF LATINOS

Two indicators that are often used to measure a population's quality of life are income and poverty. Regarding income, the economic prosperity of the 1990s missed the Latino population. The median earnings of full-time year-round Latino workers decreased as a proportion of White workers' median earnings between 1990 and 2000, from 70% to 63% respectively (Aguirre & Turner, 2001; U.S. Bureau of the Census, 2001a). Similarly, between 1995 and 1998 the median Latino household net income decreased by 24%, from $12,170 to $9,200 (Walsh, 2000). Ironically, according to Walsh (2000), "Even as the wealth of the median Latino household was falling, the Latino community's total wealth was rising . . . Latino household income (total wealth per household) rose from $61,000 in 1995 to $86,000 in 1998" (p. A16). Note that *wealth* refers to a household's total assets – houses, cars, television sets, bank accounts, etc. The decrease in Latino net income coupled with an increase in Latino household wealth suggests that *indebtedness* may have also increased among Latino households. That is, if net income is decreasing, but wealth, as measured by material possessions, is increasing, then accumulating greater debt becomes the most likely vehicle for increasing household wealth. As a result, increasing Latino household wealth may be hiding the increasing indebtedness of Latino households.

Instability in a population's economic health, especially increasing indebtedness, increases a population's chances of falling into poverty. That is, instability in a population's economic health makes it more susceptible to social forces that can increase a population's chances of becoming poor. Table 1 presents the poverty rates for the White, Black, and Latino populations. One can observe in Table 1 that the poverty rate for the White and Black populations decreased between 1990 and 2000, but remained relatively flat for the Latino population for the same time period. One can also observe that the economic prosperity of the 1990s appears to have had a greater effect on reducing the poverty rate for the Black population than for either the White or Latino populations.

Another indicator of a population's quality of life is the population's location in a society's occupational structure. In Table 2 one can observe that Latinos are less likely than either White or Black persons to have professional or white-collar occupations. In contrast, Latinos are more likely than either White or Black persons to have blue-collar occupations. In particular, more than half of Latino persons had blue-collar occupations in both 1990 and 2000. The association of professional and white-collar occupations with higher pay, more job security, and better fringe benefits suggests that the disproportionate representation of Latinos in blue-collar occupations may restrict their access to comfort factors, such as retirement plans, that could enhance their quality of life (McNamara, 1999).

Another indicator of a population's quality of life is the educational outcomes of persons in the population. One can observe in Table 3 that educational outcomes for Latinos at the high school and college levels lag behind those of

Table 1. Poverty Rates by Race and Ethnicity, 1990 and 2000.

Year	White	Black	Latino
1990	10%	31%	24%
2000	8%	24%	23%

Source: Aguirre and Turner, 2001; U.S. Bureau of the Census, 2001a.

Table 2. Occupational Distribution by Race and Ethnicity, 1990 and 2000.*

	White		Black		Latino	
	1990	2000	1990	2000	1990	2000
Occupation						
Professional	33%	33%	23%	22%	16%	14%
White-collar	21%	30%	32%	29%	19%	25%
Blue-collar	46%	37%	45%	49%	65%	61%

* Persons 16 years old and older.
Occupational Labels:
Professional = Executive, Administrative, and Managerial Occupations.
White-collar = Technical Sales and Administrative Support Occupations.
Blue-collar = Operator, Laborer, Craft, Farming, and Service Occupations.

Source: Aguirre and Turner, 2001; U.S. Bureau of the Census, 2001a, b.

Table 3. Educational Attainment by Race and Ethnicity, 1990 and 2000.*

	High School**			College**		
	White	Black	Latino	White	Black	Latino
1990	79%	66%	54%	22%	11%	12%
2000	88%	72%	57%	28%	14%	11%

* Persons 25 years old and older.
** 4 or more years.

Source: Aguirre and Turner, 2001; U.S. Bureau of the Census, 2001a, 2000.

the White and Black populations. An examination of the relative differences in educational outcomes between 1990 and 2000 shows that Latinos had the smallest increase at the high school level, but experienced a small decrease at the college level. Interestingly, the decrease in educational outcomes at the college level for Latinos is overshadowed by the increase in their outcomes at the high school level between 1990 and 2000.

The data in Table 4 also illustrate the gap in educational outcomes between the White and Black populations, and the Latino population. One can observe in Table 4 that the gap in high school completion rates between Whites and Blacks became smaller between 1971 and 2000, from 23% to 7%. By comparison, the gap in high school completion rates between Whites and Latinos remained relatively unchanged from 1971 to 2000, from 34% to 31%. The gap

Table 4. Educational Outcomes by Race and Ethnicity, 1971–2000.

Educational Outcomes	1971			2000		
	White	Black	Latino	White	Black	Latino
High School Completers	82%	59%	48%	94%	87%	63%
High School Completers With Some College	45%	31%	31%	68%	61%	52%
High School Completers With Bachelor's Degree or Higher	23%	12%	11%	36%	21%	15%

Source: U.S. Department of Education, 2001.

in rates for high school completers with some college from 1971 to 2000 became smaller between Whites and Blacks, but became larger between Whites and Latinos. The gap in rates for high school completers with a bachelor's degree or higher increased between Whites and Blacks, and Whites and Latinos. However, the gap between Whites and Latinos almost doubled from 1971 to 2000. In general, as the gap in educational outcomes from 1971 to 2000 closed between Whites and Blacks, it increased between Blacks and Latinos.

Given our characterization of quality of life indicators for the Latino population, how may one portray the Latino population in the U.S.? First, the Latino population enjoys fewer resource shares than other populations in the United States. Second, the Latino population's resource shares are an outcome of the population's location in occupations that have limited access to benefits, such as health care and retirement plans, that could improve the population's quality of life opportunities in the U.S. The Latino population's resource shares are also the result of educational outcomes that lag behind those of other populations. From a sociological perspective, there is an unavoidable association between these indicators – higher educational outcomes increase the chances of acquiring professional and white-collar occupations that enhance a population's income and access to factors that improve a population's quality of life. Conversely, weak links between the indicators increase a population's at-risk status in society by limiting the population's access to resource shares. As a result, the Latino population's limited income gains, a persistent poverty rate, its location near the bottom of the occupational structure, and lagging educational outcomes exacerbates the Latino population's precarious position in U.S. society.

THE CONDITION OF LATINO EDUCATION

Just as there are constraints on the Latino population's resource shares in U.S. society, there are innumerable challenges facing the Latino population's pursuit of educational attainment. While the absolute numbers of Latino students enrolling at educational institutions in the U.S. have increased over time, especially in the past four decades, the gap in educational attainment between the Latino and White populations has not closed. For example, the gap in high school graduation levels between Latinos and Whites increased from 29% in 1980 to 31% in 2000 (Aguirre & Turner, 2001; U.S. Bureau of the Census, 2001a). Similarly, the gap in educational attainment at the college level between Latinos and Whites increased from 9% in 1980 to 17% in 2000. As such, the gap in educational attainment between Latinos and Whites has increased over the last two decades.

The gap in educational attainment between Latinos and Whites assumes greater importance, especially at the K-12 grade levels, if one considers that Latinos are projected to comprise 54% of the students in grades K-12 by the year 2030, with Whites comprising 30% of the K-12 enrollment (Valverde, 2001). The challenge is thus to understand how social forces impact the educational condition of the Latino population. Some of the social forces we will discuss in the following pages that impact the educational condition of the Latino population are a system of racial stratification that characterizes U.S. society, the lack of a robust pipeline of well-educated Latino students coming out of the secondary schools, cultural and social gaps between Latino students and institutions of higher education, and the lack of adequate academic and financial support for Latino students at institutions of higher education.

RACIAL STRATIFICATION

Despite claims that racism has been eliminated in U.S. society, racial stratification structures and processes continue to impact the lives of Latinos. The effect of group discrimination experienced by Latinos in U.S. society is observable in a racial division of labor, public housing segregation, language barriers in the workplace, and in differential patterns and outcomes in education and the criminal justice system (Aguirre & Baker, 2000; Almaguer, 1994; Chapa & Valencia, 1993; Perea, 1998; Rodriguez, 1992). Despite social policy efforts, such as affirmative action and equal employment opportunity rules, to reduce barriers in the opportunity structure across major institutions, racial stratification persists, and continues to shape the participation of Latinos in U.S. society.

A truism in the social sciences is that educational achievement and attainment are closely associated with socio-economic status. The reason is obvious; there is greater access to more resources, e.g. resource shares, as one ascends the socio-economic ladder, from those in the household to those in the schools that the children attend. The racial division of labor generally limits the resources that Latino families can attain and the opportunities that they can pursue. Limited resources, relatively speaking, limit educational attainment, and low educational attainment limits socio-economic status. It's a mutually reinforcing process that is difficult to break once it is set in motion.

Racial stratification also impacts the perspectives, motivational levels, and identities of Latinos. Responses by ethnic minorities to American racism sometimes combine with anti-intellectual biases in the U.S. that have their roots in working-class culture, the American education system itself and in American anti-elitism (Hofstadter, 1963; Silberman, 1970). Among members of the working class are psychological defense mechanisms that not only help them rationalize their levels of relatively low educational attainment, but contribute to the low outcomes themselves. Among ethnic groups, such as Latinos, their roots also include anti-white reactions engendered by White racism. For Latinos, this bias is imbued with a need to distance themselves from things considered *White*, and Latino youth, especially as they experience the individuation process of adolescence, may come to associate academic work with Whites and consciously seek to form an authentic personal identity apart from the dominant culture. As such, Latino students who work hard to perform well in school may be stigmatized as *whitewashed*, and informal norms are invoked to nudge them back into a Latino cultural environment. While much more research is needed in this area, we know that minority responses to white racism do include oppositional cultural stances.

Unfortunately, Latino youth sometimes fail to recognize that potential for intellectual development is a key human attribute, and that all humans should strive to develop their innate capacities to their highest level. What Latino youth are reacting to, however, is the racial environment that engulfs them and limits not only their intellectual development but also their own perceptions of their academic capacities. Consequently, they may adopt anti-social behaviors (gang membership, drug use, etc.) that are not consistent with the rigors and demands of high-level intellectual growth. These behaviors are also outcomes of family environments, where educational expectations and the organization of home life frequently reflect the educational experiences of the parents and the stresses they face in everyday life (Fuller & Eggers-Pierola, 1996). There may be a lack of structure at home that effectively promotes academic behaviors (Perez & Pinzon, 1997). While Latino parents may hope for educational achievement among their children, these hopes often are not manifested in behavioral requirements and expectations that lead to academic achievement (Hurtado, Figueroa & Garcia, 1996; Hurtado & Garcia, 1994).

By the time Latino youth attend an institution of high education, anti-intellectual attitudes and behaviors are part of their academic repertoire, one that is attended by relatively poor academic skills, creating a syndrome that can only be overcome through systematic and individualized academic support by the institution. Of course, the bias is not inherent in Latino culture itself, but is a response to the racial environment that sets it in motion. The anti-intellectual attitudes and behaviors are the result of years of schooling in environments comprised of low teacher expectations and compliance-oriented, mindless pedagogical environments that constitute academic racism in K-12 systems in this country. As such, primary and secondary schools systems produce outcomes that postsecondary systems are expected to overcome if they are to promote academic achievement among Latino college students. While some states are taking steps to ensure that students and schools are held responsible for learning through minimum competency testing, this approach may have unintended consequences that could worsen the condition of Latino education (Martinez, 2001b).

LIMITED PIPELINE FROM SECONDARY SCHOOLS

The educational experiences of Latino students in the K-12 grades simply do not result in outcomes that yield robust numbers of well-educated students who can move effortlessly into institutions of higher education without requiring substantial amounts of academic support. For example, in California, a very small percent (4%) of Latinos completing high school are eligible for admission to one of the campuses in the University of California system (Tien, 1999). In contrast, nearly one-third of Asian American high school graduates in California are eligible for admission to the University of California. This difference in admissions eligibility is not only unacceptable, it is a telling outcome on the K-12 schooling process in California and, indirectly, on the rest of the nation.

The situation is actually worse than the California example conveys because the eligibility rates are based on those students who complete high school. The problem is that Latino students have one of the worst high school completion rates in the country. Nearly 50% of Latino students who begin the 9th grade do not complete the requirements for a high school diploma four years later. For example, 55% of Latino students that started the 9th grade earned a high school diploma in 1999 (Kaufman, Kwon, Klein & Chapman, 2000). Comparable figures for other populations were: Whites (82%), Blacks (73%), and Asians (88%). Consequently, the educational system fails at almost one-half of Latino students who begin high school, and most likely under educates the majority of those who persist until completion. Is it any wonder that the racial division of labor is reproduced generation after generation?

The notion of functional illiteracy became vogue in the 1980s, and connotes the mediocrity of our nation's school systems. This mediocrity is best captured by the performance of Latino students on standardized tests. Grades do not accurately reflect the performance levels of students on a universal scale. Instead, they reflect the standards of the schools and the politics of grading (Desimone, 1999). Parent involvement in school activities, for instance, is linked positively to grades, but not to scores on standardized tests. Standardized tests, on the other hand, are less place-bound in their utility and capture competencies and skills more effectively than do localized grading systems. Studies show that there is a significant achievement gap on standardized tests between Latino and White students (Campbell, Hombo & Mazzeo, 2000; Ferguson, 2001).

National Assessment of Educational Progress (NAEP) data show that between 1975, the first year that Hispanics were distinguished separately, and 1996, the "Hispanic-White gap" in reading and mathematics narrowed by 27 and 35%, respectively (Desimone, 1999). The pattern is not consistent, however, with some progress made during the 1980s, but which almost disappeared in the 1990s, when there was almost no progress. Generally, the factors that contributed to the gains in the 1980s are attributed to reduced class sizes, racial desegregation, and more demanding coursework (Grissmer, Flanagan & Williamson, 1998).

Reduced class size, among other things, is viewed as an important strategy for improving the academic performance of under-performing students. In 1998, President Clinton approved an educational spending plan that included $1.2 billion for needy schools to hire more teachers in order to reduce class size. Although researchers are not always in agreement about the generalized effects of reduced class size they tend to be clear about one thing: class sizes of 20 or less contribute to higher achievement among children from disadvantaged backgrounds and ethnic minority children, especially in the early years of schooling (Achilles, Finn, Bain & Pate, 1997–1998; Bennett, 1995). Reduced class sizes, however, must be supported by teachers who adapt their instructional approaches to smaller classes. Since discipline is somewhat easier in smaller classes, teachers must focus on meeting the needs of students through instructional reinforcement, student class participation, feedback and correction. Reduced class size must be supported through professional development among teachers, especially in schools with large numbers of students from poor families, where a disproportionate number of teachers without full credentials are struggling to promote student learning (Bowie, 2001; Grace, 2001; Sahagun & Helfand, 2000).

The desegregation of public schools during the 1960s and the 1970s reversed itself during the 1980s and 1990s. Latino students in the 1980s and 1990s were more likely than White students to attend "schools of concentrated poverty" (Orfield, Schley, Glass & Reardon, 1994). According to Orfield, Bachmeier, James and Eide (1997), segregation in America's schools has been increasing, with Latino students becoming more isolated in high poverty schools than other students throughout the country. This is a profoundly disturbing trend, as the nation appears to be moving toward the polarized society of the mid-Twentieth Century. This trend magnifies the educational needs of Latino students with limited-English proficiencies, who frequently attend schools that are limited in their capacity to address the educational needs of these students (Ruiz-de-Velasco & Clewell, 2000).

Moreover, with the expansion of high stakes testing, Latino students, as well as other minority students, may be unfairly punished for attending inferior schools (Martinez, 2001a). High stakes testing may seem like a laudable attempt to ensure that all students achieve minimum competency levels, however, unanticipated negative consequences may include increased dropout rates, with lower high school completion rates among Latino students. Treating students as equals when in fact there are structured inequalities may simply reproduce the inequities that already persist in society. The use of high-stakes testing may be inappropriate in a context where differential educational opportunities are structured along racial lines, with Latinos attending poverty schools which have fewer resources and a greater proportion of non-credentialed teachers (Lopez, 2000; Marosi & Smith, 2001). Moreover, a narrowing of the curriculum combined with the "drill and kill" instructional approaches may result in mindless educational experiences (Silberman, 1970). Finally, the courses taken by students, especially in the area of mathematics, may be more important for passing the tests than the test-taking sessions provided by teachers. Put simply, Latino students must be expected to take "gateway courses" that will develop the academic skills that will not only show on standardized tests but will prepare them for college.

ACCESS TO POSTSECONDARY EDUCATIONAL INSTITUTIONS

Latino students are concentrated in community colleges and "access universities" across the country. In the fall 1976, 55% of Latinos enrolled in postsecondary education institutions were found in two-year community colleges, compared with 34% of Whites and 42% of Blacks. In the fall 1997, the proportion of Latinos enrolled in two-year community colleges was 57%, compared with 37% of Whites and 42% of Blacks (The Chronicle of Higher Education, 2000). To put it bluntly, Latino students are concentrated at third- and fourth-tier institutions, or lower. The majority of them simply have not been academically prepared to meet the admissions requirements of more selective institutions. There are two key relationships that characterize the types of institutions of higher education that Latinos typically attend: (1) the dropout rates tend to be higher; and (2) and the graduation rates tend to be lower (Aguirre & Martinez, 1993). Not unexpectedly, Latino enrollments at institutions of higher education reflect the system of racial stratification in the larger society and, to some extent, parallel the segregation patterns of the K-12 grades.

Despite the relative lack of competitive pressure exerted by Latinos for admission to selective postsecondary education institutions, White Americans mobilized to close the admissions doors to these institutions by attacking Affirmative Action admissions programs on the basis of reverse racism and individual merit, prevailing during the last years of the 20th century by passing referenda that exclude race as a factor in the allocation of opportunities and resources (Aguirre, 2000; Harris & Naragon, 1999–2000; Tsang & Dietz, 2001). The *contested terrain* of college admissions is one in which, living in a Post-Hopwood society, Whites are the victims and minorities are the opportunists.

By arguing that group preferences, or quotas as some critics tend to call them, violate principles of individual merit, anti-Affirmative Action forces have carved out a narrow arena for attacking social policy programs intended to expand opportunities for members of groups who have been and continue to be subjected to institutional racism (Bell, 1997; Weiss, 1997). Ironically, Charles Murray (1984) and other critics refer to proponents of Affirmative Action as "the new racists," claiming that these programs subject ethnic minorities to "impressions of inferiority." This is a fascinating argument. With Latinos experiencing declines in income, increased segregation, educational racism, social injustice, police brutality, racial profiling, and nativistic movements by White Americans, the proponents of the "New Civil Rights Movement" are concerned about "impressions of inferiority."

For example, the movement to subject ethnic minorities to racial profiling by law enforcement officials brings the tension between color-blind inclusion and racial exclusion into sharp focus. The use of racial profiling techniques to target ethnic minorities undermines the argument of individual merit that emphasizes the individual and not group membership. To resist using race as a factor in addressing historical exclusion by appealing to color-blind approaches based on individual merit and then to support racial profiling is a contradictory stance that ultimately promotes the continued exclusion and oppression of ethnic minorities.

With respect to higher education, the proposed solution, which has found support in courts across the country, is to treat "historical unequals" as "equals." That is, to treat individuals who have had differential opportunities in life on the basis of racial structures as equals by making admissions decisions based on the respective merits of each individual's accomplishments through the use of common measuring instruments, such as standardized test scores. Given that academic achievement is closely linked to socio-economic status, and given that the socio-economic status of ethnic minorities is primarily the result of White racism (a group phenomenon), the solution effectively reproduces the structures of inequality that has kept ethnic minorities out of selective institutions in the first place.

How this nation addresses the tension between issues of group equality/inequality (equity) and individual merit (excellence) will determine its future relative to race relations. A starting point would be the recognition that racism is still part of this society's daily life, and that color-blind solutions ignore this fact. Additionally, the fact that racism exists at multiple levels requires that social policy programs address barriers at institutional, structural and group levels and not just at the individual level. Even the percentage admissions plans adopted by some states avoid the realities of today's racism by intentionally perpetuating its future.

CULTURE CLASH

Higher education clings to its middle-class roots and its "sink or swim" culture. Unfortunately, the cultural background of the majority of Latino youths is not aligned with the demands and approaches of institutions of higher education in general (Murdock & Hoque, 1999; Sinclair, Sidanius & Levin, 1998). For instance, working-class Latino youth have been socialized in compliance-oriented schooling and family environments where importance is accorded to events when they are told to attend or participate. On the other hand, the culture of the academy is suggestive and invitational. The professor who suggests to these students that they should attend a poetry reading will most likely be disappointed by the number of students who show up for the event. The students will most likely appreciate the invitation, but will interpret it as relatively unimportant since they were not told to attend. Had the event been important enough to warrant their attendance, then they would have been told to attend.

Interestingly, the professor is likely to feel uncomfortable "ordering" the students to attend, as s/he most likely prefers the middle-class culture that is suggestive and values personal initiative among the students themselves. Seldom is the problem understood in terms of a cultural clash. Instead, the professor will conclude that the students are disinterested and lazy. Yet, the students may genuinely want to learn. They simply are not experienced at making crucial decisions about education, and they probably feel uncomfortable within the academy anyway. The faculty and the students, then, are "like ships passing in the night."

This cultural gap can be addressed by systematically aligning the "front years" of the college educational experience with the culture of the students coming into the institution. That is, providing a structured learning environment where students are required to engage in and participate in specific activities. As the students progress through the institution they also are taught middle class values and culture, and the behavioral norms they are expected to adhere to during the junior and senior years. By addressing the cultural gap directly and explicitly, communications between students and faculty improve and students develop a better sense of their own educational experiences. (Gloria & Rodriguez, 2000; Rendon, 1999).

LACK OF ACADEMIC SUPPORT

The academic support needs of Latino and other working-class students often overwhelm the resources of the institutions of higher education they attend. Not only do many of them require remediation in basic skill areas, but those who do not often require academic support beyond the level of remediation. Unfortunately, policymakers have prohibited some colleges and universities from providing students with the remedial support that they need. The underlying view is to "force" secondary schools to graduate students with better academic skills. However, until that occurs, those students without the requisite skills to perform satisfactorily in colleges and universities will become the casualties of an educational system that fails to address their educational needs.

Academic support requires substantial resources. Math, writing, and advising centers, for instance, require trained staff members, computer labs, diagnostic tools, resources to follow through on individualized academic improvement plans, and the capacity to remain open extended hours. The capacity of 3rd and 4th tier institutions, where Latino college students are concentrated, to meet the academic needs of students is limited by resource constraints. The massification of higher education that occurred during the second half of the 20th Century increased the number of public institutions and the diversity of students, but the post-massification period is characterized by budgetary retrenchment and increased stratification of higher education itself (Zemsky, 1998).

Over the past two decades, state governments have substantially reduced the relative share of revenues they contribute to higher education (McPherson & Schapiro, 1999). Regarding Latino students, relative decreases in state funding for higher education ignore the fact that increasing the numbers of college educated Latinos is an economic investment not an economic liability (Sorensen, Brewer, Carroll & Bryton, 1995). This has forced institutions of higher education to press forward with tuition increases as much as they are allowed. The current situation, then, is one where Latino students face increasing tuition rates and limited academic support at the institutions they attend. Investments by the federal government in financial aid and in institutional capacity building, especially with the shift away from need-based tuition aid, are not sufficient to meet the educational needs of the masses of students seeking a college education. The net result of all of these changes, according to McPherson and Schapiro (1999), is that today's American system of finance for higher education "is highly responsive to the demands of middle- and upper middle-income families for help, but much less equipped to respond to the needs of lower-income families for assistance with their college investments" (p. 2). If this trend persists, it is difficult to envision improvements in the educational attainment levels of the Latino population over the next several years.

CONCLUDING REMARKS

Dramatic increases in the number of Latino persons in U.S. society have created tremendous pressures for change across American institutions, pressures that will intensify throughout the 21st century if Latinos are successful in improving their quality of life opportunities. By the middle of the 21st century, Latinos are expected to comprise the majority of the students in elementary and secondary education institutions. The entry of Latinos into postsecondary education institutions, however, will continue to be slow. Latinos are not to blame for their limited progress through educational institutions in U.S. society. Rather, educational institutions have not been able to effectively transform themselves to meet the educational needs of Latino students.

Despite numerous initiatives by federal and state governments, philanthropic foundations, and businesses, educational institutions remain White and Eurocentric in their institutional culture. The organizational culture in educational institutions is shaped by forces of social and cultural resistance that are fueled by conservative nativistic sentiment in society. If this country is to produce generations of well-educated Latino students that can contribute substantively to a vibrant national economy, one that is integrated within a global economy, then educational institutions must overcome their racially exclusionary and repressive practices that prevent Latino students from learning at the highest levels possible.

At the level of higher education, tensions between equity and excellence must be resolved by removing structures and altering practices that limit the participation of Latino students. American society needs to recognize that these structures and practices occur at multiple levels, including individual, institutional, and group levels. The current emphasis on promoting individual merit through a color-blind approach ignores the persistence of racism and the benefits gained by White persons in U.S. society. A vision of an American society in the 21st century free of racial bias utilizes the racial legacy of the past and the persistence of racism in the present to transform its racialized social fabric.

Finally, the future for Latinos in 21st century U.S. society is clouded largely due to their limited resource shares in society and stagnant educational attainment. The Latino population's precarious position in U.S. society needs immediate attention; it needs transformation not transition. We have argued in this essay that increased access to resource shares and higher educational attainment are vital to improving a population's quality of life opportunities. Improving the Latino population's quality of life opportunities would help it raise its self-awareness, especially its desire to seek inclusion in U.S. society. More importantly, improving the Latino population's quality of life opportunities will raise the population's confidence, and feeling of self-worth, in challenging U.S. society to meet its needs and expectations. On the other hand, the inability to improve the Latino population's quality of life opportunities will continue the population's subordinate position in U.S. society. As such, increasing numbers of Latinos in U.S. society will not serve to challenge U.S. society. Instead, they will simply enhance the Latino population's vulnerability to prejudice and discrimination in everyday life and in educational institutions.

REFERENCES

Achilles, C. M., Finn, C. M., Bain, J. D., & Pate, H. (1997–1998). Using class size to reduce the equity gap. *Educational Leadership, 55*, 40–43.

Aguirre, A., Jr. (2000). Academic storytelling: A critical race theory story of affirmative action. *Sociological Perspectives, 43*, 319–339.

Aguirre, A., Jr., & Turner, J. (2001). *American ethnicity: The dynamics and consequences of discrimination* (3rd ed.). New York: McGraw-Hill.

Aguirre, A., Jr., & Baker, D. (Eds) (2000). *Latinos in the criminal justice system. The Justice Professional, 13* (special issue).

Aguirre, A., Jr., & Martinez, R. (1993). Chicanos in higher education: Issues and dilemmas for the 21st century. *ASHE-ERIC Higher Education Report No. 3*. Washington, D.C.: The George Washington University, School of Education and Human Development.

Almaguer, T. (1994). *Racial fault lines: The historical origins of white supremacy in California.* Berkeley, CA: University of California Press.

Bell, D. (1997). Protecting diversity programs from political and judicial attack. *The Chronicle of Higher Education* (April 4), B4–B5.

Bender, S. (1996). Consumer protection for Latinos: Overcoming language fraud and English-only in the marketplace. *American University Law Review, 45,* 1027–1109.

Bennett, N. (1995). Class size and the quality of educational outcomes. *Journal of Child Psychology and Psychiatry, 39,* 797–804.

Bowie, L. (2001). Group issues school report, study finds poor sites have high number of novice teachers. *The Baltimore Sun* (May 6), 1B.

Branch-Brioso, K. (2001). Mexican Americans fueled growth in Hispanic population data show. *St. Louis Post-Dispatch* (May 10), A2.

Bustos, S., & Mathis, D. (2000). Small towns shaped by influx of Hispanics. *USA Today* (May 23), 10A.

Campbell, J., Hombo, C., & Mazzeo, J. (2000). NAEP 1999 trends in academic progress: Three decades of student performance. *Education Statistics Quarterly, 2,* 31–36.

Chapa, J., & Valencia, R. (1993). Latino population growth, demographic characteristics, and educational stagnation: An examination of recent trends. *Hispanic Journal of Behavioral Sciences, 15,* 165–187.

Cornell, D., & Bratton, W. (1999). Deadweight costs and intrinsic wrongs of nativism: Economics, freedom, and legal suppression of Spanish. *Cornell Law Review, 84,* 595–695.

DePalma, A. (1997). Migrant worker debate heats up. *The Press Enterprise (Riverside, CA)* (May 24), A1, A8.

Desimone, L. (1999). Linking parental involvement with student achievement: Do race and income matter? *Journal of Educational Research, 93,* 11–30.

Doyle, M. (1997). Deportations up over last year. *The Press Enterprise (Riverside, CA)* (May 14), A3.

Dreazen, Y. (2000). Racial wealth gap huge. *The Press-Enterprise (Riverside, CA)* (March 15), A1, A10.

Feigenbaum, R. (1999). Racial disparity in loans/minorities rejected more often than whites. *Newsday* (September 16), A7.

Ferguson, R. F. (2001). Test-score trends along racial lines, 1971–1996: Popular culture and community academic standards. In: N. J. Smelser, W. J. Wilson & F. Mitchell (Eds), *American Becoming: Racial Trends and their Consequence.* (Vol. 2, pp. 348–390). Washington, D.C.: National Academic Press.

Fuller, B., & Eggers-Pierola, C. (1997). Rich culture, poor markets: Why do Latino parents forgo preschooling? *Teachers College Record, 97,* 400–418.

Garaway, G. B. (1995). The equity/excellence dialectic: Pluralism and the impact of educational reform. *Equity & Excellence in Education, 28,* 65–72.

Gearty, R. (2000). Beat victims tell tale, Mexicans thankful to be alive. *Daily News (N.Y.)* (Swptember 20), 13.

Gloria, A. (1997). Chicana academic persistence. *Education & Urban Society, 30,* 107–121.

Gloria, A., & Rodriguez, E. (2000). Counseling Latino university students: Psychosociocultural issues for consideration. *Journal of Counseling & Development, 78,* 145–154.

Grace, M. (2001). Teachers ducking certificates, fear being assigned to bad schools. *Daily News (New York)* (April 3), 2.

Greenhouse, S. (2000). Major change in labor force. *The Press Enterprise (Riverside, CA)* (September 4), A1, A6.

Gregory, S. T. (2000). Strategies for improving the racial climate for students of color in predominately White institutions. *Equity & Excellence in Education, 33,* 39–47.

Grillo, T. (2000). Study documents subprime targets minority, low-income borrowers found likeliest to get costly mortgages. *The Boston Globe* (November 19), H1.

Grissmer, D., Flanagan, A., & Williamson, S. (1998). Why did the black-white test score gap narrow in the 1970s and 1980s? In: C. Jencks & M. Phillips (Eds), *The Black-White Test Score Gap* (pp. 182–226). Washington, D.C.: Brookings Institution Press.

Harris, L., & Naragon, U. (1999–2000). Affirmative action as equalizing opportunity: Challenging the myth of preferential treatment. *National Black Law Journal, 16,* 127–143.

Hofstadter, R. (1963). *Anti-intellectualism in American life.* NewYork: Knopf.

Horton, H. W. (2000). Perspectives on the current status of the racial climate relative to students, staff, and faculty of color at predominantly White colleges/universities in America. *Equity & Excellence in Education, 33,* 35–37.

Hurtado, A., Figueroa, R., & Garcia, E. (Eds) (1996). *Strategic interventions in education: Expanding the Latina/Latino pipeline.* Oakland, CA: Office of the President, University of California Latino Eligibility Study.

Hurtado, A., & Garcia, E. (Eds) (1994). *The educational achievement of Latinos: Barriers and successes.* Oakland, CA: Office of the President, University of California Latino Eligibility Study.

Kaufman, P., Kwon, J., Klein, S., & Chapman, C. (2000). Dropout rates in the United States: 1999. *Education Statistics Quarterly, 2,* 37–42.

Kent, N. J. (1996). The new campus racism: What's going on? *Thought & Action, 12,* 83–94.

Lopez, N. (2000). The missing link: Latinos and educational opportunity programs. *Equity & Excellence in Education, 33,* 53–58.

Lowe, E. Y., Jr. (1999). Promise and dilemma: Incorporating racial diversity in selective higher education. In: E. Y. Lowe Jr. (Ed.), *Promise and Dilemma: Perspectives on Racial Diversity and Higher Education* (pp. 3–43). Princeton, NJ: Princeton University Press.

Marosi, R., & Smith, D. (2001). Study of schools cites inequities for minorities. *Los Angeles Times* (May 15), 8B.

Martinez, R. (2001a). High-stakes testing and Latino students. *The Hispanic Outlook, 11,* 21–23.

Martinez, R. (2001b). High-stakes testing and Latino students: A focus on Texas and Colorado. Paper prepared for presentation at the 15th Annual Conference of the Hispanic Association of Colleges and Universities, October, San Juan, Puerto Rico.

McNamara, M. (1999). For Latinos, retirement years not always so golden. *Los Angeles Times* (November 2), E1, E5.

McPherson, M. S., & Schapiro, M. O. (1999). *Reinforcing stratification in American higher education: Some disturbing trends.* Stanford, CA: Stanford University, National Center for Postsecondary Improvement.

McWhorter, J. H. (2000). Explaining the Black education gap. *Wilson Quarterly, 34,* 72–90.

Murdock, S. H., & Hoque, Md., N. (1999). Demographic factors affecting higher education in the United States in the twenty-first century. *New Directions for Higher Education, 108,* 5–13.

Murray, C. (1984). Affirmative Action: How preferential treatment works against blacks. *The New Republic* (Dec. 31), 18–23.

Murray, G. J. (2000). Class size: Major implications for school leaders. *NASSP Bulletin, 84,* 108–113.

Orfield, G. (1999). The resegregation of our nation's schools: A troubling trend. *Civil Rights Journal, 4,* 8–12.

Orfield, G., Bachmeier, M. D., James, D. R., & Eide, T. (1997). Deepening segregation in American public schools. *Southern Changes, 19*, 11–18.

Orfield, G., Schley, S., Glass, D., & Reardon, S. (1994). The growth of segregation in American schools: Changing patterns of separation and poverty since 1968. *Equity and Excellence in Education, 27*, 5–8.

Perea, J. (1998). American languages, cultural pluralism, and official English. In: R. Delgado & J. Stefancic (Eds), *The Latino Condition: A Critical Reader* (pp. 566–573). New York: New York University Press.

Perez, M., & Pinzon, H. (1997). Latino families: Partners for success in school settings. *Journal of School Health, 67*, 182–184.

Ramphele, M. (1999). Equity and excellence – Strange Bedfellow? A case study of South African higher education. In: E. Y. Lowe, Jr. (Ed.), *Promise and Dilemma: Perspectives on Racial Diversity and Higher Education* (pp. 145–161). Princeton, NJ: Princeton University Press.

Rendon, E. (1999). Creating successful opportunities for Latinos/Latinas in academia. *Latino Studies Journal, 10*, 75–99.

Rodriguez, H. (1992). Population, economic mobility, and income inequality: A portrait of Latinos in the United States, 1970–1991. *Latino Studies Journal, 3*, 55–86.

Ruiz-de-Velasco, J., & Clewell, B. C. (2000). *Overlooked and underserved*. Washington, D.C.: The Urban Institute.

Sahagun, L., & Helfand, D. (2000). ACLU sues state over conditions in poor schools. *Los Angeles Times* (May 6), 1A.

Silberman, C. E. (1970). *Crisis in the classroom: The remaking of American education*. New York: Random House.

Sinclair, S., Sidanius, J., & Levin, S. (1998). The influence between ethnic and social system attachment: The differential effects of hierarchy-enhancing and hierarchy-attenuating environments. *Journal of Social Issues, 54*, 741–757.

Sorensen, S., Brewer, D., Carroll, S., & Bryton, E. (1995). *Improving Hispanic participation in higher education: A desirable public investment*. Santa Monica, CA: The RAND.

Soto, L. (1997). The treatment of the Spanish language and Latinos in education in the southwest, in the workplace, and in the jury selection process. *Texas Hispanic Journal of Law and Policy, 3*, 73–90.

The Chronicle of Higher Education (2000). Almanac issue (September 1), 2000/2001.

Tien, C.-L. (1999). What a university can learn and teach about conflict and difference. In: E. Y. Lowe, Jr. (Ed.), *Promise and Dilemma: Perspectives on Racial Diversity and Higher Education* (pp. 193–198). Princeton, NJ: Princeton University Press.

Tobar, H. (2001). A lotta cultures goin' on. *Los Angeles Times* (May 16), A1, A16.

Tobar, H. (1999). Farm belt delivers the frijoles. *Los Angeles Times* (September 16), A1, A16.

Tsang, C., & Dietz, T. (2000). The unrelenting significance of minority statuses: Gender, ethnicity, and economic attainment since affirmative action. *Sociological Spectrum, 21*, 61–80.

U.S. Bureau of the Census (2001a). *The Hispanic population in the United States: March 2000*. Washington, D.C.: U.S. Government Printing Office.

U.S. Bureau of the Census (2001b). *Black Population in the United States: March 2000*. Washington, D.C.: U.S. Government Printing Office.

U.S. Bureau of the Census (2000). *Educational attainment in the United States: March 2000*. Washington, D.C.: U.S. Government Printing Office.

U.S. Bureau of the Census (1991). *The Hispanic population in the United States: March 1990*. Washington, D.C.: U.S. Government Printing Office.

U.S. Department of Education (2001). *The condition of education 2001*. Washington, D.C.: National Center for Education Statistics.

Valverde, L. (2001). The current state of Hispanic students in higher education. Paper presented at the Hispanic Border Leadership Institute Conference (May), University of California-Riverside.

Walsh, M. (2000). Latinos' net worth shrinking despite boom times. *Los Angeles Times* (March 25), A16.

Weiss, K. (1997). UC law schools' new rules cost minorities spots. *Los Angeles Times* (May 15), A1, A23.

Zemsky, R. (1998). Labor, markets and educational restructuring. *The ANNALS of the American Academy of Political and Social Science, 559*, 77–90.

THE CROSSOVER TO COLLEGE

TRANSITION POINTS FROM HIGH SCHOOL TO COLLEGE

Toni Falbo, Helen Contreras and Maria D. Avalos

INTRODUCTION

The goal of this chapter is to delineate the transition points from high school to college for American youth, in general, and for Latino high school students, in particular. We will be attempting to explain why the Latino population in the U.S. is much less likely to attain a bachelor's degree than are other Americans and what can be done to improve the educational attainment of Latino youth in the U.S.

There are several key transition points during any students' high school career that send them toward or away from participation in higher education. Three such transition points will be the focus of this chapter: full participation in high school, college preparation coursework, and college decision-making.

First of all, students need to attend classes in high school, earning credits toward graduation, for about four years before they obtain the diploma that makes them eligible for college admission. Second, in order to be successful in college, high school students need to take challenging courses as well as engage in extracurricular activities that prepare them for participation in higher education. Third, high school seniors need to learn how to select post-secondary educational institutions that meet their needs, apply to these institutions, and gain admission. Along this pathway, there are many points where students can leave the educational pipeline that conveys them toward college entrance.

Latinos in Higher Education, Volume 3, pages 59–72.
Copyright © 2003 by Elsevier Science Ltd.
All rights of reproduction in any form reserved.
ISBN: 0-7623-0980-6

For Latino students, there is substantial evidence that completing high school has been a major obstacle in the pathway to higher education. According to a recent report of the U.S. Census (Therrien & Ramirez, 2000), the Hispanic population (hereafter referred to as Latinos) is much less likely to have completed at least four years of high school than are other Americans. Overall, in 2000, 57% of the Latino population 25 years of age or older had completed at least four years of high school, while 88.4% of the non-Hispanic White (hereafter referred to as Whites) population had attained this level of education. Within the overall Latino population, there was substantial variation in completing at least four years of high school: Cuban Americans (73%), Central and South Americans, and Puerto Ricans (64.3%) and Mexican Americans (51%).

The gap in high school completion between Latino and the general U.S. population in 1999 was huge, ranging between 15 to 31 percentage points (U.S. Census Bureau, 2000). Thus, for Latinos, failure to graduate from high school is a major turning point. Any plan to increase the number of Latino students in higher education must address this problem.

Then, there is the problem of course taking in high school. There is a series of college preparatory that students must take in order to have the skills needed for successful participation in higher education. In American high schools, students are often assigned to different sequences of courses based on their standardized test scores. Because Latino youth, on the average, score lower on these tests than other students, then they are more likely to be placed in courses that do not prepare them for success in higher education (San Miguel & Valencia, 1998). There are many consequences of this tracking, including lack of academic preparation for college and discouragement from school personnel about aspirations for college. Thus, any plan to improve the rates of Latinos in higher education will have to address the problem of college preparation in American high schools.

Finally, the junior and senior year of high school for college bound students is a time for planning for college applications and decisions about which college to attend. The common American pattern is for parents to guide their children through the process of selecting which colleges to apply to, prepare for college admission tests, and complete college applications. Although there are guidance counselors at high schools, they have too many students assigned to them to provide the kind of day-to-day guidance that middle class parents typically provide. Guidance counselors can be key to helping a few, highly motivated and able Latino students select, apply, and gain admission to colleges, but in general, they cannot help the majority of Latino youth who need guidance in navigating the pathway to college. Thus, any plan to improve the rates of Latinos in higher education will have to address the problem of guidance for college planning.

THE BIG PICTURE

It is important to keep in mind that the majority of Americans have not completed a bachelor's degree. In the U.S. in 2000, only 28.1% of the White population, 25 years or older, had completed four years of college or more (Therrien & Ramirez, 2000). This means that the bulk of the American population has educational levels somewhere between high school diploma and bachelor's degree. Among Americans, there is substantial variation by race and ethnicity in terms of completing four years or more of college. For whites, in 1999, 25.9% had completed four or more years of college, 42.4% of Asian or Pacific Islanders and 15.4% of Blacks had completed this level of education (U.S. Census, 2000).

Given the relatively low percentage of Latino youth graduating from high school, it is not surprising that the percentage of Latinos who have completed four years of college is much smaller than the percentage for other groups. In 1999, only 10.9% of Latino overall had completed four years of college. However, the percentage for Cuban Americans (24.8%) was similar to that of the total American population. Unfortunately, the percentage for Puerto Ricans (11.1%) and Mexican Americans (7.1%) were much lower than the national average in 1999 of 25.2% (U.S. Census Bureau, 2000).

Since parents are key to guiding most college bound students through the college decision-making process, it is not surprising that students whose parents have attended college are more likely to attend college. College educated parents know more about the college decision-making process and know that they need to guide their children through it. Parents who never completed high school, let alone attend college, are less likely to know how to navigate the college admission process. For Latino youth in general, a significant increase in the number attending college will require that they get effective guidance through the college decision-making process from people other than their parents. Other adults, including school personnel and community leaders, will have to serve this guidance function. The Hispanic Scholarship Fund (Yachnin, 2001) has been organizing such community outreach programs for Latino high school students and has been raising money for scholarships for Latino students.

FULL PARTICIPATION IN HIGH SCHOOL

Latino youth are much more likely to leave high school before graduation than White youth. According to a recent report from the National Center for Education Statistics (Kaufman et al., 2000), several national studies of youth indicate that Latinos are at greater risk of dropping out than Whites. This report indicated that Latinos had a dropout rate of 7.8%, compared to a 4.0% for White students.

Information about the percentage of young adults who have less than a high school education has been collected since 1972, and throughout this period, the percentage of Latino young adults who do not have a high school credential is substantially higher than that of Blacks and Whites. During this time period, about 30% of Latinos, aged 16–24, lacked a high school credential. In contrast, the percentage of Whites that did not have a high school credential dropped from about 13% in 1972 to about 7% in 1999 (Kaufman et al., 2000).

These high dropout rates for Latinos can be attributed partially to the fact that many young immigrants from Mexico come to the U.S. without a high school education (Brown et al., 1980; Bennici & Strang, 1995; Strang et al., 1993; Kaufman et al., 1999). Latino youth who were born outside the U.S. are more likely to drop out of high school than Latino youth born in the U.S. (Kaufman et al., 2000). According to a study of foreign-born Latino youth (McMillen, 1995), many who were counted as dropouts had never enrolled in a U.S. school. They migrated to the U.S. in order to find employment, not to get an education.

The topic of dropping out of high school has been well researched in the educational, psychological and sociological literature of the past few decades. The variables that influence dropping out among ethnic minority students and Mexican American students in particular are very complex and interrelated. Low academic achievement has been found to play a significant role. In a recent study on this issue, Battin-Pearson et al. (2000) found that low academic achievement was the strongest predictor of dropping out of school before the 10th grade for all students. According to a recent report issued by the National Commission on the High School Senior Year (Barth et al., 2001), only 1 in 30 Latino 17 year-olds could comfortably perform multi-step problem solving and elementary algebra – as compared to 1 in 10 Whites. Furthermore, by their senior year Latino students have math and reading skills that are comparable to those of White 8th grade students.

Another main factor that has been repeatedly found to influence Latino students' academic success is socioeconomic status (SES). Students who come from low SES backgrounds are more likely to live in communities with poor housing conditions, inadequate public and social services, and schools that are severely overcrowded and under-funded (Gonzalez & Padilla, 1997; Perez & Salazar, 1997). Not surprisingly, academic achievement is significantly related to SES. In general, children from lower SES families achieve less academically than children from middle or upper SES. For example, students who are in high-poverty schools have shown very little academic progress in terms of achievement on national tests (Riley et al., 2001).

The quality of education can also be influenced by the quality of teachers in schools. For example, in a recent study by Rumberger and Thomas (2000) they found that schools in which students report a higher quality of teachers (more supportive and understanding) have a lower dropout rate than schools in which students report just an average quality of teachers. Several scholars who have conducted qualitative studies on Mexican American high school students have found that they perceive inequalities in terms of how they are treated in school. Suarez-Orozco and Suarez-Orozco found that school personnel were oftentimes "indifferent or hostile to the linguistic and other cultural needs of Mexican-origin families" (Suarez-Orozco & Suarez-Orozco, 1995). Furthermore, these students reported that they were the targets of racial prejudice by their White classmates, teachers, and other school personnel. In her qualitative study on a predominantly Mexican American high school in Houston, Texas, Valenzuela (1999) found that students often felt that many teachers were simply uncaring and unsupportive.

The issue of under-qualified teachers has also been addressed by many studies. Students in high poverty schools are more likely than other students to be taught by teachers without even a minor in their fields (Barth et al., 2001). According to the report, 40% of the teachers in high poverty schools were found to be under-qualified to teach math as compared to 28% teachers at higher income schools. In regards to predominantly minority high schools, the situation is more bleak; for example, in math and science only about half of all the teachers in schools with 90% or greater minority enrollments even meet their states' minimum requirements to teach those subjects. The disparity is evident in that 86% of teachers in schools with over 90% White students are certified in their fields with almost 70% of them holding a B.A. or B.S. in those fields.

Other factors that play a role in the propensity for Latino youth to drop out of school is lack of English proficiency and the lack of parental involvement in their children's education. Many limited English proficient and bilingual students do not receive adequate resources in school and receive instruction by teachers who lack the proper credentials (White House Report December, 2000). Many Mexican-origin parents do not have the necessary school experience and "know-how" in order to advocate for their children in schools (Romo & Falbo, 1996; Romo, 1984).

Other researchers believe that parents who have higher levels of education are better equipped to help their children succeed in school. Gandara reports: "middle and upper-class parents who have been successful in school understand the 'hidden curriculum' of schooling and know how to coach their children in appropriate responses to the system" (Gandara, 1995, p. 26). Here parents are teaching their children how to "deal with the system" so to speak.

According to Trueba (1990), many researchers who attempt to explain the lack of academic achievement among Latinos and other ethnic minority youth point to cultural deficits – in other words there is something inherently wrong within the students' culture. Likewise Suarez-Orozco and Suarez-Orozco (1995) report that some scholars have accused Latino families of not valuing education and have pointed to their lack of fostering independence and individualism among their children – which are framed as prerequisites for achievement.

The culture deficit theory has been upstaged by the recent trend in the past decade of examining school and education inequalities as a source of ethnic minority school underachievement and school attrition. More recently, considerable attention has been given to sociological based theories of social inequalities within schools, namely social and cultural capital theories and the role of schools in maintaining social class differences. Proponents of this view argue that ethnic minority children do poorly in school because of the class structure of capitalist society (Valdez, 1996).

Stanton-Salazar and Dornbusch (1995) examined social capital in terms of the relationships that students form with individuals in schools:

> As used here, social capital refers to social relationships from which an individual is poten-
> tially able to derive institutional support, particularly support that includes the delivery of
> knowledge-based resources, for example, guidance for college admission . . . Working class
> youths have vastly less social capital than do middle-class youths (p. 119).

Social capital within schools is a reflection of the society as a whole whereby "social distance, distrust, and latent – and not-so-latent – antagonisms rooted in our stratified society can and do manifest themselves in subtle ways in the interpersonal relationships between minority children and adolescents and institutional agents" (Stanton-Salazar, 1997, p. 14). Schooling inequalities between the dominant culture students and ethnic minority and lower SES students are seen to be rooted in social class differences.

College Preparatory Coursework

The term "tracking" has been used to define the common educational practice of sorting high school students into college bound and not college-bound. This sorting is usually done on the basis of standardized tests. These tests claim to be objective measures of the skills of students and they also claim to be predictors of a child's potential. For example, the Manual accompanying the Iowa Test of Basic Skills claims that there is a strong correlation, ranging from

0.70 to 0.80, between fourth graders' ITBS scores and their twelfth-grade ITBS scores (Scannell, 1958). Consequently, scores on these tests have been used by high schools to ". . . reflect the extent to which pupils can profit from later instruction" (Hieronymus & Hoover, 1986, p. I).

In general, children from lower SES backgrounds score lower on such norm-referenced tests than White children. In particular, Mexican American children score below Anglo children on standardized tests (Keith & Litchman, 1994; Okagaki et al., 1998; San Miguel & Valencia, 1998). According to data from the National Assessment of Educational Progress, between 1975–1996, Latino students on the average scored well below Anglo students in mathematics, reading and science (San Miguel & Valencia, 1998). As a result, White children are more likely to be sorted into the college bound group, while Latino children are more likely to be sorted into the not college bound group (Alexander et al., 1978; San Miguel & Valencia, 1998).

The consequences of being sorted into the not college bound group are profound. Often these students take low level courses that have a "dumbed down" curriculum that does not prepare them for further education. Academic tracking has been found to have negative affects specifically on the academic achievement of Mexican origin students in low SES high schools (Valenzuela, 1999; Romo & Falbo, 1996). According to Barth et al. (2001), "students who take the SAT are reporting higher and higher GPAs over the last decade, yet scores have systematically declined across all GPA categories" (p. 15). For example, based on their statistics, in the past decade the percentage of students with A+ GPAs has risen by 3% yet their SAT scores have fallen by 15 points. Furthermore, they report that the situation is worse in schools that are predominantly made up of minority and poor students where many students receive As for doing mediocre school work.

Another consequence is the reduction in the high school students' educational aspirations. Teachers treat college bound students very differently than they treat non-college bound students (Oakes, 1985; Romo & Falbo, 1996). Although this differential treatment can be subtle, most students eventually get the message that they are not the type of student that "benefits" from a higher education. Even high school students who thought that they were going to college begin to regard themselves as not worthy or qualified because their teachers regard them as NOT college bound (Harris & Rosenthal, 1985; Jussim, 1986; Rosenthal, 1985; Snyder, 1984).

What courses should high school students be taking to prepare for college? In general, high school students should be taking four years of English and Social Studies and at least two years of a foreign language. High school students should be writing papers in high school. They should be taking challenging mathematics courses, such as Algebra, Geometry, Trigonometry, Pre-Calculus, and Calculus. They should take Chemistry and some form of Physics.

Although high school students are supposed to be responsible for their own schoolwork, many high school students rely on their parents for some sort of assistance, either in the form of homework help or participation as a booster in extracurricular activities (Falbo et al., 2000). It is difficult for parents who have not completed high school to help their children with their homework. These parents never took the courses their children are taking. Furthermore, high school students whose parents were born outside the U.S. have no clue how to help their children with their U.S. History projects or their English assignments. In contrast, parents who have bachelor's degrees are more likely to have the skills and the time flexibility to help their children with school projects and assignments. Furthermore, such parents are more likely to have the resources to provide their children with home computers with Internet access (Technology Counts, 2001).

How does this affect Latino students? As reported above, Latino adults in the U.S. are much less likely than other adults to have completed a high school education. They are likely to be foreign-born. They are much less likely to have a bachelor's degree. Thus, Latino parents of high school students are less likely, on the average, to be able to provide the type of support students need to succeed at challenging coursework. This makes it harder for Latino students, on average, to succeed in the challenging courses involved in a college prepara-tory sequence of high school courses. While after-school tutoring and computer labs at school can help Latino students, these students have to have the drive to stay at school to do this work, when more advantaged students can do their work in the comfort of their homes.

In recent years there has been increased interest in having all high schools provide at least a few Advanced Placement (AP) courses. If a student takes such a course and passes the AP test, then the student gets college credit. Do students need to be taking pre-AP or AP classes in order to be prepared for college? No, AP courses are not college preparation courses; they are college courses. AP courses are college course taught in high school. State officials often encourage high schools to offer AP courses because this demonstrates to outsiders, at least, that some of the students in that high school are capable of doing college-level work.

Another form of college in high school is "dual enrollment" (Gehring, 2001). This term means that a high school student is taking some courses in high school and some courses in college. College faculty use high school classrooms during regular school hours to provide college level courses. Or, a high school student travels a few miles during his or her school day to a community college to take a course.

There are positive effects of taking AP or dual credit courses. First, at least a few high school students have the chance to be challenged at the college level. Second, if they are successful, then this should give these high school students more confidence that they are capable of college. In fact, students taking and passing AP classes or dual enrollment college courses are doing college work, while still high school students. Third, the fact that at least some students have passed college level courses should help them gain acceptance into more competitive colleges.

College Decision-Making

Traditionally, for the college bound, the junior year in high school includes the taking of the PSAT and the beginnings of consideration of which colleges are the best ones for the student to attend. Middle class parents study college guidebooks to try to find the right type of post-secondary institution for their child. Colleges and universities throughout the U.S. offer summertime tours of their campuses so that prospective applicants can get the feel of the campus and information about what constitutes a successful application. Middle class parents consider this exploration an essential part of their teen-ager's growing up. In the U.S., middle class parents expect their 18-year-olds to leave home and they want to find the right environment for their child.

During the fall of the senior year, students take their college admission tests, and begin the process of applying to the colleges that seem appropriate to them. This process of selecting, evaluating, and applying to colleges is time-consuming and expensive. Although low-income applicants can get some fees waived, they still have to pay some of the costs involved in making college applications. More competitive colleges require the applicants to write several essays in addition to completing the application. Applicants to competitive colleges need to have good grades and good college admission tests scores. They also need to have accumulated a record of extracurricular activities that matches the special features of the college. For example, a student applying to a religiously affiliated school will gain points if he or she has participated in youth activities organized by that religious group. Or, a college that emphasizes the fine arts will prefer an applicant who has taken many arts courses during their high school years.

Colleges and universities look over the high school transcripts of applicants to make sure the student has taken college preparatory coursework. Colleges are interested in the student's grade point average because this correlates strongly with the likelihood that a student will be successful in college (Zwick, 1999). Although a few universities have made college admission test scores optional, most colleges and universities require that the student provide a set of college admission scores. Colleges vary in terms of their use of these scores. Some have minimum scores, particularly minimum scores combining the math and verbal sections. Others expect to admit only students with high scores.

In terms of the Latino high school student, what is wrong with the picture painted above?

Because Latino high school students are less likely to have parents who have attended college, they are less likely to receive the parental guidance they need. Students who have parents with very little education and no English language skills are at a major disadvantage in completing college applications. Counselors and teachers can be helpful to a few students, but ultimately, they do not have the time and motivation to dedicate to each senior's college decision-making as do most college-educated parents.

The value of having college-educated parents has been noted by several recent studies. According to Wallace et al. (2000) students who have parents, family members, and friends who have gone to college have a major advantage in their pursuit of a college degree. These students have the benefit of having live-in or close contact role models to guide them through the college planning and decision process. Similarly, Galotti and Mark (1994) reported that students whose parents were highly educated relied on their parents more as a source of information than did students with less educated parents. Thus, the fact that Latino high school students are more likely to have parents who do not have a college degree puts these students at a disadvantage in the college decision-making process.

Fortunately, some Latino high school students are able to gain admission to college and even go on to complete post-graduate education, although their parents had little education. Gandara (1995) studied Latinos who had completed graduate degrees and found that although their "parents had few resources and relatively little experience with schooling themselves, most of what they could offer their children was verbal support and encouragement for their educational undertakings" (p. 39). Another major type of support given by their parents was the instilling of values of hard work and persistence. For many who made it through college, parents indirectly influenced their educational experience by placing them in "better schools" that had more college preparatory courses. Sometimes, Latinos who make it through college indicated that teachers, counselors, and older siblings also served as guides through the college decision-making process.

In a similar study, Galindo and Escamilla (1995) interviewed two successful Mexican American students and likewise found that families provided the students encouragement and support along with the motivation to succeed academically. Although the parents had not often participated in school activities or functions, the students reported that their parents were supportive in the home by monitoring school attendance and schoolwork.

One of the key challenges facing Latino students in the college decision-making process is standardized tests. The most commonly used college admission test is the Scholastic Aptitude Test (SAT). In order to be admitted to a competitive college, an applicant needs to have relatively high college admission test scores.

On the average, Latino high school students score lower on these tests than White or Asian high school students (Lemann, 1999). Furthermore, among seniors in 1998, Blacks, Hispanics, *and* Native Americans accounted for only about one in twenty of those who had very high scores, scores commonly found among students admitted to highly selective universities (Borman et al., 2000).

These relatively low scores make it less likely that Latino applicants will gain admission to competitive colleges. Affirmative action allowed college admission officers to accept Latino applicants who did not have admission test scores that were as high as those of White or Asian students. However, the demise of affirmative action in states with large Latino populations makes it difficult for Latino high school seniors to gain admission to competitive public institutions of higher education.

The feedback that Latino high school seniors receive from college admission scores can be discouraging for students who aspire to college. Such students may have decent grades in a college preparatory program of coursework, but if they receive relatively low college admission scores, then these students may question whether they are really "college material." Most colleges, even those not competitive in admissions, post average SAT scores of their students as a guide for potential applicants. It is not uncommon for a Latino student to aspire to a college only to find out that his or her SAT scores are below what is considered average or minimum by the college they wish to attend. This leads some Latino students to think that they may not deserve to go to college.

Community colleges appear to attract Latino students because these colleges accept students with lower grades and lower college admission scores (Andrews & Fonseca, 1998). Community colleges even accept students who do not have high school diplomas, but have a GED instead. Additional advantages of community colleges include the fact that they are widely distributed so that students can attend college classes without having to leave home, they are less expensive to attend, and they provide students with college credits that they can use to transfer to a university offering bachelor's degrees. Community colleges are accustomed to having part-time students, allowing them to work part-time and attend classes part-time. Unfortunately, most students who attend community colleges do not transfer to four-year institutions (Tienda & Simonelli, 2001).

Increasing the Numbers

Throughout this chapter, we have mentioned ways of increasing the numbers of Latinos with bachelor's degrees. To summarize, in order to arrive at a time when Latino youth are earning bachelors' degrees at a rate comparable to that of Whites, we need to increase the numbers of Latino students graduating from high school, increase the number of Latino students taking challenging courses in high school, and increase the number of Latinos who complete the college planning process with admission to college. Along this perilous pathway are many obstacles. Most American youth do not make it all the way to a bachelor's degree. Those who do earn a bachelor's degree usually have received substantial parental support throughout their educational career. Parents who have not completed high school or attended college are at a great disadvantage in helping their children make it through to completion of the bachelor's degree. It is possible for other adults to provide the guidance, encouragement, and support needed to increase the number of Latino students earning a bachelor's degree. However, it will take enormous community organization and leadership, as well as other resources, to provide Latino youth with what they need to make the journey from high school freshman to college graduate.

REFERENCES

Alexander, K. L., Cook, M. A., & McDill, E. L. (1978). Curriculum tracking and educational stratification: Some further evidence. *American Sociological Review*, *43*, 47–66.

Andrews, A. C., & Fonseca, J. W. (1998). *Community colleges in the United States: A geographical perspective. George Mason University.* Retrieved May 31, 2001 from: http://www.zanesville.ohiou.edu/geography/communitycollege/default.htm

Barth, P., Haycock, K., Huang S., & Richardson, A. (2001). Youth at the crossroads: Facing high school and beyond. *National Commission on the High School Senior Year.* The Education Trust, Inc.

Battin-Pearson, S., Newcomb, M. D., Abbott, R. D., Hill, K. G., Catalano, R. F., & Hawkins, J. D. (2000). Predictors of early high school dropout: A test of five theories. *Journal of Educational Psychology*, *92*(3), 568–582.

Bennici, F., & Strang, W. (1995). *An analysis of language minority and limited English proficient students from NELS:88.* Washington, D.C.: U.S. Department of Education.

Borman, G. D., Stringfield, S., & Rachuba, L. (2000). *Advancing minority high achievement: National trends and promising programs and practices.* Retrieved May 25, 2001 from: http://www.collegeboard.com

Brown, G., Rose, N., Hill, S., & Olivas, M. (1980). *The Condition of Education for Hispanic Americans.* Washington, D.C.: U.S. Department of Education.

Falbo, T., Lein, L., & Amador, N. (2000). Family resources and the transition to high school. Unpublished manuscript. Population Research Center, University of Texas, Austin.

Galindo, R., & Escamilla, K. (1995). A biographical perspective on Chicano educational success. *Urban Review, 27*(1), 1–29.

Galotti, K. M., & Mark, M. C. (1994). How do high school students structure an important life decision? A short term longitudinal study of the college decision-making process. *Research in Higher Education, 35*(5), 589–607.

Gandara, P. (1995). *Over the ivy walls: The educational mobility of low-income Chicanos.* Albany: New York.

Gehring, J. (2001). Dual-enrollment programs spreading. *Education Week* (April 25), 17–18.

Gonzalez, R., & Padilla, A. M. (1997). The academic resilience of Mexican American high school students. *Hispanic Journal of Behavioral Sciences, 19*(3), 301–317.

Harris, M. J., & Rosenthal, R. (1985). Mediation of interpersonal expectancy effects. *Psychological Bulletin, 97*, 363–386.

Hieronymus, A. N., & Hoover, H. D. (1986). *Manual for school administrators, levels 5–14, 77.* Iowa City: University of Iowa.

Jussim, L. (1986). Self-fulfilling prophecies: A theoretical and integrative view. *Psychological Review, 93*, 429–445.

Kaufman, P., Klein, S., & Frase, M. (1999). *Dropout rates in the United States: 1997, NCES 99–082.* Washington, D.C.: U.S. Department of Education.

Kaufman, P., Kwon, J. Y., Klein, S., & Chapman, C. D. (2000). *Dropout rates in the United States: 1999, NCES 2001–02.* Washington, D.C.: U.S. Department of Education.

Keith, P. B., & Litchman, M. V. (1994). Does parental involvement influence the academic achievement of Mexican American eighth graders? Results from the National Education Longitudinal Study. *School Psychology Quarterly, 9*(4), 256–272.

Lemann, N. (1999). *The big test: the secret history of the American meritocracy.* New York: Farrar, Straus and Giroux.

McMillen, M. (1995). *Dropout rates in the United States: 1995, NCES 97–473.* Washington, D.C.: U.S. Department of Education.

Oakes, J. (1985). *Keeping track: How schools structure inequality.* New Haven: Yale University Press.

Okagaki, L., Frensch, P. A., & Gordon, E. W. (1995). Encouraging school achievement in Mexican American children. *Hispanic Journal of Behavioral Sciences, 17*(2), 160–179.

Perez, S. M., & Salazar, D. D. (1997). Economic, labor force, and social implications of Latino educational and population trends. In: A. Darder, R. D. Torres & H. Gutierrez (Eds), *Latinos and Education: A Critical Reader* (pp. 45–79). New York: Routledge.

Report on the White House strategy session on improving Hispanic student achievement (2000). (December.)

Riley, R. W., Winston, J. A., Ginsburg, A. L., & Takai, R. T. (2001). *High standards for all students: A report from the national assessment of Title I on progress and challenges since the 1994 reauthorization* (January). Washington, D.C.: U.S. Department of Education.

Romo, H. (1984). The Mexican origin population's differing perceptions of their children's schooling. *Social Science Quarterly, 65*(2), 635–650.

Romo, H., & Falbo, T. (1996). *Latino High School Graduation: Defying the Odds.* University of Texas Press: Austin, TX.

Rosenthal, R. (1985). From unconscious experimenter bias to teacher expectancy effects. In: J. B. Dusek, V. C. Hall & W. J. Meyer (Eds), *Teachers' Expectancies* (pp. 37–65). Hillsdale, NJ: Erlbaum.

Rumberger, R. W., & Thomas, S. I. (2000). Urban and suburban schools. *Sociology of Education, 73*, 39–67.

San Miguel, G., & Valencia, R. R. (1998). From the Treaty of Guadalupe Hidalgo to Hopwood: The educational plight and struggle of Mexican Americans in the Southwest. *Harvard Educational Review, 68*(3), 353–398.

Scannell, D. P. (1958). Differential prediction of academic success from achievement test scores. Unpublished doctoral dissertation, University of Iowa.

Snyder, M. (1984). When beliefs create reality. In: L. Berkowitz (Ed.), *Advances in Experimental Social Psychology* (Vol. 18, pp. 247–305). New York: Academic Press.

Stanton-Salazar, R. D. (1997). A social capital framework for understanding the socialization of racial minority children and youths. *Harvard Educational Review, 67*(1), 1–40.

Stanton-Salazar, R. D., & Dornbusch, S. M. (1995). Social capital and the reproduction of social inequality: Information networks among Mexican-origin high school students. *Sociology of Education, 68*(2), 116–135.

Strang, W., Winglee, M., & Stunkard, J. (1993). *Characteristics of secondary-school-age language minority and limited English proficient youth.* Washington, D.C.: U.S. Department of Education.

Suarez-Orozco, C., & Suarez-Orozco, M. (1995). *Transformations: Migration, family life, and achievement motivation among Latino adolescents.* Stanford, CA: Stanford University Press.

(2000, May 10). Technology Counts 2001: The New Divides. *Education Week,* Retrieved from www.edweek.org/tc01/.

Therrien, M., & Ramirez, R. R. (2000). The Hispanic Population in the United States: March 2000, *Current Population Reports,* P20–535, U.S. Census Bureau, Washington, D.C.

Tienda, M., & Simonelli, S. (2001). Hispanic students are missing from diversity debates [The Chronicle Review]. *The Chronicle of Higher Education* (May 29), B13.

Trueba, H. T. (1991). From failure to success: The roles of culture and cultural conflict in the academic achievement of Chicano students. In: R. R. Valencia (Ed.), *Chicano School Failure and Success: Research and Policy Agendas for the 1990s* (pp. 151–163). New York: Falmer Press.

U.S. Census Bureau (2001). Current Population Reports, P20–528, Tables No. 249 & No. 251 *Statistical Abstract of the United States: 2000.* Washington, D.C.: Author.

Valdez, G. (1996). *Con respeto: Bridging the distances between culturally diverse families and schools.* New York: Teachers College Press, Columbia University.

Valenzuela, A. (1999). *Subtractive schooling: U.S.-Mexican youth and the politics of caring.* Albany: State University of New York Press.

Wallace, D., Abel, R., & Ropers-Huilman, B. (2000). Clearing a path for success: Deconstructing borders through undergraduate mentoring. *The Review of Higher Education, 24*(1), 87–102.

Yachnin, J. (2001). Group Suggests Ways to Increase College-Going Rates of Hispanic Students. *The Chronicle of Higher Education.* Retrieved May 24, from: http://chronicle.com/daily/2001/05/2001052405n.htm

Zwick, R. (1999). Backdoor affirmative action. *Education Week* (February 10), 56.

BEYOND STIGMA: SOCIAL IDENTITIES AND THE EDUCATIONAL ACHIEVEMENT OF CHICANOS

Aída Hurtado, Eugene Garcia, Luis A. Vega and Reynold Gonzalez

INTRODUCTION

The evidence on the effects of social identity on academic achievement among minority students is mixed. In some instances, the effects are negative (Fordham & Ogbu, 1986; Steele, 1990), in others the effects are positive (Allen, 1992), and in others the effects are nulled (White, 1988). The reasons for these contradictory results are not well known and very few studies have attempted to address them (Bernal, Saenz & Knight, 1991). In this chapter we first propose that it is different conceptualizations of social identity that account for the differences of results. Next, we review the contradictory evidence on social identity and academic achievement. Finally, we empirically test what we consider to be a correct conceptualization of social identity and its relation to academic achievement in a Chicano college sample.

Latinos in Higher Education, Volume 3, pages 73–84.
© 2003 Published by Elsevier Science Ltd.
ISBN: 0-7623-0980-6

WHAT IS SOCIAL IDENTITY?

According to Tajfel (1974), social identity is "that part of an individual's self-concept which derives from his knowledge of his membership of a social group (or groups) together with the emotional significance attached to that membership" (p. 69). Social identity theory posits that an individual's group memberships influence behavior and relations with members of an individual's own group, as well as relations with other groups. Two processes can explain how this occurs. One is social categorization, or the process of systematically grouping together social objects in order to make sense of the world (Tapel & Turner, 1979); the other is social comparison, or the process of defining one's group by some standard (Festinger, 1954). Through these two processes, individuals develop views of themselves and others in the social environment.

For minority students, a social identity approach takes into account cultural discontinuities (i.e. mismatch) and cultural context in the explanation of academic achievement (Bernal et al., 1991; Ogbu, 1987). Academic achievement among minority students can be more accurately understood by identifying the social identities of students (Hurtado, Gurin & Peng, 1994), including associated expectations and behaviors (Bernal et al., 1991). Once social identity dimensions are identified, their evaluative content must be determined (Bernal et al., 1991). This view suggests that social identity is a multi-dimensional construct having a differential effect on academic achievement.

Thus, it is possible that different social identities could have a negative effect on academic achievement, and still others a positive effect. This can explain why different studies have found conflicting results in the relationship between social identity and academic achievement. In fact, a close look at several of these studies supports such a view.

A REVIEW OF THE STUDIES

Two processes are said to account for the negative effects of social identity on academic achievement among minority students – the emergence of an oppositional identity (Ogbu, 1987) and disidentification (Steele, 1990). On the one hand, an oppositional identity is the result of cultural inversion, where cultural pressures impel minority students to act against the dominant group's frame of reference (e.g. getting good grades) (Ogbu, 1987). Under this process, school success is equated with identification with the majority, hence the negative effects of social identity on academic achievement (Fordham, 1988; Fordham & Ogbu, 1986). On the other hand, Steele (1992) argues that "pressure to disidentify with school can come from the already demoralized as well as from racial vulnerability in the [school] setting" (p. 75, emphasis ours). This in turn can affect academic success in minority students because to do well in school is to act "white" – a potential stigma for many minority groups (Steele, 1990, 1992). An example of dis-identification can be seen in an article from the Washington Post written by Dorothy Gilliam (February 15, 1982) and quoted by Fordham and Ogbu (1986, p. 176):

> My friend was talking to her son, who is 20, when he blurted out a secret half as old as he. It was the explanation for his ambivalence toward success. It began, he said, in his early school years, when a fifth-grade teacher questioned whether he had really written the outstanding essay he'd turned in about the life of squirrels. It ended when the teacher gave him a grade that clearly showed that she did not believe the boy's outraged denial of plagiarism. Because the young man is black and the teacher is white, and because such incidents had happened before, he arrived at a youthful solution: "I never tried again"...

Under disidentification, to do well in school is equated with betraying the minority ethnic group, and hence the negative effects of social identity on academic achievement.

Both processes of disidentification and the emergence of an oppositional identity assume that social identification is unidimensional, and both assume an inverse relationship of social identification to academic achievement. A similar analysis can be made for those studies which find positive effects of social identity on academic achievement (Cross, 1978), and where a positive social identity is associated with academic success. These studies have been done in traditionally black colleges, where it is argued that a nurturing environment for one's social identity leads to academic success (Fleming, 1984).

Those studies which show no effect of social identity on academic achievement posit other variables as responsible for the poor performance of minority students in college. For example, White (1988) shows that high school grade point average, a college student identity, and education aspirations are some of the most important predictors of academic achievement for minority students. Also, other studies implicate the extent of positive relationships minority students have with faculty (Allen, 1992), the perception of job ceilings (Fordham & Ogbu, 1986), and level of self-esteem (Hare, 1987) in the academic achievement of minority students.

THE PRESENT STUDY

Given that most studies have not carefully delineated a clear definition of social identity (one that includes a multidimensional definition), its relationship to academic achievement is tenuous. One exception is the study by Bernal et al. (1991), where a social identity approach is discussed, and where a multidimensional conceptualization of social identity is introduced. However, this paper is theoretical and it does not empirically test the relationship of social identity to academic achievement. In this study we empirically test this relationship and, in addition, statistically control background variables which can directly and indirectly influence academic achievement (White, 1988).

Because the population we used in this study is of Mexican American descent, the composition of its social identity necessitates two clarifications. First, the social identity of Mexican Americans is one that has historical influence (Alvarez, 1973), both in time and place. Second, various modes of entry into the U.S. render the Mexican American population very heterogeneous, and their social identity includes many aspects, including language, family, race, class, and ethnicity (Hurtado, Gurin & Peng, 1994). However, because we adopt a multi-dimensional definition of social identity, both of these concerns are taken into account in this study.

PROCEDURES

Sample

The sample used in this analysis is taken from a survey of 523 Chicano college students in a South Texas public university. This university is located near the U.S.-Mexican border, about four hours south of San Antonio. Approximately 76% of the students are of Mexican descent. The majority of these students come from low-income areas, in what is known as the Rio Grande Valley and what is considered to be "the poorest region in the U.S." (Gibney, 1987). The sample is broken down into two groups: the full sample of 523 students, and a partial sample of 298 students for which grade point averages were also obtained. The full sample of college students consists of 327 (63.5%) females and 191 (36.5%) males. The average family income is $17,834 (SD = $537) and approximately 67% of respondents are underclassman (freshmen and sophomores). There is a wide representation of areas of study; among the most popular majors within the full sample were education (29%), health professions (15%), social sciences (14%), business/commerce (14%), and community service (includes law) (12%). Just under half (46.5%) of the full sample are third generation Americans (respondents who were born in the U.S. and for whom at least one parent was also born in the U.S.). Approximately 45% (45.1%) are second generation, and only 8.4% are first generation (all of whom came to the U.S. before the age of 12). Ninety percent (90%) of respondents were born in the U.S.

Measures

The background variables included age, gender, family income, father's education, mother's education, father's occupation, mother's occupation, and student classification. Age, father's education, and mother's education were asked in number of years in an open-ended question format. Gender, father's occupation, mother's occupation, and student classification were measured via choice questions. Occupation ranged from a 1 ("unskilled") to 4 ("self-employed/owner of business"). Student classification options ranged from 1 ("Freshman") to 5 ("graduate/special student"). Family income was also a choice question, with responses ranging from 1 ("less than $2,000") to 16 ("$30,000 and above").

The ethnic identity measures were derived from factor analyzing 29 labels which respondents endorsed, or did not endorse as self-descriptive. Responses to endorsement ranged from 1 ("not me") to 5 ("very important"). The labels referred to ethnicity, gender, class, work, and family roles. From previous studies where these labels have been used (Hurtado, Gurin & Peng, 1994), we know that seven dimensions should be present in a data sample that comes from Chicanos who are second generation. Consequently, in this analysis we sought to replicate previous work, while deriving the ethnic identity measures for the present work.

Using the SPSS computer package, we conducted a principal component analysis of the 29 labels. We used the Kaiser criterion, which extracts for rotation the number of factors with eigenvalues of one or higher, as well as varimax rotation. The original solution produced nine factors, but in order to replicate the Hurlado, Gurin, and Peng (1994) results, the solution was forced into seven factors (see Table 1).

The seven factor solution was similar in structure to the Hurtado, Gurin, and Peng (1994) solution, with the exception of two modifications. First, a factor tapping into the identity of working class had to be dropped because of low reliability. This made sense because the Hurtado, Gurin and Peng (1994) study was based on heads of households, and not students, who might conceivably not have a strong worker identity. Second, the label "White" was dropped from the farmworker identity. This was done because the label did not conceptually go with the other two labels (immigrant and farmworker). Additionally, the results of an item analysis indicated that dropping that label would improve reliability of the factor.

The six factors from the analysis provide a social identity measure which gives a score on each of the six dimensions. Weighted averages were constructed using the labels that loaded within each of the six dimensions. The score on each dimension can be interpreted on a scale that ranges from a low of 1 ("not me") to a high of 5 ("very important").

The six dimensions can be interpreted as follows: The political raza dimension included thinking of oneself in terms of the Chicano movement, involving the political labels Raza, Chicano, Mestizo, Latino, Brown and Pocho. The labels of poor and Spanish speaker also loaded in this dimension and it is consistent with earlier work (Hurtado, Gurin & Peng, 1994). The bicultural dimension is a continuum contrasting American, on one end, with American of Mexican descent, on the other. This dimension also included U.S. citizen, U.S. native, and English Speaker. The mobile ethnicity dimension included labels which denote economic advancement and traditional cultural labels. The labels were Hispanic, Mexican, Mexican American, Catholic, and Middle Class. The family dimension included seeing oneself in terms of gender, sibling, and son or daughter. The head of household identity involved seeing oneself as a parent, spouse, and breadwinner. The last dimension, farmworker, involved thinking of oneself as Immigrant and as Farmworker. All six dimensions had acceptable reliabilities (see Table 1).

Finally, grade point average (GPA) was measured on a scale that ranged from 0 (F grade) to a 4.0 (A grade). The results that follow are based on 220 respondents for whom all the data were complete. Also, except for the farm-worker identity, which had excessive positive skewness, all variables met normality assumptions. The farmworker identity was normalized by applying the inverse in a transformation of the variable.

RESULTS

Seven simultaneous regression runs were done to assess the effect of the background variables and the six ethnic identities on GPA (e.g. direct effects), and the effect of the background variables on each of the six ethnic identities (e.g. indirect effects).

Table 2 shows the standardized coefficients for each of the seven regression analyses, as well as the R-square for each regression run. To aid in the interpretation of the direct and indirect effects, Fig. 1 displays only the signif-icant coefficients of the predictor variables on the criterion variable(s).

As can be seen in Fig. 1, only three dimensions of ethnic identity had significant direct effects on GPA: the family, mobile ethnicity, and head of household iden-tities. Specifically, thinking of one's self in terms of family was associated with a higher GPA. However, thinking of one's self in terms of a mobile ethnicity and as a head of household was associated wfth a lower GPA.

Also, only two of the background variables had significant direct effects on GPA: income and class level. Thus, a high income and a higher class level were associated with a higher GPA (see Fig. 1).

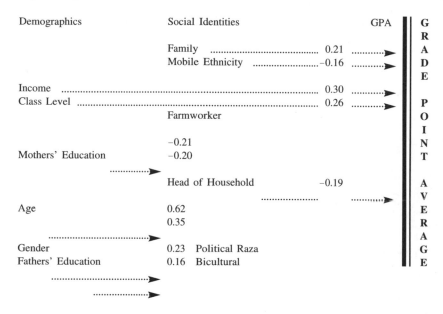

Fig. 1. Direct and Indirect Effects of Demographics and
Social Identities on GPA.

In addition, there were two indirect effects that were significant. Mother's education and age influenced GPA through the identity of head of household. The more education the respondents' mothers had, the less likely the respondents saw themselves in terms of an identity of head of household, which could negatively influence GPA. However, the older the respondents were, the more likely they were to see themselves in terms of a head of household identity, and the more likely they would have lower GPAs (see Fig. 1).

Finally, four background variables had significant intermediate effects on three of the ethnic identity dimensions. An intermediate effect is defined as a direct effect of a background variable on a social identity, with no direct or indirect effects present on GPA. First, the more education the respondents' mothers had, the less likely the respondents saw themselves in terms of a farmworker identity. Second, the older the respondents were, the more likely they would see themselves in terms of a political raza identity. Third, being a man was associated with a higher political raza identity. Finally, the more education the respondents' fathers had, the more likely the respondents saw themselves in terms of a bicultural identity.

Table 1. Rotated Factor Loadings for Social Identity Scales.

Label[1]	Political Raza	Bicultural	Mobile Ethnicity	Family	Head Household	Worker	F
Raza	0.75						
Chicano/a	0.74						
mestizo/a	0.61						
Latino/a	0.53						
Brown	0.51						
Poor	0.43						
Pocho/a	0.36						
Spanish Speaker	0.34						
U.S. Citizen		0.80					
American		0.72					
U.S. Native		0.67					
Am. of Mex. Descent		0.53					
English Speaker		0.46					
Hispanic			0.71				
Mexican			0.66				
Mexican American			0.60				
Catholic			0.58				
Middle Class			0.40				
Daughter/Son				0.77			
Sister/Brother				0.73			
Woman/Man				0.68			
Mother/Father					0.85		
Wife/Husband					0.81		
Family Breadwinner					0.64		
Working Class						0.66	
Blue-collar						0.63	
White							0.61
Immigrant							0.56
Farmworker							0.51
Percent Variance	15.7%	12.0%	6.5%	5.6%	5.0%	4.4%	4.0%
Cronbach's alpha	0.75	0.72	0.65	0.68	0.73	–	0.64

Note: $n = 523$.

Table 2. Regression Beta Coefficients of the Independent Variables on Grade Point Average (GPA).

Variable	Political Raza	Bicultural	Mobile Ethnicity	Family	Head Household	Farmworker	GPA
Political Raza							0.08
Bicultural							0.03
Mobile Ethnicity							-0.16*
Family							0.21*
Head of household							-0.19*
Farmworker							-0.12
Father's Education	-0.12	0.16*	0.05	0.08	0.07	0.04	0.08
Mother's Education	-0.09	0.00	-0.12	-0.11	-0.20*	0.21*	-0.07
Family Income	-0.10	0.08	0.10	-0.04	0.10	0.11	0.30*
Father's Occupation	0.02	-0.07	-0.04	0.04	-0.03	0.08	-0.03
Mother's Occupation	0.08	0.04	0.03	0.06	0.04	-0.14	-0.06
Class Level	0.01	0.01	0.03	0.05	-0.07	-0.04	0.26*
Age	0.35*	0.09	-0.11	0.09	0.62*	-0.06	0.01
Gender	0.23*	0.03	0.04	-0.04	0.09	-0.12	-0.06
R square	0.26	0.05	0.02	0.02	0.47	0.10	0.22

$p < 0.05$.

DISCUSSION

Consistent with a multidimensional definition of social identity (Tajfel, 1981), the results showed that only some dimensions of social identity affect the academic achievement of Chicanos. The same is true for background variables, of which some had significant direct and indirect effects on academic achievement (White, 1988). These results can help explain why many studies have reported mixed effects of social identify on the academic achievement of minority groups.

First, only two dimensions of social identity were found to negatively affect academic achievement-mobile ethnicity and a head of household identity. As outlined in the results section, a mobile ethnicity included labels which denote economic advancement and traditional cultural labels. Because the university from which the respondents came was predominantly a commuter school, viewing oneself as economically well off involved having to work more, leaving less time to invest in school courses. This would explain the negative effect this dimension had on academic achievement. Likewise, for the second dimension, viewing oneself as a head of household also meant more responsibilities outside of school, which then translated into low grades.

Both of the above results are inconsistent with the oppositional identity and disidentification literature (Ogbu, 1987; Steele, 1990). This is the case because viewing oneself in terms of a mobile ethnicity and head of household is the result of having to work more, having children, and having less time to study – all situationally driven. The political raza dimension, viewing one's self in highly ethnic terms, and the one dimension which would have supported the oppositional identity and disidentification literature, did not affect academic achievement. In addition, the indirect effects of mother's education and age on academic achievement, through the dimension of head of household, also attest to situational influences on academic performance. In specific, the older the respondents were and the less education the mothers of these respondents had, the more likely these respondents would view themselves in terms of head of household and would be less likely to do well academically.

Second, the results also account for those studies which have shown a positive effect of social identity on academic achievement (Fleming, 1984). For example, viewing one's self in terms of a family dimension had a positive effect on academic achievement. This can be explained in terms of being in a nurturing environment, and receiving support from others in one's group (Keefe & Padilla, 1987). Consistent with Hurtado's (in press) analysis of the Latino family, the family does not hinder individual action nor is a familial orientation a liability, as assimilationists would have us believe.

Third, the effects of the background variables on academic achievement help explain why some studies have found null effects from social identity to academic achievement (Allen, 1992). A high income does affect how well one does in school, independent of any social identification one might have, and income did have a significant positive effect on academic achievement here. The other background variable which also had a positive direct effect on academic achievement was class level, and this would be expected, as the university from which we sampled had an open admissions program. This would mean that low grades from high school would only get better as the students adjusted to the university setting.

Other effects on academic achievement are consistent with what one would expect in a Chicano college sample. For example, the more education the respondents' mothers had, the less likely the respondents were to see themselves in terms of a farmworker identity. Being older and male contributed to viewing one's self in terms of a political raza dimension, and perhaps having a higher sense of ethnic consciousness (Hurtado, 1994, Chap. 1). Finally, the more educated the fathers of the respondents were, the more likely the respondents were to view themselves in terms of bicultural identity. This is the case because more educated parents usually have higher incomes and a higher social class, and hence more exposure to both Mexican and American cultures.

POLICY IMPLICATIONS AND CONCLUSIONS

Several policy implications emerge from this study. The most important is that academic achievement among Chicano students is situationally driven and context dependent. Academic achievement was not adversely affected by any social identification based on ethnicity, as has been shown in other studies of disidentification and oppositional identities (Ogbu, 1987; Steele, 1990). It is possible to be academically successful and at the same time be a proud Chicano. It is not as easy to be a head of household and academically successful, nor is it easy to be academically successful while overworking to achieve economic advancement.

Social policy needs to address the needs of students over and beyond what their ethnic affiliation would suggest. Perhaps providing more child care could improve the academic achievement of those students who are heads of households. Those students who emphasize work more than college courses could perhaps benefit from a lighter course load. Perhaps more needs to be done to emphasize the benefits of an education and a college degree to those students who must work. Nonetheless, the need for more financial aid to these students is a must – else these students will continue to spend more time in the work setting than in a classroom-the only place where grades will improve.

NOTE

1. There were 32 labels but three were dropped because of low endorsement. These labels were Foreign (8.6% endorsement), Indian (7.2% endorsement), and Cholo (2.0% endorsement).

REFERENCES

Allen, W. R. (1992). The color of success: African-American college student outcomes at predominantly white and historically Black public colleges and universities. *Harvard Educational Review, 62*, 26–44.

Alvarez, R. (1973). The psycho-historical and socioeconomic development of the Chicano community in the United States. *Social Science Quarterly, 53*, 920–942.

Cross, W. E. (1978). The Thomas and Cross models of psychological nigrescence: A literature review. *Journal of Black Psychology, 4*, 13–31.

Festinger, L. (1954). A theory of social comparison processes. *Human Relations, 7*, 117–140.

Fleming, J. (1984). *Blacks in college*. San Francisco: Jossey-Bass.

Fordham, S. (1988). Racelessness as a factor in Black students' school success: Pragmatic strategy or pyrrhic victory? *Harvard Educational Review, 58*, 54–84.

Fordham, S., & Ogbu, J. U. (1986). Black students' school success: Coping with the "Burden of 'Acting White.'" *The Urban Review, 18*(3), 176–206.

Gibney, F. J. (1987). In Texas, a grim new Appalachia: Desperate lives in the nation's poorest region. *Newsweek* (June 8), 27–28.

Hare, B. R. (1987). Structural inequality and the endangered status of Black youth: The Black child's home environment and student achievement [Special Issue]. *Journal of Negro Education, 56*, 100–110.

Hurtado, A., Gurin, P., & Peng, T. (1994). Social identities-A framework for studying the adaptations of immigrants and ethnics: The adaptations of Mexicans in the United States. *Social Problems, 41*(1), 129–151.

Hurtado, A. (in press). Variations, combinations, and evolutions: Latino families in the United States. In: R. E. Zambrana & M. Baca Zinn (Eds), *Latino Families: Developing a Paradigm for Research, Practice, and Policy.* Thousand Oaks, CA: Sage.

Hurtado, S. (1994). *Latino consciousness and academic success.* University of California Project on Latino Eligibility Monograph. Santa Cruz, CA: University of California.

Keefe, S. E., & Padilla, A. M. (1987). *Chicano ethnicity.* Albuquerque: University of New Mexico Press.

Ogbu, J. U. (1987). Variability in minority school performance: A problem in search of an explanation. *Anthropology and Education Quarterly, 18*, 312–334.

Ogbu, J. U. (1986). Cross-cultural study of minority education. Contributions from Stockton Research, 23rd annual J. William Harris Lecture, School of Education, University of the Pacific, Stockton, CA.

Steele, C. (1990). Protecting the self: Implications for social psychological theory and minority achievement. Unpublished paper presented at the annual meeting of American Psychological Association, Boston, MA.

Steele, C. (1992). Race and the schooling of Black Americans. *The Atlantic Monthly* (April), 68–78.

Tajfel, H. (1981). *Human groups and social categories.* Cambridge, England: Cambridge University Press.

Tajfel, H. (1974). Social identity and intergroup behaviour. *Social Science Information, 13*, 65–93.

Tajfel, H., & Turner, J. C. (1979). The social identity theory of intergroup behavior. In: W. G. Austin & S. Wotchel (Eds), *The Social Psychology of Intergroup Relations.* Monterey, CA: Brooks Cole.

White, C. L. (1988). Ethnic identity and academic performance among Black and white college students: An interactionist approach. *Urban Education, 23*(3), 219–240.

"BEING THERE FOR US:" LATINO STUDENTS AND THEIR FIRST-YEAR EXPERIENCES IN URBAN COMMUNITY COLLEGES

Romero Jalomo, Jr.

INTRODUCTION

Throughout the decade of the 1990s, colleges and universities in the U.S. experienced increased student enrollments driven in part by a baby boom echo effect and rise in the number of students who were the first in their family to attend college. Among these "new majority" students were many from Latino backgrounds. The rise in Latino college participation rates was a result of primary and secondary school enrollment growth that began more than a decade earlier (Rendón & Hope, 1996). In observing the rise of Latino student participation in all aspects of the American educational system, Nora and others (1997) stated that they were among "the youngest and fastest growing segments of the population, yet severely underrepresented in higher education" (p. 2).

Despite gains in enrollment, Latino students continue to exhibit moderate attrition rates that begin in secondary school and extend into college (Aguirre & Martinez, 1993; Carter & Wilson, 1994; Duran, 1983; Hurtado & Garcia, 1994; Jalomo, 1995, 2000; Rendón & Hope, 1996; Rendón & Nora, 1988). This trend significantly limits the number of Latino high school graduates and students participating in postsecondary education. Further complications such

Latinos in Higher Education, Volume 3, pages 85–105.
Copyright © 2003 by Elsevier Science Ltd.
All rights of reproduction in any form reserved.
ISBN: 0-7623-0980-6

as unmet college subject requirements, low college entrance exam scores, and low grade point averages prevent many Latino students from enrolling in four-year colleges and universities directly upon high school completion (Duran, 1983; Hurtado & Garcia, 1994; Nora, 1993; Rendón & Nora, 1988). For many Latinos, choosing to attend a local community college rather than a four-year college or university upon high school completion is not inconsequential.

During the past decade Latinos made gains in their high school graduation rate but their attrition rate remained high in urban areas. The acute Latino attrition rate has reached 50% in many urban high school districts across the country (Nora & Cabrera, 1992; Rendón & Hope, 1996). Nora and Cabrera (1992) documented instances in which high attrition rates (often 50% or more) were exceptionally acute in large metropolitan school districts. The researchers found that an additional 10% of African American and Latino students left high school during their senior year. Consequently, Latinos were the only major racial or ethnic group with a larger percentage of non-high school graduates than completers for adults age 25 or over in 1990 (Aguirre & Martinez, 1993). Due in part to these troubling findings, critics argue that Latino students are participating in an educational system that often perpetuates their limited educational attainment (Olivas, 1986).

In light of the attrition problem in secondary schools, Latino student enrollments are expected to rise in the K-12 sector during the first decade of the 21st century (Jalomo, 2000). Similarly, the Latino college participation rate is also expected to increase in both two-year and four-year colleges. Both estimations follow trends established during the previous two decades. For example, among the major ethnic and racial minority student groups, only Asians experienced a higher rate of increase in four-year college participation than Latinos during 1982–1992. In the same period, Latinos posted the largest percentage increase of any major ethnic or racial group attending two-year colleges (O'Brien, 1993).

In 1980, there were 249,800 Hispanic students enrolled in public community colleges in the United States. By 1999, Hispanic student enrollment grew to 704,500 nationally (Chronicle of Higher Education, 2001). During the twenty year period 1980–1999, the number of Latino students enrolled in public community colleges increased by almost one-half million students (454,700). Continuing the trend of the past two decades, community colleges remain a popular institutional choice among Latino college students.

During the 1999–2000 academic year, over 5.6 million students attended two-year colleges in the U.S. (Chronicle of Higher Education, 2001). This figure constituted 44% of the approximately 12.7 million undergraduate students enrolled in colleges and universities in the U.S. In 1999, nearly three-quarters of one million (735,100) Hispanic students were enrolled in public and private two-year colleges. Three years earlier Hispanic student enrollment in two-year colleges exceeded the Hispanic proportion of the overall population in 41 states (Cohen & Brawer, 1996). The total number of Hispanic students attending two-year colleges represented over 60% of the group's undergraduate enrollment in postsecondary education during the 1999–2000 academic year. In contrast, among the major ethnic and racial student groups in the U.S., only American Indians enrolled a majority of undergraduates in two-year colleges (54%). During 1999–2000, approximately 46% of African American (678,700) and 45% of Asian (355,800) undergraduate students were enrolled in two-year colleges compared to slightly more than 41% (3,670,400) of Caucasian students (Chronicle of Higher Education, 2001).

Perhaps no other group can benefit most from a critical analysis of the community college experience than Latino students. Because of their historically high enrollment rate in these institutions and expected growth in the future, the need to investigate the issues surrounding Latino student participation in community colleges is vital. While Latinos have benefited from the open door policy of community colleges, as a group they have experienced inconclusive educational outcomes. The problem of Latino student persistence in college leaves cause for concern among educators, legislators, community activists, internal and external stakeholders, and other interested groups (Aguirre & Martinez, 1993; Jalomo, 1995, 2001; Nora, 1993; Nora et al., 1997; Rendón, 1994; Nora & Rendón, 1990).

This chapter is concerned with the plight of Latino college students enrolled in community colleges for several important reasons. First, the growing Latino student population continues to significantly impact the nation's educational system. Second, unlike White, Asian, and African American college students, the majority of Latino college students continue to enroll in community colleges. Third, there remains a need to study the postsecondary experiences of Latino students in order to address the influences that affect their persistence and success in college. Policymakers and educators agree that Latino students must find a satisfying and rewarding first year college experience if they are to persist and achieve their educational goals (Jalomo, 2000).

LATINO STUDENT PERSISTENCE IN COMMUNITY COLLEGES

Recent studies of Latino student persistence continue to focus on student preparation for and performance in college (Aguirre & Martinez, 1993;

Jalomo, 1995, 2000; Nora, 1993; Nora et al., 1997; O'Brien, 1993; Rendón & Hope, 1996). While Latino students appear better prepared for college success than the generation that preceded them, their persistence in college leaves cause for concern. Despite inconclusive findings, Latino student outcomes continue to draw the attention of external constituencies such as policymakers, local and state legislators, district boards, higher education associations, Latino professional organizations and internal constituencies such as campus administration, faculty, student services personnel, counselors and the like (Jalomo, 2001).

Latino student persistence in college occurs as a result of the interaction of student factors and institutional elements among other influences (Aguirre & Martinez, 1993; Nora, 1993; Rendón & Nora, 1988; Rendón, Jalomo & Garcia 1994; Valadez, 1993). Among the documented student factors that influence persistence is a student's socioeconomic background. Factors such as unemployment and socioeconomic status were found to lower student persistence (Aguirre & Martinez, 1993; Valadez, 1993). Other student influences found to limit persistence include insufficient academic preparation in high school, inadequate study habits, diffuse academic goals, self-doubt, low self-esteem, anxiety, and cultural separation (Rendón & Nora, 1988; Rendón et al., 1994).

Institution-related influences on Latino student persistence remain a central focus for campus administration, faculty and student services personnel (Padrón, 1994; Rendón et al., 1994). These factors are often classified as either academic or student services in nature. Among the prominent academic hindrances to Latino student persistence are few Latino faculty, limited office hours, a curriculum that minimizes multicultural perspectives, inadequate teaching styles, restricted tutoring assistance and excessive enrollment in remedial coursework (Nora, 1993; Rendón & Nora, 1988; Valadez, 1993). Some of the noted student services hindering Latino persistence include rising tuition costs, inadequate financial aid offerings, limited counseling or advising services, minimal bilingual student services, few student life opportunities for commuting and evening students including those with childcare needs, and an over-reliance on student initiated involvement in college (Jalomo, 1995; Rendón et al., 1994).

In addition to the many influences on student persistence in college, the literature on nontraditional student retention further suggests that the degree of student success is dependent on how well students negotiate multiple influences during their transition to college. This is especially true for first-generation students. The following section elaborates on these persistence factors.

Negotiating the Transition to College

Research suggests that the transition to college is different for traditional and nontraditional students (London, 1989; Rendón, 1994; Terenzini, Rendón, Upcraft, Millar, Allison, Gregg & Jalomo, 1994). For traditional students (i.e. recent high school graduates, those who enter college with a lapse of less than two years, students from an upper or middle class background or those from a family that has attended college) their transition from high school to college is often expected. For nontraditional students, college attendance is a new experience that warrants assistance from a high school counselor, relatives, friends or neighbors who have previously attended college and can provide valuable information on college participation. For nontraditional students, choosing to attend college may have been a delayed decision made late in high school or sometime after secondary school completion. The process of enrolling in college can prove to be confusing, frustrating and challenging (Terenzini et al., 1994). Many first-generation Latino college students find the transition to college to be a major disjunction in their life course, because the precedent of attending college has not been previously established in their family (Jalomo, 1995; Rendón, 1992).

In a study of first-year college students, Terenzini and others (1994) found that the transition from high school or work to college is a complex process that varies according to several important influences: a student's social, family, and educational background; the nature and mission of the institution attended; the student's educational aspirations; the people encountered in college; and the complex interaction of these influences. These findings support Nora's (1993) assertion that community college students bring diverse socioeconomic, academic and social characteristics to college that continuously influence their academic progress. For many first-year students with little or no family experience with college-going behaviors and practices, these factors become magnified as many students become overwhelmed, confused, and discouraged with their first-year college experience (Jalomo, 1995; Rendón, 1994; Terenzini et al., 1994; Zwerling, 1992). The dilemma of an overwhelming first-year experience can eventually lead some students to consider leaving college altogether.

Nearly a decade ago Rendón (1992) reported that a growing number of Latino students had broken past family "traditions" of non-college participation when they sought to pursue a postsecondary education. The college-going experience for these first-generation Latino college students meant encountering difficult issues such as identity development, resocialization into a new culture, being perceived as different, maintaining or redefining friendships with those who chose not to attend college, family separation or breaching family codes of loyalty and unity among others (Rodriguez, 1982; Rendón, 1992). The result of confronting these issues often caused stress, anxiety, depression and loneliness among these first-year college students.

Many first-year students who are the first in their families to attend college often struggle with living between two worlds during their college experience: their home and campus environments (London, 1989; Rendón, 1994; Rodriguez, 1982; Terenzini et al., 1994). Many fear that they will not be fully accepted in either environment (Weis, 1985, 1992). However past studies of the "breaking away" process report that changing former behavioral norms can foster a heightened self-concept, improved self-esteem, and reinforced identity (London, 1989). Conversely, negative implications of the breaking away process are feelings of isolation, alienation, self-doubt, and psychological distress. These factors can have a detrimental impact on a student's self-concept, persistence and attainment of educational goals (Rendón, 1992, 1994; Rodriguez, 1982; Terenzini et al., 1994; Weis, 1985, 1992). This is especially true for many first-year students who confront the dualism of attending college while attempting to maintain family roles and relationships, friendships and other personal obligations (Jalomo, 1995; Rendón, 1992, 1994).

According to numerous studies examining student involvement in college, academic and social influences such as student-faculty and student-peer interactions, student participation in campus activities and student organizations, and frequent utilization of campus services lead to an increased likelihood for success in college (Astin, 1985; Pascarella & Terenzini, 1991; Schlossberg, Lynch & Chickering, 1989; Terenzini et al., 1994). Conversely, students who become disconnected to vital campus mechanisms and social networks are more likely to encounter academic or social difficulties which can lead to their eventual departure from college (Astin, 1985; Carter & Wilson, 1994; Kuh, Schuh, Whitt and Associates, 1991; Nora, 1993; Pascarella & Terenzini, 1991; Tinto, 1987, 1993). For example, Anderson (1981) found that community college students who were employed (excluding work study) and lived off-campus (but not with their parents) were more likely to leave college during their first and second year than were students in other institutional settings.

Summary

Latino students often bring to college diverse background and pre-college experiences that are not directly addressed in existing models of postsecondary teaching and learning. These students face the challenge of adapting to a college experience that often is quite different from the environment from which they come (Jalomo, 1995; Rendón, 1992, 1994; Terenzini et al., 1994). The apparent difference between students who are satisfied with their college experience and achieve their educational goals and those who become bewildered or leave after their first year may be due to the nature of their transition to college and first-year experience. There remains a need for students to form connections with campus agents and utilize vital institutional mechanisms in order to have a satisfying and rewarding first-year experience in college (Jalomo, 1995). The following section details findings from an analysis of Latino first-year student experiences that focused on student transitions to college and the degree to which they formed connections to various aspects of the campus life.

AN ANALYSIS OF LATINO FIRST-YEAR STUDENT EXPERIENCES IN COMMUNITY COLLEGES

This section will report findings from focus group interviews with 44 Latino first-year students attending community colleges in California, Texas and New York. The focus of this analysis was to learn more about the nature of students' transition to college and the influences on their first-year college experience. In addition, this project sought to gain a greater understanding of these two dynamics in order to address policies and practices that could help improve Latino student persistence in community colleges.

Data analyzed for this project were taken from three separate case studies of urban community colleges in California, Texas and New York. The first two case studies were undertaken as part of the In- and Out-of-Class Experiences Project for the National Center on Postsecondary Teaching, Learning, and Assessment, funded by the Office of Educational Research and Improvement, United States Department of Education. The third case study analyzed the first-year student experience in an urban community college in New York. A Research Challenge Grant sponsored by the Steinhardt School of Education at New York University funded the project. The focus of each study was to examine students' transition to college and the expectations they formed about campus life during their first year in college. The intent was to capture these dynamics from student voices to determine the variation of experiences and to provide insights relative to how students perceive these dynamics.

An Overview of the Research Project
Although many approaches have been used to study student experiences in college, a focus group design was adopted for this project because it allowed for eliciting multiple perspectives of student life in and out of the classroom

environment. Focus group research is a popular social science approach that has been particularly effective in providing information about why people think or feel the way they do (Krueger, 1988). Given the exploratory nature of this study, the focus group technique was considered a suitable approach to uncover the dynamics associated with negotiating the transition to college. Of particular concern was the use of student voices that provide richness, nuance and candidness.

Each college was selected because of its location to predominant Latino communities, which is reflected in the colleges' composition of the student body. One college is located in a suburb of southern California that has historically been the center of Latino political and economic development in the region. As one of nine campuses comprising the Los Angeles Community College District, its Latino student population consists of significant numbers of Mexican American and Central American students. The second college is located in a west Texas city with a predominant Mexican American population and has been recognized for its international importance along the U.S. and Mexico border. The third college, located in New York City, is a campus within the City University of New York, and enrolls a significant number of Puerto Rican and Dominican students. In addition to the diversity among Latino students who participated in this project, each college offered variation in student characteristics (e.g. first-generation status, gender, family background, socioeconomic level) and institutional traits (e.g. size, curricular emphasis, geographical location). Fictitious campus names were employed to ensure anonymity.

A Profile of Latino Community College Students
As mentioned previously, 44 Latino students participated in nine focus group interviews for this project. Three focus group interviews were conducted at each campus. Each interview session was conducted with four to six students during their second semester in college. The number of students interviewed at each campus was: 17 at West Coast Community College (WCCC), 13 at Southwest Community College (SCC) and 14 at Big Apple Community College (BACC). Two of the 14 Big Apple students self-identified as biracial with one at least one parent being from a Latino background. Among the 44 Latino students, 19 were male and 25 were female. Therefore, 43% of all respondents were male while 57% were female. The gender distribution of the study was nearly representative of the distribution at all three campuses where approximately 55% of the student population was female.

While most students participating in this study entered community college immediately following high school, others had taken time off to enter the military, workforce, or became parents. The average age of the student participation was 20. The oldest student was 41 years of age. Thirty-four students were of traditional college age (18–24 years) while 10 were over 24 years of age.

Most students interviewed at each campus had set high aspirations for themselves. For example, when asked to name their career interests, students at all three campuses spoke of becoming electrical engineers, college faculty, psychologists, historians, paleontologists, entrepreneurs, commercial artists, computer programmers, lawyers, high school teachers, medical doctors, professional musicians, and various types of legal and law enforcement professionals. Some of these students were already on the path of attaining success while serving as college recruiters at their former high schools, role models to younger family members and friends, nursing home volunteers, and student leaders on campus. The following section describes student background characteristics in greater detail including students' educational objectives, employment status, enrollment status, and first generation student status.

Educational Objectives

The majority of student participants in this study were enrolled in traditional, transfer-related academic programs. Students at each campus conveyed their desire to achieve more than an Associate of Arts or Associate of Science degree. Thirty-nine of 44 students conveyed that they were enrolled in transfer programs leading to a baccalaureate degree. Among the most popular transfer-related majors were biology, computer science, education, engineering, and political science. The popular Associate degree programs mentioned were: administration of justice, general studies, law enforcement, and nursing.

Employment Status

The findings regarding employment status for students participating in this study conveyed mixed results. The number of students who were employed (23) was slightly more than those who were unemployed or not seeking work (21). While the majority of students at West Coast (11) and half the students at Big Apple (7) were unemployed, the majority of students at Southwest (13) and half the students at Big Apple (7) indicated they were employed at least on a part-time basis.

A total of 11 students at West Coast were unemployed during their second semester in college. Six students were employed at least part-time. Five of the six conveyed that they were working at least 20 hours per week. Two students were working in excess of 30 hours per week, with one student stating that he was "working more than full-time" (40+ hours per week).

Eight Southwest students were employed at least part-time, while five were unemployed. Two of the eight students who were employed mentioned that they were working full-time, while another was working a minimum of 35 hours per week. Five students were working on a part-time basis.

A total of seven students were employed at least part-time at Big Apple while another seven were unemployed or not seeking work. Among those who were working, six of the seven students were working between 20 and 30 hours per week. The other student mentioned that he was working between 31 and 40 hours per week.

Enrollment Status

Nearly all students interviewed were attending college on a full-time basis (42 of 44 students). At Southwest, all 13 students reported that they were attending college on a full-time basis. At West Coast, 16 of 17 students mentioned that they were attending full-time. At Big Apple only one student was attending on a part-time basis while 13 were enrolled full-time. The one student attending West Coast on a part-time basis was a young woman who was working full-time. Several students who were attending college on a full-time basis revealed that they were also parents with infant children, including one mother of six.

First Generation Student Status

For the most part, the students interviewed at both campuses reflected the profile of what is known about first-generation working class community college students. At Southwest Community College an overwhelming majority (77%) of students were the first in their family to attend college while the remainder (23%) were the second in their family to attend college.

At West Coast Community College, a majority of the students were split between those who were the first and those who were the third in their family to attend college. The college participatory breakdown for students attending West Coast were: 35% were the first in their family to attend college; 18% were second; 41% were third; and 6% were the fourth member of their family to attend college.

At Big Apple, 12 of the 14 students were the first in their family to attend college. This number represented 86% of all Big Apple participants. Only two students conveyed that another family member had previously attended college. In both cases a sibling was identified as the family member who had entered college previously. One Latino male student had two older brothers who attended college previously. Another student had enrolled at Big Apple at the same time as her brother and mother.

The demographic characteristics and educational background of students participating in this study appear typical of many Latino community college students. While most were traditional age students there were a notable number over 24 years of age. While the majority attended college on a full-time basis, almost half of the participants were working at least part-time and off-campus. Despite the challenges posed by their first-generation status the majority of students aspired to enter professional career fields and had transferable educational goals. Nonetheless, the success and satisfaction with the first-year college experience hinged on transitional issues encountered by each student.

Findings Related to the Transition to College

In this second section attention is focused on how students negotiated the transition to college. The themes presented in this section are derived from accounts provided by students including descriptions of their own experiences. Uncovering cultural realities through the use of student voices provides an important context for understanding the issues involved in making the transition to college. The following section details students desire for academic rigor; varying opinions of college coursework; expectations of academic intensity; receiving assistance from family, friends, and faculty; and the impact of the first-year experience on relationships.

Students Desire for Academic Rigor

Because student expectations can often mediate first-year college experiences, we sought to understand what students expected from their collegiate experience within and outside of class. An analysis of focus group transcripts revealed that there were multiple instances within each campus where students shared similar expectations of college. A majority of students in this study identified academic rigor in coursework, among peers and faculty, as their primary expectation of college. In learning about the expectations students held, we also discovered how they developed their expectations and addressed the disjuncture between their expectations and their experiences during their first year in college.

One continuous theme resonating throughout each focus group was the expectation students held of their collegiate peers. Overall, students expected to meet academically like-minded peers who were serious, mature, and academically supportive. Instead, students often described their peers as "kids," "young," with an "immature attitude," and "probably grown up in age but not in mind." A few students elaborated on these phrases by recounting how students they met did not appear serious about their academic work. It should be noted that a majority of the students who participated in this study were traditional age undergraduate students, and many had entered college immediately after their graduation from high school. Students explained, however, how they drew a very clear distinction between their peers who attended college during the day and those who attended during the evening. Students in each focus group consistently described their peers who attended evening courses as "more mature," "serious," and "dedicated" toward their education.

Nonetheless, some students indicated that they met some peers who were serious about their coursework. For example, Yolanda and Julia, two traditional age Big Apple students, expressed their feelings about the academic quality of their collegiate peers:

> *Yolanda*: There are a lot of people that really want to try and really are trying. They want to transfer and they have goals. But there are others who come to hang out.
> *Julia*: But you can find friends in class who will study with you.

On the other hand, Tamara, a Big Apple student, shared a poignant story that reflected her hopes and disappointments about the academic seriousness of her fellow students:

> I came to this school and I'm thinking, okay, I can find friends that are mature. Because from high school to college it's a totally different scene. You want it to be a mature crowd. You want to talk about sophisticated things, and you don't want to gossip, talk about sex and stuff. And that's what it's all about in this school. I have a friend that goes to NYU. In his school there is a group he studies with and it's not about making friends, it's about studying Shakespeare together. He says, "We're all collaborating so when we take the test, we know what we're doing." And it's like, you can't do that here because people look at you like you're weird, or you're trying to be something you're not.

Although some students suggested that their expectation of meeting serious-minded peers had gone unmet, others shared how they worked proactively to seek out such students. For instance, Raymond and Robert, traditional age Southwest students, believed the classroom and campus atmosphere during the day was too immature for them and therefore enrolled in evening classes.

During our interviews, students shared how they handled disruptive students in class in order to maintain their academic focus. For instance, when Laura, a West Coast student discussed the distractions she experienced in classes when other students talked out of order, entered late, or failed to complete class assignments, a male student in the group confirmed her observations and frustrations. Enrique later shared the coping mechanisms he had taken to eliminate similar distractions in class such as speaking to the instructor after class, sitting toward the front of the classroom, and avoiding group work with those not serious about learning. These students' experiences imply that they believed it is each student's responsibility to stay focused on their academic needs and purposes for attending college. Carina, a Southwest student shared her belief that, "It is up to the individual to take responsibility for his or her academic success in college."

Varying Opinions of Community College Coursework

Students in this study addressed the issue of community college coursework. Most categorized their studies as "hard" as in academically challenging, or "easy" as in academically unchallenging. Students suggested that they often used their classroom experiences in high school as a comparison for what they expected from their college coursework. For instance, Javier, a Big Apple student, expressed his expectation for academic rigor in college courses: "I would expect the level of work to be to be a little tougher than it was in high school."

Expectations concerning the academic rigor of college coursework seemed to be influenced by students' belief that the college experience is supposed to be difficult; by the reputation each community college had among students' family or peers; or by prior conversations with friends. For instance, Carlos conveyed how he expected the academic work at Big Apple to be difficult because of conversations he had with friends in college: "I expected a lot of work, a lot of hard work. Like what all my friends that are in college tell me."

While almost half of the students interviewed conveyed that they felt their courses were "hard," many shared the opinion that their courses were "easy." It was noted that among students who felt their academic coursework was "easy," most were enrolled in at least one remedial course. For example, Sandra, a West Coast student shared her disappointment and frustration when revealing that she was placed in a remedial course where she felt unchallenged. She shared her opinion that the course had not helped prepare her for passing an exam that would allow her to enroll in a transferable English composition course.

For students who shared the opinion of an academically unchallenged first year, most conveyed that their beliefs were formed in part from the reputation that the college held among their friends and family members. For instance, Lucy, a Big Apple student, shared that through discussions with family members she was told that Big Apple fostered a social environment not conducive for students: "My generation, like my younger brothers, think of [Big Apple] as a big hang out [place]. They don't think that you are serious when you come here."

Students expressed that they were sometimes teased by friends or family members for electing to attend a community college. While some students stated that they were not offended by such taunting others affirmed that their impression of community college education had been influenced by others' opinions at the start of their first year in college. Javier, a Big Apple student, shared how he based his opinion of the academic quality of Big Apple on what others had told him previously about the similarity between college life and his experiences in high school: "Before I came to this college, a lot of people told me that it was going to be just the same as high school." Javier's comment was typical of those we heard from students who were told that community colleges were unchallenging. However, most students shared that by the end of their first year in college, they felt their coursework was as difficult as they expected.

While some students conveyed that they believed their courses were "easy," others shared that they felt their courses were challenging. A Southwest student confirmed that his coursework was "real work" when asked to compare his courses to those offered at the university level. When asked about the quality of courses at Southwest Community College, Ricardo, a transfer student, stated, "The academics at [Southwest] are really excellent."

For most students in this study who shared that their first language is not English, college courses were not identified as "easy." Lucy, a Big Apple student, stated: "I have found it [Big Apple coursework] more difficult than high school. Learning English has been very difficult." Lucy's comments regarding the difficulty of learning English at the college level underscores one of the several challenges identified by students during their first year in college. In addition, approximately 66% of all students participating in this study self-identified themselves as the first in their family to attend college. This fact suggests that without the assistance of various campus agents some students would experience difficulty transitioning to the demands of college coursework and the first-year college experience.

Obtaining Assistance from Family, Friends, and Faculty

The group interviews were designed to uncover helpful and unhelpful elements during students' transition to college. At each campus, students eagerly shared how individuals helped and supported them throughout their first year. This help most often came from family members, specifically their parents, but also significant others, on- and off-campus friends, and faculty.

The assistance provided by students' families was direct, such as providing financial assistance for tuition and related expenses, childcare, removing of household responsibilities, and in one case, receiving academic tutoring from a father. Though many students shared that they received financial assistance from their parents, several students identified their siblings or extended family members as being helpful during their first year in college. Most often, financial assistance and household support were noted as helpful. When asked who was the most influential person in his life, Nestor, a West Coast student stated: "My grandmother is very important in my life because she allows me to live with her and feeds me so that all I have to do is go to school and get good grades."

Students who had parents or siblings who attended college before them also spoke of the helpful nature of their family members' advice in regards to selecting academic majors, securing financial aid, choosing classes, preparing for exams, and reconciling students' expectations during their first year in college. David, a West Coast student stated that his brothers were helpful during his first year: "I was lucky, I had two brothers who went to college before me and they've really helped me out."

Assistance from family members also came in the form of emotional support. Students reported how family members inspired, motivated, encouraged, and supported them. For example, a Southwest student shared how her son's graduation from college inspired her to pursue a college education with his support. In addition, Lorena, a West Coast student, described how her mother inspired her to set goals for herself and to fight to obtain them. Lorena shared her motivation to follow in her mother's footsteps by not giving up her desire to earn a baccalaureate degree in Psychology: "My mother taught me to fight for everything. She has always set goals and reached them. To me, it's important to follow her footsteps. She says that when you desire something, you have to go after it. She tells me that if you fail, that it is not a reason to give up but a reason to keep going."

For those students who were parents, most acknowledged the help they received from their children. One student shared that her children were willing to "be good and quiet when I study." Sonya, a Big Apple student, restated what many students said they felt about their families: "They are there for me. We are a very united family and they are always there for me."

Similar sentiments were also expressed about friends, on and off campus. Friends on campus were most often recognized as being helpful when they provided academic assistance or rendered encouragement. One Southwest student stated: "My friends help me if I have problems with my studying." Whereas on-campus friends were recognized as helpful when they provided academic support and encouragement, off-campus friends were described as helpful when they provide emotional support and motivation. Irene, a Big Apple student who had dropped out of high school 15 years earlier, stated: "My best friend is really glad I'm in school. When people want to talk to me, she tells them, 'Not right now because Irene has to get to class.' She'll walk me to school and I'll meet her on my break."

While on campus, students communicated that they recognized and appreciated the help, support, and encouragement provided by faculty and counselors. For instance, three students enrolled in West Coast's Puente Project, a retention program promoting Latino student transfer to the University of California, shared examples of how their Puente counselor provided academic guidance and advice about life outside of college. Other students shared how faculty "reached out" to them when they missed class due to illness or a crisis. One student stated that she simply appreciated how a faculty member was able to help her become self-reflective about her life. Students also conveyed that faculty were more willing to help them when they demonstrated effort in class. One group of Southwest students agreed that it was imperative they performed well on class assignments so they could garner help from their professors.

The Impact of the First-Year Experience on Relationships

Students made it clear that family and friends were instrumental in helping and supporting them during their first year college experience. However, since the college experience has the potential to create psychosocial changes in students, the interview questions were designed to elicit information on the changing nature of student relations with family and friends. Responses from students in this study revealed that community college attendance often improved family relations, although it limited the amount of time students could spend with family members. Few students commented that a family member trivialized their college experience. College attendance appeared to affect friendships in more complex ways than did family relations, including the termination of some friendships that could not be sustained after students enrolled in college.

Students in this study beamed with pride when they recounted the positive changes in their relationship with family members, particularly with parents. They shared numerous stories on how their parents "bragged about them" to friends or extended family members, treated them differently, giving them more attention and even more "respect." A few students reported their parents interpreted their college attendance as a sign of maturity or responsibility. In addition, students offered stories on how their parents were "happy" about their college enrollment, as did Irene, a Big Apple student: "The relationship with my parents has gotten better. They are really happy that I'm going to school because I was a high school dropout. I'm pretty old, 32, I have not been in school for about 15 years. My family members are really happy that I'm going to school."

Although students experienced positive changes in their relationship with their parents, many shared the frustration at having limited time to spend with family members. Sandra, a Southwest student who previously shared the support she received from her nine-year old daughter, also lamented the drawback of attending college: "I do not spend as much time with my daughter anymore. I feel badly about that. I come home at 11 p.m. and she is already in bed; she leaves me little notes to catch me up on what happened during the day. It's like we are ships passing in the night. I miss being there for my family and friends."

However, students in this study who felt similarly distressed, offered that they reconciled their distress with the belief that they were working toward a "greater good," "to improve themselves," for the "future of their children," or the ability to "care for parents."

While relations with family members generally improved, several students commented that their relationships with friends seemed more tenuous as social roles were renegotiated and their loyalty to former friendships was tested. Julia, a Big Apple student, revealed how her friendship had been impacted by her enrollment first year in college: "I only have one best friend. She's the total opposite of me, she's not in college. I know she respects me but she feels intimidated that I'm in college."

While these students were searching for and finding ways to maintain their friendships with those outside of their college experience, others felt their relationships with friends had become impaired. When elaborating on her friendships with those who chose not to attend college, Tamara, a Big Apple student, stated: "The phone calls have stopped and the hanging out has stopped too."

For those who commented on their impaired relationships with friends, most attributed this outcome to the lack of available time needed to nurture friendships and the growing difference in common interests. Some students, however, suggested that they did not seek to maintain their former friendships with those who had negative influences on their lives or because they trivialized their college enrollment. Whether friendships were stable, in flux, growing, or diminishing, most students discussed reevaluating their relationships with off-campus friends in order to determine the effect on them during their first year in college.

The Uniqueness of the First-Year Community College Experience

When students were asked about the "specialness" of their first year in college, one group of Big Apple students stated that they felt their first year was unique because they had an opportunity to reflect upon and plan their future. Another Big Apple student group shared that they sought to clarify their academic goals.

Yet other students at all three campuses conveyed that they enjoyed the fact that they "came up to speed," took remedial courses for free, or repeated classes without penalty. A group of West Coast students agreed in viewing their first year in community college as an opportunity to "redeem themselves," providing a second chance to fulfill their educational goals. Most students conveyed that they used their time on campus for multiple purposes and felt the responsibility of faculty and staff was to help students fulfill their educational and career goals.

Student responses in each focus group interview provided a glimpse into their transition from high school or work to college. These students conveyed that despite their previous educational experiences or socio-economic status, they were proud to have the opportunity to earn a college degree. They also made extraordinary observations as to the role of the urban community college. Sonya, a Big Apple student, appeared to have summarized the feelings of many students at all three campuses when she commented that her college needed to "be there for us."

RETENTION IMPLICATIONS

Although this study was exploratory in nature, its findings may prove beneficial to educators, policymakers and others interested in a better understanding of the first-year experiences of 44 Latino community college students. The findings from this study may also prove useful to those interested in further examining several important influences on student transitions to college. Although this was not a study of student retention, it was aimed toward gaining greater insights into transition issues and the first-year experience so that community college policymakers and practitioners might consider using the study's findings to address student support services to enhance first-year student retention rates.

Community colleges have made inroads in understanding the needs of nontraditional first-year students. However, they must continue to assist these students in negotiating the transition to college and enhance their opportunities to form connections with campus agents and institutional offerings. Rendón (1994) suggested that additional research is needed to explore how in- and out-of-class experiences influence these dynamics in college, especially during the critical first year. Moreover, a special focus is needed to address the Latino student experience, given the group's high rate of attrition in community colleges. By examining the the first year experience of Latino community college students, transitional issues may be uncovered and evaluated in an attempt to curb the historically high attrition rate for this student group.

ACKNOWLEDGMENTS

The author wishes to thank Ms. Monica Martinez and Mr. Nelson Reynoso, doctoral candidates in the Higher Education Administration program at New York University who served as Research Assistants on the project. A word of thanks is also in order for Mr. Adrian Trejo, EOP&S Counselor at Monterey Peninsula College who provided assistance with the review of the research literature on student persistence in college.

REFERENCES

Aguirre, A., & Martinez, R. (1993). Chicanos in higher education: Issues and dilemmas for the 21st Century. *ASHE-ERIC Higher Education Report No. 3*. Washington, D.C.: The George Washington University.

Anderson, K. (1981). Post-high school experiences and college attrition. *Sociology of Education*, *54*, 1–15.

Astin, A. (1982). *Minorities in American higher education: Recent trends, current perspectives and recommendations*. San Francisco: Jossey-Bass.

Astin, A. (1985). *Achieving educational excellence: A critical assessment of priorities and practices in higher education*. San Francisco: Jossey-Bass.

Carter, D., & Wilson, R. (1994). *1993 Twelfth annual status report: Minorities in higher education*. Washington, D.C.: American Council on Education, Office of Minorities in Higher Education.

Cohen, A., & Brawer, F. (1996). *The American community college* (3rd ed.). San Francisco: Jossey-Bass.

Chronicle of Higher Education (2001). Almanac issue (Volume 48, No. 1, August 21). Washington D.C.: The Chronicle of Higher Education.

Duran, R. (1983). *Hispanics' education and background: Predictors of college achievement*. New York: College Entrance Examination Board.

Hurtado, A., & Garcia, E. (1994). *The educational achievement of Latinos: barriers and successes*. Santa Cruz, CA: Regents of the University of California.

Jalomo, R. (1995). Latino students in transition: An analysis of the first-year experience in the community college. Unpublished doctoral dissertation, Arizona State University, 1995.

Jalomo, R. (2000–2001). Assessing Minority Student Performance in Community Colleges. In: S. Aragon (Ed.), *New Directions for Community Colleges: Increasing Retention and Learning Success for Minority Students* (Winter, pp. 7–18). San Francisco, CA: Jossey-Bass Publishers.

Jalomo, R. (2001). Institutional Policies That Promote Persistence among First-Year Community College Students. In: B. K. Townsend & S. Twombly (Eds), *Community Colleges: Policy in the Future Context* (pp. 261–281). Stamford, CT: Ablex Publishing.

Krueger, R. (1988). *Focus groups: A practical guide for applied research*. Newbury Park, CA: Sage Publications.

Kuh, G., Schuh, J., Whitt, E. & Associates. (1991). *Involving colleges: Successful approaches to fostering student learning and development outside the classroom*. San Francisco: Jossey-Bass.

London, H. (1989). Breaking away: A study of first generation college students and their families. *American Journal of Education, 97*(February), 144–170.

London, H. (1992). Transformations: Cultural challenges faced by first generation students. In: S. Zwerling & H. London (Eds), First generation students: confronting the cultural issues. *New Directions for Community Colleges No. 80, 20*(4), 5–12.

Mow, S., & Nettles, M. (1990). Minority student access to, and persistence and performance in, college: A review of the trends and research literature. In: J. Smart (Ed.), *Higher Education: Handbook of Theory and Research* (Vol. 6, pp. 35–105). New York: Agatha Press.

Nora, A. (1993). Two-year colleges and minority students' educational aspirations: Help or hindrance? In: J. Smart (Ed.), *Higher Education: Handbook of Theory and Research* (Vol. 9, pp. 212–247). New York: Agatha Press.

Nora, A., & Cabrera, A. (1992). A theoretical framework for the study of minority undergraduate student persistence. Research paper presentation at the Hispanic Association for Colleges and Universities' (HACU) National Conference on the Retention of Hispanic College Students, Boulder, CO.

Nora, A., Castaneda, M., & Cabrera, A. (1993). College persistence: Structural equations modeling test of an integrated model of student retention. *Journal of Higher Education, 64*(2), 123–139.

Nora, A., Kraemer, B., & Itzen, R. (1997). Persistence among non-traditional Hispanic college students: A causal model. Research paper presentation at the annual meeting of the Association for the Study of Higher Education (ASHE). Albuquerque, NM (November 4).

Nora, A., & Rendón, L. (1990). Determinants of predisposition to transfer among community college students: A structural model. *Research in Higher Education, 31*, 235–255.

O'Brien, E. M. (1993). *Latinos in higher education.* Research Brief. Vol. 4, No. 4. American Council on Education, Division of Policy Analysis and Research, Washington, D.C.

Olivas, M. (1986). *Latino college students.* New York: Teachers College Press.

Padrón, E. (1994). Hispanics and Community Colleges. In: G. Baker (Ed.), *A Handbook on the Community College in America.* Westport, CT: Greeenwood Press.

Pascarella, E., & Terenzini, P. (1991). *How college affects students: Findings and insights from twenty years of research.* San Francisco: Jossey-Bass.

Rendón, L. (1992). From the barrio to the academy. Revelations of a Mexican American scholarship girl. In: S. Zwerling & H. London (Eds), First generation students: Confronting the cultural issues. *New Directions for Community colleges No. 80, 20*(4), 55–64.

Rendón, L. (1994). Validating culturally diverse students: Toward a new model of learning and student development. *Innovative Higher Education, 19*(1), 23–32.

Rendón, L., & Hope, R. (1996). *Educating a New Majority: Transforming America's Educational System for Diversity.* San Francisco: Jossey-Bass.

Rendón, L., Jalomo, R., & Garcia, K. (1994). The University and Community College Paradox: Why Latinos Do Not Transfer. In: A. Hurtado & E. Garcia (Eds), *The Educational Achievement of Latinos: Barriers and Successes* (pp. 227–258). Santa Cruz, CA: Regents of the University of California.

Rendón, L., & Nora, A. (1988). Hispanics students: Stopping the leaks in the pipeline. *Educational Record, 68*(4), 79–85.

Richardson, R., & Skinner, E. (1992). Helping first generation minority students achieve degrees. In: S. Zwerling & H. London (Eds), First generation students: Confronting the cultural issues. *New Directions for Community Colleges No. 80, 20*(4), 29–44.

Rodriguez, R. (1982). *Hunger of memory.* Boston: David R. Godine Publishers.

Schlossberg, N., Lynch, A., & Chickering, A. (1989). *Improving higher education for adults.* San Francisco: Jossey-Bass.

Terenzini, P., Rendón, L., Upcraft, L., Millar, S., Allison, K., Gregg, P., & Jalomo, R. (1994). The transition to college: Diverse students, diverse stories. *Research in Higher Education, 35*(1), 57–73.

Tierney, W. (1992). An anthropological analysis of student participation in college. *Journal of Higher Education, 63*(6), 603–618.

Tinto, V. (1993). *Leaving college: Rethinking the causes and cures of student departure* (2nd ed.). Chicago: University of Chicago Press.

Upcraft, L., & Gardner, J. (1989). *The freshman year experience.* San Francisco: Jossey-Bass.

Valadez, J. (1993). Cultural capital and its impact on the aspirations of nontraditional community college students. *Community College Review, 21*(3), 30–43.

Weis, L. (1985). *Between two worlds: Black students in an urban community college.* Boston: Routledge and Kegan Paul.

Weis, L. (1992). Discordant voices in the urban community college. In: S. Zwerling & H. London (Eds), *First Generation Students: Confronting the Cultural Issues: New Directions for Community Colleges No. 80, 20*(4), 13–28.

Zwerling, S. (1992). First generation adult students. In: S. Zwerling & H. London (Eds), First generation students: confronting the cultural issues. *New Directions For Community Colleges No. 80* (Vol. 20, No. 4, pp. 45–54). San Francisco, CA: Jossey-Bass.

SUCCESSFUL TRANSITIONS OF LATINO STUDENTS FROM HIGH SCHOOL TO COLLEGE

Harriett Romo and Joanne Salas

INTRODUCTION

This paper looks at key issues that affect the successful transitions of Latino students to postsecondary educational programs. The authors pay special attention to successful transition to college in Texas. The paper explores ways to promote successful college entry and earned degrees for Latino students. Examples are drawn from interviews with first-generation college attendees enrolled at a major research university in Texas and the authors' experiences in teaching in some of the programs discussed. The student interviews illustrate the difficulties students encounter because of poor high school preparation for postsecondary education and parents' lack of knowledge in education. The student interviews shed light on the importance of the availability of high quality colleges and universities, the affordability of higher education, and programs that help students make timely progress toward completing degrees. Successful institutional strategies, such as freshman seminars, learning communities, and 2 + 2 collaborations between community colleges and four-year institutions are discussed.

Latinos in Higher Education, Volume 3, pages 107–130.
© 2003 Published by Elsevier Science Ltd.
ISBN: 0-7623-0980-6

THE STATUS OF THE CURRENT SITUATION

The ethnic breakdown in the nation's universities in 1996 was 79.6% Caucasian, 13.3% African American, and 6.6% Hispanic. The enrollment of Hispanics has been increasing, but still lags behind the proportion of non-Hispanic White and Black students who enroll in post-secondary education. During the last ten years, African Americans have shown a 63.1% increase, Hispanics a 53.3% increase, and Caucasians a 6.6% increasing college enrollments (ACT Program et al., 1997). The distribution of fall enrollment of Hispanics in degree-granting institutions increased from 4% in 1980 to 8.6% in 1997 (National Center for Education Statistics, 2001:19), but a 1998 summary of first time-full-time students in public U.S. universities indicated that 82.6% of those freshman students were Caucasian, 7.2% were African American, 1.8% were American Indians, 7.3% were Asian, and 1.4% were Hispanic (American Freshman Survey, 1998). The increases, while positive, do not reflect the Latino distribution in the U.S. population, which is approximately 12%.

Latino distribution in the K-12 student population is even higher. Data from the University of California Latino Eligibility Task Force suggests that Hispanic K-12 enrollments are growing by more than 200,000 students per year and are expected to reach over five million in 2005 (University of California, 1997). That represents about a 130% increase since 1987. The number of Hispanic participants in higher education has not kept pace with the growing Hispanic K-12 school age population and the rapidly increasing numbers of Hispanic high school graduates (Garcia, 2001, p. 197). In California, approximately 9% of Hispanic high school graduates applied to the University of California in 1997–1998 compared to 10.2% in 1989–1990 (Garcia, 2001, pp. 197–198). An analysis of similar data led researchers Nevarez-la Torre and Hidalgo (1997) to conclude that the number of Hispanic students in higher education is dismal. Studies have also shown that increasing enrollments in higher education have not produced significant increases in Hispanic graduation rates (Guzman, 1996).

Measuring Up 2000, a report prepared by the National Center for Public Policy and Higher Education examined how effective each state in the United States has been in providing its residents with opportunities for education and training beyond high school. Many states with high percentages of Latino students received low grades. In Texas, 81% of the young adults earn a high school diploma or GED by age 24. However only a fair percentage of Texas' high school students enroll in upper-level math and science courses. Texas received a D in Participation because a very low percentage of students go on to college immediately after high school (32%) and only a fair percentage (30%) of young adults ages 18–24 are enrolled in college-level education or training.

The *Measuring Up* report did not break down these figures by ethnic group. If it had, the results might have been even more striking because large gaps persist between the successful transition of Latino and African American students from high school to college and the success rates of such transfers for Whites.

Census numbers regarding the Latino community have broad implications for improving higher education opportunities (Center for Educational Statistics, 1996). The current college enrollment of 15 million for all students is expected to climb by 3.3 million by 2015. Latino students are expected to comprise 40% of that enrollment growth. Unless we are prepared to make the transitions to college successful ones, the large gap that presently exists between Hispanics and non-Hispanic Whites and Blacks in high school graduation and college completion will persist. According to a report in *Hispanic Outlook* (Alicea, 2001, pp. 21–22), the 2000 Census found that 57% of Hispanics 25 and over had graduated from high school, compared to 88% of non-Hispanic Whites in the same age category. Only one in 10 Hispanics (10.6%) had a college degree. Among non-Hispanic Whites, 28.1% had a college degree. Garcia (2001) found similar gaps. Hispanics were less than half as likely to graduate from college as Whites. Only 13% of the 25–28-year-old Hispanics had earned a bachelor's degree or more, compared to 30% of Whites (Garcia, 2001, p. 196).

Four states, New Mexico with 42% Latino population, California and Texas with 32% Latino population each, and Arizona with 25% Latino population, account for a very large percent of the Latino students in schools. New York and Florida with 15.1% and 16.8% Latino population respectively account for an additional large number of the growing Latino population.

One of the most important findings of the report *Measuring Up 2000* was how widely the opportunities for higher education varied from state to state. There are also extreme variations from city to city and from school district to school district. Thus, the place where a person resides affects his/her chance of enrolling in and completing college. This ultimately affects one's life chances – and cumulatively affects the prosperity of the United States and individual states, cities, and neighborhoods.

Of course, other factors in addition to where one lives also influence opportunities. School organizational factors, courses and quality of instruction available, personal financial resources, ethnicity, gender, age, and personal drive and motivation all affect positive transitions from high school to college. In organizing this paper, the authors focus on categories of performance that the *Measuring Up* report found to be especially important. Those categories are: (1) preparation for educational success beyond high school; (2) participation in post secondary programs; (3) availability of high quality colleges and universities; and (4) affordability. The categories of performance identified in the *Measuring Up* report are critical because they are susceptible to influence by city and state policies, corporate concern and attention, and by the intervention of groups and individuals.

APPROACH

Data are drawn from existing studies, census reports, and interviews conducted by the authors. Harriett Romo interviewed ten freshman students from diverse backgrounds who successfully completed a university freshman seminar she taught. Students were asked a series of open-ended questions about their experiences at college, their high school experiences, and their first semester course work. Joanne Salas interviewed eight Mexican origin first-generation college students from working class backgrounds who had made successful transitions to a major research university in Texas. She asked open-ended questions about high school preparation, mentors, and experiences at the university. All interviews were tape-recorded and transcribed. These interviews provide the perspectives of students who have made successful transfers from high school to college. The authors also draw from their teaching and counseling experiences to discuss programs that promote successful transitions from high school to college.

HOW WELL ARE WE PREPARING LATINO STUDENTS TO BENEFIT FROM EDUCATION AND TRAINING BEYOND HIGH SCHOOL?

The level of preparation of high school students for college is uneven and not as excellent as it could and should be. Among Latino college students, the range of writing and other college readiness skills varies. Many Latino students have not taken high level math or English courses in high school to prepare them for high scores on the SAT exams or for college level work. First generation college-bound students know little about the tutoring and preparation courses available outside of the school context to help them in college preparation; moreover, few have the financial resources to access such courses.

Extensive research in the late 1980s showed clearly that course taking patterns have a strong relationship with persistence and achievement in college. Researchers analyzing the *High School & Beyond* data set looked at course-taking patterns in secondary schools and the relationship of course-taking patterns to student characteristics (Lee & Bryk, 1988; West, Miller & Diodato, 1985). Hispanic students represented only about 9% of the math concentrators relative to their overall representation of 16% in the population. Hispanic students were over-represented in the non-participant (not taking high level math courses) categories. Yet high percentages of the Latino students in the general education program expected to complete a four or five-year BA degree and almost 11% expected to earn a MA degree or above. The authors of the study questioned whether this was possible given their course taking patterns. The authors found that in general, educational expectations of students were consistent with their high school course taking patterns. A higher percentage of students who participated intensely in math, science, or computer science expected to attain at least a four-year or five-year college degree. Vocational education and general education students were more likely to end formal education with high school or to include vocational track or business schools in their future plans. Students who had participated in more intense level math, science and computer science classes earned higher overall grade averages and scored higher on tests designed to measure vocabulary, verbal and math abilities. The reverse was true for vocational education and general education participation. Students who participated more intensely in math and science were more likely than other students to have taken part in school extra-curricular activities that enhanced academic skills, such as the school newspaper, yearbook, honor society, service clubs, or varsity athletics. It is difficult, but not impossible, to make up for skills lost in earlier years of education. But to make sure that that loss does not continue, high schools must emphasize factors that contribute to higher levels of preparation.

Jeannie Oakes (1985) in a study of 25 junior and senior high schools found that the practice of dividing students into instructional groups on a criterion of assumed similarity of academic attainment is widespread. Students may be "tracked" for only a few classes or for an entire range of school-based learning. Research has shown that dividing a class into different level ability groups and singling out some students for special attention also creates socially significant classifications on the basis of which others respond differentially. When instruction is applied differentially in tracked classes or groups, and research has shown convincingly that it is (Oakes, 1985; Oakes, Ormseth, Bell & Camp, 1990; Rist, 1979), substantial learning differences are produced.

Rist's work shows how teachers often make very early assessments of students' academic ability based on sociocultural factors that have little relationship to academic ability. For example, in Risk's 1979 study of kindergarten teachers' grouping practices, he found that teachers used children's appearance, use of non-standard English, and other non-academic factors to make determinations about their academic potential and skills. Although teachers sometimes view tracking as a way of reducing student variability and thus making teaching more manageable, tracked classes still have a wide range of ability and often prevent efforts to meet individual academic needs and differences. Oakes and other researchers (Adelman, 1999; King, 2000) have found that one of the best predictors of both enrollment and success in college is the rigor of the high school curriculum. The availability of a full range of higher-level classes is not equally distributed in our various high schools. Efforts to expand the training programs for teachers to prepare them to offer more high-level classes are underway in many states, but there is still a great disparity in course offerings in U.S. high schools.

A report by the U.S. Department of Education (Condition of Education, 1996) found several patterns among students who enrolled in four-year colleges. They were academically prepared (had completed at least one advanced math course). They had received help in completing the college application process, a type of help provided more frequently in Advanced Placement (AP) and Honors courses than in low track courses. They were more likely to have participated in extracurricular activities in high school. They had discussed school-related matters with their parents, and they were more likely to report that all or most of their friends planned to attend college. The family and friend criteria are also related to being in advanced level courses. Many of the students taking AP or Honors courses are not taking the courses because they have exceptional ability. Many of them have parents who know of the importance of advanced courses and insist that their children be placed in those courses (Useem, 1992). Parents who are unfamiliar with the ways U.S. schools are organized do not have such information and may not be aware that they can request placement of their children in higher level courses.

Moreover, the research on tracking has shown that the student-to-student relationships and student-to-teacher relationships in higher level classes are more likely to be positive and supportive than such relationships in lower level classes. Students tracked together with the same group of peers over several classes have more opportunities to make friends with those students than with others in different tracks. Students often receive more information and are more highly influenced in a number of important areas related to high school and academic work by peers than by either parents or teachers (Steinberg, Brown & Dornbusch, 1996). Still, even when Latino students are tracked into college preparatory classes, the rigors of those classes in small rural high schools or in urban high schools in largely minority communities may not prepare them adequately for college. Bright Latino students who made good grades in their high school courses with little effort frequently do not learn the study skills necessary for challenging college courses.

Salas (2000) found that only two of the eight first-generation Mexican American college students she interviewed had school counselors who helped them prepare for college entrance or helped them apply to college. For example, Jason, a first time college student had difficulties in making decisions about college. Rudy, another first-generation college student, discovered that in spite of what he thought was excellent academic preparation in high school, he was not prepared for the rigors of college. Lupe attended a high school designed to prepare students for science careers, but discovered that college classes were especially challenging.

Jason knew he wanted to go to college and applied to a Catholic college in a town away from his hometown because he had a friend whose parents recommended the college as an excellent school. He received a scholarship and attended a summer program at the college to ease the transition. But Jason discovered that he was not prepared for college life away from home. He explained: "I didn't know a soul. It was too hard for me. I couldn't deal with being alone. I couldn't deal with not having somebody there. I was just so depressed, so alone, I couldn't deal with it. So I came home that same summer."

Jason enrolled at a small public university in his home town but discovered that the student population there were mostly older, non-traditional students who commuted to college classes and worked full time. After a year, he transferred to a local community college where most of his friends attended. He took the initiative to write to a four-year university to find out the requirements for a major in pharmacy and planned his course work at the community college to prepare for the transition to the pharmacy program. At the time we interviewed him, he was in his second year at the four-year university. He was receiving financial aid and working part-time. Jason's situation illustrated the difficulties, and sometimes delays, that students experience when they have poor assistance in planning for college. Jason initially made college choices that did not work for him. Tenacity, goal directedness, and a determination to find a program that suited him helped him negotiate a system that many first-generation college students find difficult.

Rudy attended a very poor elementary school and middle school with a high teacher-turnover rate. He attended an exclusive college preparatory school on an athletic scholarship. He told us that he struggled to overcome the low expectations and poor academic rigor that he had experienced in his elementary and secondary schools. He explained: "In college I initially felt like there was something wrong with me. I felt like I had a learning disorder because I worked ten times harder than the person who got an A and would get a B. It was disturbing to me. It was like, 'Man, I thought I knew everything.' I worked hard but still ended up with that same grade."

Rudy's mother, a Mexican immigrant, and his elderly father had no expectations that Rudy would attend college. For them, having a son graduate from high school was a major accomplishment. They had no knowledge to help him through the college application process. Rudy discussed his difficulties with the Scholastic Aptitude Test (SAT).

> To tell you the truth, I took it twice and I barely got into college. My parents didn't know anything about it. I didn't know a whole lot about it. My counselors did not talk to me about it. I didn't even know there were prep courses or books to help you prepare. I just took it and I did bad. I mean really bad! I looked at my score and I didn't even know how to calculate it. I talked to a friend and he told me just add those numbers, the verbal and the math, and I was like 'Oh, God.' I was ashamed but I knew that my best work was not in something like an exam, or like a one-shot thing. I knew it was not an indication of how intelligent I am. I mean, my grades were good, and that was an indication of, you know, I'm a hard worker. But, my SAT was horrible and I was embarrassed. But I was going to college. I told my parents and they said, 'Sure, whatever you want to do, estamos contigo.' But even today, I don't think they even vaguely know what this is about. But hopefully during graduation, I'll give them a tour. First time and the last time.

Lupe attended a magnet school designed to prepare students for college, but she struggled with college level work her first year. Even though she had taken four years of math in high school, including calculus, she ended up taking a college algebra class at the community college to help her pass college science and math courses. An A student throughout high school, she earned primarily C's her first semester in college. She explained,

> I did read a lot in high school, but never the way you read in college, never. They give you worksheets in high school and you don't really have to read. You just look for the main points. And then you study off the worksheet and you make a good grade. And at college they don't have worksheets or anything like that.

When students are not adequately prepared for college in high schools, the colleges must offer remedial instruction. College level assistance programs, such as those that help students with study skills, writing mechanics, and other problems they may encounter in the transition to college, have proven to be very effective if the students take advantage of the services. However, it is often demoralizing and discouraging to students admitted to college to be told that they have not arrived with adequate reading, writing, and computing skills needed to be successful. Students become frustrated when they are placed in remedial classes that do not count toward a degree. Some have taken out loans or received financial aid that is expended on tuition for the remedial courses that contribute no progress toward their degree. This is particularly true for math classes.

One non-traditional student, previously a teacher in a Head Start preschool program for low-income three and four-year-olds, received a fellowship from the Head Start program to pursue a teaching credential. We interviewed Rosemary before she began her first semester of classes at a local college. When we asked about her anxieties about returning to school, she responded, "I didn't have high school. I'm afraid I will be behind the other students in the classes." We were expecting anxieties about college algebra or science or writing skills, and had not imagined that she had missed all the high school years. Rosemary had dropped out of school at the beginning of the 9th grade because of family and boyfriend problems. At the time, she had been an A student. When she enrolled in college, she would be in the same classrooms with students who had completed four years of high school, many of whom had taken college preparatory or advanced placement high school courses. Her college advisor assigned her a philosophy class, a history class, and two remedial courses – one in math and one in English. She did not know what philosophy was.

At the end of the first semester, we interviewed her again. She had done well in her courses. She made an A in the history class and an A in the two remedial classes. She made a B in Philosophy. She was angry that she had been assigned to the remedial courses. A large portion of her fellowship had been used to pay the tuition for the remedial courses that did not count toward her degree. She argued strongly that she could have handled the material in the regular classes. A less determined student might have been discouraged by this delay. The frustration level is especially high for older returning students who must juggle work and family responsibilities as well as school. Most feel that time lost toward the degree is a tremendous setback in their efforts to complete course requirements for graduation. This particular student did not enroll in any additional remedial courses and went on to earn a B.A. degree and a teaching credential. She made good use of counseling and tutoring services on the college campus and attended an adult education center in the evenings where she received additional tutoring and assistance with her college assignments.

A younger student enrolled in freshman classes experienced a similar situation. She was assigned two remedial courses and two regular courses in her major area. When she realized that she would not receive credit toward the BA degree for the remedial courses and her financial aid would be used for the tuition costs of those courses, she dropped out of college. The most unfortunate part was that she did not seek help from her professors or persons at the student services offices; she just stopped attending classes.

Research has clearly demonstrated that early intervention programs are more effective than remedial programs in preparing students for college (Fenske, Geranios, Keller & Moore, 1997). Among the most successful early intervention programs are school-college collaborations. Effective intervention programs require coordination between local school districts and college and university systems, particularly with regard to admission standards, to facilitate a seamless transition from one level of education to the other. By providing opportunities for K-12 students to get an early glimpse of college life, programs, and resources, the transitions to higher education are less daunting. Student services personnel, particularly academic advisors and admissions staff, can present a clear picture of the information and competencies that students require to successfully persist through higher education. With many experiences on a college campus and reinforcement of information from both college staff and K-12 personnel, once the student has reached the point of enrollment in college, the actual experience will seem more like a continuation than a shocking break in the continuum of education. The benefits of such a collaboration will be the improved readiness of entering freshmen.

An example of a program that involved Latino high school students in group projects that built cognitive, interpersonal, and communication skills needed in college is the Student Voices project. The project involved Latino students in research and public information dissemination to raise voter awareness and increase citizen participation in the voting process. The projects involved teamwork and marketing strategies. In a demonstration of final projects, students presented their work to the public at a local college campus. Projects receiving the highest number of points on criteria that included soundness of research, involvement of multimedia, evidence of a wide range of participation of team members and teamwork, significant content, and creativity won grants for their school's social studies program. Some students created a glossy magazine of student essays on issues such as maintenance of public parks, neighborhood safety, noise pollution, smoking in public places, access to library materials, and other concerns. Students created web pages in which mayoral candidates addressed questions the students posed. Teams held mock elections, conducted polls of students' knowledge of candidates and issues, and created photo-journalism displays of comparisons of neighborhoods' potholes, parks, and public spaces. The students in these classes demonstrated a wide range of preparation, but all learned skills that served them well in college. Teachers prepared students to discuss and understand varying perspectives of issues, to think critically, to use highly technical media skills, and to work with colleagues to solve problems. Programs such as this focus student energies on issues that concern them in their daily lives. In action-oriented research, they develop high level thinking skills. They improve their writing and oral communication skills as they devise ways to present their findings to a wider audience. The students search for materials and references and learn to compile and analyze data. These learning activities are much better preparation for college level work than the worksheets described in the student interview cited above.

Upward Bound is another program that brings high school students to college campus environments and assists them in preparing for college enrollment. The program helps families and high school students understand the prerequisites and pathways to higher education. Many Latino parents simply do not understand the U.S. educational system, even though they are firm in their desire that their children obtain as much formal schooling as possible. Goldberg et al. (2001) found that families benefit from clear information about how to interpret grades and other school communication, and from finding out what their children's college options are, what courses students should take in high school, and what grants, scholarships, or mentoring and advising might be available to help them. These researchers suggested that K-12 educators and community workers in schools with Latino children should actively pursue partnerships and collaboratives with colleges and universities to provide parents and students with this information on a systematic and ongoing basis.

PARTICIPATION IN POST SECONDARY EDUCATION: TO WHAT EXTENT DO WE OFFER OPPORTUNITIES TO ENROLL IN COLLEGE LEVEL PROGRAMS?

It became obvious from the college student interviews and from talking to elementary and middle school students about college that few first-generation college children of working class Latino parents know what college is about or what it takes to get there. The questions asked by elementary and middle school students and the reflections of college students were enlightening.

Harriett Romo addressed a group of young students touring a college campus and a sixth grade student asked, "Do you have to walk in line in college?" A classmate asked, "What are the hours of college?" A middle school student asked, "How long does college take?" The sixth grade student had never been on a college campus before, although he lived several blocks from a four-year university. No one in his family had attended college. He had no idea how classes were organized, what was expected of college students, or how college students organized their lives. His classmate was thinking of the work experiences of his parents. Some worked evening shifts or long irregular hours. His question also demonstrated that he had little understanding of the organization of college or the independence expected as students planned their own course schedules. The third student also lacked information about the organization of post secondary education. He was shocked when Dr. Romo explained that college usually required four years, and perhaps longer for many who worked or took reduced course loads. The student responded, "NO WAY!" and generated loud laughter from his friends. All the high school students Harriett Romo interviewed in a study of Latino high school graduation (Romo & Falbo,

1996) expressed a desire to go to college and to have professional careers, such as doctors or lawyers, but few of them knew anyone, besides their teachers, who had attended college. Few students interviewed had any understanding of the requirements for enrolling in college, what a degree plan might entail, or the academic preparation required for college success.

These questions are not unusual for many first-generation, college-bound students. They know few people who have attended college and their parents cannot help them prepare for the transition to post secondary schooling. Middle school students' questions are especially insightful because it is at these middle school grade levels that students must begin thinking about planning a college oriented high school program and making decisions about course-taking and extracurricular activities that have serious consequences for a positive transition to college. Many students make decisions based on peers' suggestions or best friends' choices. Rudy, a first generation college student explained:

> No one ever really told me, 'Well, Rudy, you're going to go to college.' No one ever said, 'You should go to college' or like helped me out or took me by the hand, you know, showed me a college or whatever. But I think a part was that everyone else was doing it. And I applied to three schools.

Rudy's example demonstrates another advantage of students being placed in college preparatory classes or attending a school that has a large number of students who go on to college. They begin to think about college and take appropriate SAT exams and make applications because "everyone else is doing it." Lisa, a successful honor student in college, had similar experiences. She explained how she applied to college:

> I saw what my friends were doing, so I did it too. A lot of them were doing the applications, the scholarship applications and stuff like that. So I would just sort of watch what they were doing and then I would say, 'Oh, where did they get that? I'm going to get one too.' It was never a counselor. My parents were, 'You're going to go to college,' but it was assumed I was going to the local college. It was just mostly watching my friends and doing it on my own. I applied for a scholarship and I received a four-year scholarship which pretty much covered all the tuition.

These successful students exhibited a number of non-cognitive characteristics that are significant predictors of academic performance, particularly for Latino students. Student persistence in college is related to a complex set of factors, including student involvement, gender, age, place of residence, and many factors which they bring with them, such as high school achievement. High school grades and rank remain significant predictors of academic performance and for minority students are often more reliable predictors of academic success at college than SAT scores. Self confidence, ability to deal with racism, availability of strong support networks, successful leadership experiences, a university-based community that is supportive and welcoming, and Hispanic mentors have been noted as effective in retaining Hispanic students in college (Sedlacek, 1996; Tracey & Sedlacek, 1987). However, academic self-concept consistently emerges as a reliable and perhaps the single best, non-cognitive predictor of academic success (House, 1994). Each of the students interviewed for this study had the confidence that they could do high level college work and that they would be successful in college, despite low test scores, lack of support from teachers or family, and financial need. Other non-cognitive predictors of success include adjustment and integration into the campus environment.

AVAILABILITY OF HIGH QUALITY COLLEGES AND UNIVERSITIES

The availability of high quality colleges and universities is closely related to the availability of high quality public K-12 schools. Much research on school finances has shown the large disparities in funding for educational programs across school districts, particularly in states that depend primarily on property taxes to support public schools. Districts with larger tax bases are less dependent on the state when it comes to building more schools, lowering class sizes, paying teachers' salaries, or expanding college preparatory programs. Limited tax bases make it difficult for districts to raise money to build new schools as population growth increases. Budgets in small districts afford the districts less flexibility to move people around and fewer resources to accommodate growth. As suburban areas experience increased subdivision of ranch or farm land, the districts experience increases in the numbers of children to educate, but no new industry to feed the district's tax bases. In one rural area between Austin, the state capital, and San Antonio, a major city in Texas, developers are building large manufactured home communities. These communities are appealing to working class Latino families because of their low cost. The resulting population increases mean that school districts have little time to order new school buses to transport the new students, to build classrooms to accommodate them in the existing schools, or to design and build new schools or programs.

In San Antonio, a small district of about 3,000 students on the predominantly Mexican-origin Southside of the city has experienced a 48% growth rate. In comparison, the city of San Antonio independent school district experienced a three percent decline in student enrollment during the same year. The first district, with the largest growth rate, had the lowest property wealth per student during the 2000–2001 school year at $41,549. This rate reflects a considerable gap when compared to the highest property wealth per student district, Alamo Heights, which had $660,771 property wealth per student in the same period

(Hughes, 2001). The population in Alamo Heights is predominantly non-Hispanic White.

In terms of availability of post secondary level educational opportunities, major urban areas, such as Los Angeles, San Antonio, and New York have a variety of community colleges, private liberal arts colleges and religious colleges, and public universities that allow students different options for completing a college degree. Some 84% of the students in Texas attend public universities. Texas has concentrated its funding in two major flagship universities and other campuses have been poorly funded or neglected by the state university system. A legal suite filed by the Mexican American Defense and Education Fund (MALDEF) in Texas [Richards et al. v. League of United Latin American Citizens (LULAC) et al., 1993] challenged the distribution of post-secondary educational resources in Texas. MALDEF claimed that the border area and South Texas, where Mexican population is heavily concentrated, had not received a fair share of educational resources and challenged the virtual absence of higher education opportunities in South Texas. The lawsuit was originally filed in 1987 to challenge the under enrollment of minority under-graduate students, the high attrition rates of minority college students, and the denial of access to graduate and professional education, especially in South Texas.

Following a seven-week trial in Brownsville, Texas in 1991, the jury found that the State of Texas had in fact denied Hispanics in South Texas access to graduate and professional education and had failed to provide Hispanics with equal access to a "university of the first class" as required by the Texas Constitution and that the state had also failed to provide and maintain an "efficient system" of public universities (Mexican American Legal Defense and Educational Fund Litigation Docket, 1991–1992). The jury found that the state had not engaged in intentional discrimination against Hispanics. The last finding was significant because in May of 1992, the Texas Supreme court allowed the state to take a direct appeal to the Supreme Count on the basis that the state officials had not intentionally discriminated against Hispanics in South Texas and effectively voided the District Court's judgment of unconstitutionality. MALDEF argued that that single verdict did not undercut the many other findings of unconstitutionality. In June 1992 MALDEF and representatives of the major population areas in the border region of Texas offered a plan as a settlement to *LULAC v. Richards*. The proposed ten-year plan called for the development of comprehensive research universities and professional schools in El Paso, San Antonio, the Rio Grande Valley, and the Costal Bend area. The attention to the unequal distribution of higher education resources caused state legislators from those areas to pressure the University of Texas system to provide more funds to schools such as the University of Texas at San Antonio and the University of Texas at Brownsville and UT Pan American, all universities serving large numbers of Hispanic students.

The California University system has done better than Texas in distributing its higher education resources and assuring that there are several high quality, research-level public universities in the state. California has a system of state colleges and one university system. The University of California System includes, Berkeley, Los Angles, and San Diego, all major flagship universities, and also supports centers of excellence and graduate level programs at eleven other campuses, such as Riverside, Irvine, and Davis. California, of course, has several well-known, highly selective private universities as well, such as Stanford, California Institute of Technology, the Pomona colleges, and religious institutions that also provide access to university studies, although tuition at the private universities is considerably more than tuition at public institutions.

Two-year community college programs are somewhat less expensive than a four-year institution and tend to provide remedial assistance, counseling and advising services that may not be as readily available at four-year universities. Hispanics are more likely to be attending two-year colleges than other groups – 52% Hispanic, 36% blacks, and 36% Whites (Weiser, Ramirez & Linde, 1994). Low SES Hispanic students are less likely to transition immediately to college than their upper-SES peers, and Hispanic students are far less likely to finish high school than either Whites or African Americans. Many students who do not enroll in college immediately after high school eventually do enter higher education, particularly through community colleges. The vast majority of these late enrollees are likely to be women (King, 2000). However, a major factor in accessibility to higher education concerning Latinos is the low rate of transfer from two-year community colleges to four-year colleges and universities.

THE AFFORDABILITY OF HIGHER EDUCATION

Texas earns a C in this category. Although the state tuition in public universities is among the lowest in the country, Texas makes a very limited investment in financial aid for low-SES students and families. Low tuition, in reality, subsidizes families who can afford to pay. Tuition is only one of the costs of higher education. Since Latino parents work in poorly paid occupations, they cannot afford tuition even if it is low. This forces Latino college students to work and take out loans while pursuing their college degrees.

Opportunities to enroll in college have been increased by many generous individuals and corporations that fund scholarships. Interviews with students demonstrate clearly how sometimes even a few hundred dollars in scholarships can provide the incentive to participate in higher education. However, financial disadvantage continues throughout the college years and often creates difficult burdens for students who must juggle work and school. Many Latino students see other students with more resources who are insensitive to the financial hardships low-income students face. Latino students often feel guilty about being away from family members who have depended on their assistance during high school or from families who also suffer financial difficulties.

Few of the students interviewed had experienced overt racial or ethnic discrimination, although they were conscious of being among the minority on the college campus they attended. They often drew strength from the hardships their ancestors had overcome. One student, LaQuita, a freshman, explained, describing the hardships members of her ethnic group had encountered, "I think it is just the struggle that we've been through and how we are trying to overcome a lot of things, just everything, the pressure, trying to get through. Just bringing each other up, just overcoming a lot of different things. I think that's important about my life." This student continued to explain how isolated she sometimes felt because of the few Latino and Black students enrolled at the university, "Being at this university is kind of difficult to deal with because when you come, maybe two other faces are like yours or similar to yours. Then it is kind of difficult to feel like you fit in, but then when you get around your peers, you know that you're not alone. It's hard to go out into the world and say, 'I feel comfortable' knowing that someone else is other than my own racial background, but among my peers it is OK."

For most of the students interviewed, socioeconomic differences were more prevalent in their college experiences than racial or ethnic differences. Lisa worked as a dorm resident advisor to pay room and board expenses. She wanted to live in an apartment, but was trying to save money for graduate school tuition. She realized that other students had economic advantages that she lacked. She explained,

Well, if the money issue was bad in high school, I mean, it is really bad now. You really see, not the race differences, class differences. A lot of time it angers me because my parents work really hard and it is sad that they have to work just to have the basic requirements for life, while other people, to me it seems like they squander their money . . .. One time there were these two girls sitting next to me and they were sorority girls. I heard one saying that she had spent so much money shopping that she didn't have any more money in her account, so she called her dad up and he put $1,000 into her account. I was thinking, 'Wow. My parents don't, probably together don't have that much in their savings account. Yet this person can just call up her father or whoever and the money is there for her.' That's great for them, but it just seems really unfair. You can't help but feel some resentment, because, why can't everyone, you know, be well off? I see the opportunities that they can have. And when you don't have those kinds of networks and contacts and things like that, you're starting at zero and trying to get up there to where they are when they already have this huge head start.

Veronica, another successful college student interviewed by Joanne Salas, experienced a series of family problems as she was preparing for college. The emotional and financial burden of helping her family made college more difficult. She assumed family and work responsibilities and struggled to keep focused on college. Research has shown that working a full-time job has been negatively associated with completion of a bachelor's degree, a good college GPA, preparation for graduate school, graduating with honors, knowledge of field or discipline and almost every area of satisfaction with the university environment (Astin, 1993). Veronica confirmed this as she told us:

> My senior year in high school my dad had a accident and was hospitalized and partially paralyzed. And right before my junior year my grandmother died and my mom went into a really deep depression. My brother started having trouble in school. My sister was going through some stuff with her husband so I was helping her take care of her kids. I thought, 'Oh God, my college plans are all screwed up.' But then I thought, 'well, if it takes me forever, that's still my goal.' I wish I had had parents that had said, 'Just go to college, don't worry about anything. Don't work.' But it wasn't like that. I had to go to school full time and work full time. I was having to take school and the family responsibility. It was like I was dealing with everything and it was really hard. I had to get a car because how else was I going to get to school and work? And I had to have a job to pay for the car. You know, dealing with school and work and family, it's hard. And all I wanted to do was go to school.

Eddie, a college freshman, experienced socioeconomic differences that made him uncomfortable, but he took pride in the accomplishments that brought him to college and the struggles that his family had gone through to provide basic necessities in Mexico and in migrant worker camps. His family came to the U.S. as migrant workers from Mexico. His mother dropped out of high school and raised him as a single parent by working in restaurants or in tomato fields. Eddie told us that his family's experiences helped him keep things in perspective and kept him from getting caught up in campus problems. He explained:

> I don't get caught up in my life because life to me on campus is like, a lot of the worries and stuff just really aren't that big a deal. I think my background has helped me keep that in perspective. I think about my mom and my grandparents and it really helps keep me grateful and humble and appreciative . . . The majority of bad experiences I've had have had to do with socioeconomic background. People make a lot of comments. The majority of people here are from a higher socioeconomic background than I am. A lot of times I hear something and it bothers me. I wanna say something, but I can't just go around interjecting all the time. Sometimes I do say something. It is a chance for me to show them that there is another side to things. A lot of them come from backgrounds, suburban high schools, where everyone has had the same kind of experience. If something isn't right, they will say, 'That's ghetto.' If a car doesn't look nice, they'll say, 'That's ghetto.' I really

have a problem with that because these people are so removed from any type of experience
like that. They look down on anything that is associated with low socioeconomic status. I
don't feel that it should be looked down upon. It is just different than what they are used
to. The way they use "ghetto" carries a very bad connotation.

All of these students overcame financial hardships and succeeded in college.
Their experiences demonstrate clearly, however, that financial barriers are not
just problems of lack of money. Latino students from low socioeconomic
backgrounds may come from families that continue to face economic, health,
social or legal problems that prevent them from providing emotional, academic
or financial support to the college student. Students who juggled work and
school often found themselves having to take time off from college to catch
up financially or to resolve a family crisis. Worries about finances distracted
them from their academic work. These students demonstrated strong motivation
to continue their college studies despite financial hardships. They recognized
the inequities in resources, but drew upon their families and friends for
emotional support.

There are many opportunities in place on college campuses that help Latino
students establish support networks. Freshman seminars provide beginning
students with small classes that allow them to get to know their professors and
other students in a more personal context. These programs have been very
successful in keeping students enrolled and focused on college. A large-scale
research project by Alexander Astin (1993) revealed that what had the most
significant impact on student achievement and development was student-student
interaction. This empirical finding strongly suggests that freshmen seminars that
promote meaningful collaboration among students should make a significant
contribution to Latino student achievement, particularly in the first year of
college and for first-generation college students. Learning Communities also
block students with similar interests into the same cluster of classes so that they
can form friendships and study groups. Cluster groups in dorms help students
form support groups and peer learning opportunities. These programs are
designed to produce a sense of group identity and social cohesiveness. Activities
include having groups participate in ice-breakers when they are first formed
and providing groups with explicit suggestions and concrete recommendations
for promoting cooperation and teamwork (e.g. phone-number exchange, group
review of class notes, and study group formations, etc.). The educational
objective of these activities is to create a social-emotional climate conducive
to the development of an esprit de corps and sense of intimacy among group
members, enabling them to feel comfortable in future activities that may require
them to express personal viewpoints, disagree with others, and reach consensus
in groups. Explicit attention to the social and emotional foundations of effective

small-group interaction serves to increase students' social integration into the college community and promotes student retention (Pascarella & Terenzini, 1991).

Participation in extra curricular activities also builds strong bonds to the university. Not only traditional activities, such as sports and student government, but ethnic professional and social organizations – such as the Hispanic Student Engineers, the Hispanic Student Business Association, the Bilingual Education Student Organization, etc. – allow students to work together in teams on common projects, to acquire additional professional skills, and to form personal relationships with peers, professors and professionals in areas of career interest. Often these programs can provide mentoring and emotional and academic support that families cannot provide.

There is a substantial body of research that supports the idea that both retention and student development are positively related to involvement in college activities outside the classroom. Off campus work negatively impacts a student's time and opportunities to connect with faculty and peers on the college campus. Latino students who must work a large number of hours off campus have less out-of-class contact with faculty and have fewer opportunities to become involved with clubs and organizations. Research has shown a marked decrease in participation in campus activities when students are employed 30 hours or more per week. Students who work more than 30 hours per week are also more likely to report that financial worries negatively impacted their studies on a regular basis (Furr & Elling, 2000). Students become less connected to the institution as they become more involved in off campus employment. On-campus employment may provide more opportunities for students to engage in projects with professors. Students working on campus frequently work in their major department and may have more opportunities to interact informally with faculty and staff and to learn more about academic opportunities outside the classroom.

MAKING TIMELY PROGRESS TOWARD COMPLETION OF DEGREE PROGRAMS

Due to many of the problems associated with financial need, lack of adequate preparation for college work, and family responsibilities, Hispanic students take longer to complete college than non-Hispanic White students. In 1990, 72% of the White students enrolled in college graduated in five years or less, while 73% of the Hispanic students graduated in six years or less (Garcia, 2001, p. 196). Only 31% of Hispanic students graduated in four years or less, compared to 44% of non-Hispanic White students (National Center for Educational Statistics, 1998).

Two-year community colleges normally offer the first two years of a standard four-year-college curriculum and a selection of terminal vocational programs. A large percentage of college-bound Latino students enter two-year colleges because they are less expensive, are located closer to the students' home, or because two-year colleges have less rigorous admission requirements. Students of color are much more likely than White students to enroll in a community college, with 50% of all students of color who were enrolled in postsecondary education enrolled in community colleges, compared to 38% of White students (Kent, 1997). These colleges provide important post-secondary education opportunities for many Latino students.

However, nationwide the transfer rate from two-year colleges to four-year colleges is low (Nora, Rendon & Caudez, 1999). A study of the state of California system of higher education found that the transfer rate from community colleges to the University of California system was only 2% of the total Hispanic high school graduating cohort two years earlier (Garcia, 2001, p. 198). Studies of students who do transfer to four-year colleges suggest that community college students across academic disciplines did as well, or better, academically than direct entry high school students (Bell, 1995).

A key factor in the successful transition from community colleges to four-year institutions is transfer of credits. Academic core courses completed at a two-year college are usually transferable for credit at a four-year college or university, but there are problems of poor or nonexistent articulation agreements between community colleges and universities. In 1993, The Center for Career Development in Early Care and Education at Wheelock College, in a survey of early childhood programs at two- and four-year schools of higher education, found that only seven states guaranteed acceptance of transfer credits among the public institutions statewide (Morgan et al., 1993). For example, community colleges offer AA degrees (Liberal Arts or General Education coursework) and AAS (degrees in Applied Arts and Sciences). In some fields, such as child development, an area of study that is attractive to Latinas interested in becoming preschool teachers, access to four-year institutions of higher education have been denied unless the students are willing to begin their higher education anew. These AAS degrees in early childhood education require some 30 hours of courses in pedagogy and other classroom related skills. If students decide to transfer to four-year institutions to earn a bachelor's degree in education or a teaching credential, many of those lower level courses do not transfer into a major at the four-year institution, except as electives. Articulation agreements between the two-year college and the four-year college may allow as few as three credit hours to as many as 64 hours of credit to transfer and often the courses accepted by the four-year schools are general education courses and not the professional courses taken at the community college (Cassidy et al., 2001). Since many baccalaureate degree majors require a concentration of courses in the major at the upper division level, students with the AAS degree in child development found themselves having to take the same courses again at the upper division level at the four-year institution and others lost a large number of credit hours that would not transfer to the four-year major. Clearly, the existence of an articulation agreement between a two- and four-year institution does not ensure that a community college student will receive adequate credit for the completion of a degree at a community college. There is a great deal of variability in quality in the transfer agreements. Needless to say, this has caused students much anguish and frustration. This situation of transferability of credits is not limited to child development, but has affected a number of community college majors.

Administrative agreements between two-year and four-year institutions, often referred to as 2 + 2 articulation agreements, and state legislation requiring the transferability of core courses have helped facilitate transfers from community colleges to four-year institutions, but have not completely resolved the problem. A stronger articulation of degree plans, collaboration in academic advising, and better informed students and staff at both institutions are necessary to promote positive transitions from community colleges to four-year degree plans.

CONCLUSION

Support for Latino student success in college must be widespread across K-12 programs, community college and four-year institutions of higher education, families, and community. To successfully focus on positive transfers from high school to college, all constituents must be involved in a meaningful and supportive way. Key approaches and strategies essential to addressing Latino student success include:

- more rigorous high school preparation and higher expectations of all students;
- collaboration between K-12 institutions and post-secondary institutions in making clear the requirements for success in college, the enrollment and admission process, and prerequisite courses and skills;
- financial aid support for students so that they do not have to work excessive hours;
- programs that build a sense of community and commitment to the college institution, such as freshman seminars, learning communities, and other team-building activities;
- recognition and support for non-cognitive factors that promote success in students, such as positive academic self-concept;

- articulation and coordination between two-year and four-year colleges to facilitate credit transfer and smooth transitions;
- recognition that first-generation college bound Latino students need support and mentoring from faculty at secondary and postsecondary institutions.

Embracing student success is a comprehensive task that must involve many people in many institutions. Research has demonstrated that community-building programs and out-reach programs that provide information and access to colleges and universities can be successful in promoting positive transitions to higher education for Latino students. Effectively introducing success initiatives can serve the needs of Latino students, enrich the working environment of staff and faculty, and focus the energies of our schools and universities on educational excellence.

REFERENCES

American College Testing program (1997). Unpublished tabulations, 1987, derived from statistics collected by the U.S. Bureau of the Census; and U.S. Department of Labor, College enrollment of high school graduates, various years (July). Cited in Peltier, Laden, and Matranga, 1999.

American Freshmen Survey (1998). Cooperative Institutional Research Program, American Council on Education.

Adelman, C. (1999). The answers are in the toolbox. Washington, D.C.: U.S. Government Printing Office.

Alicea, I. P. (2001). Latino Perspective on Census 2000. Hispanic Outlook, (September 10).

Astin, A. (1993). What matters in college? Four critical years revisited. San Francisco: Jossey-Bass.

Bell, S. (1995). The college-university linkage: An examination of the performance of transfer students in the faculty of arts at York University: 1987–1992. Toronto: York University.

Cassidy, D., Linda H., Peggy T., & Springs, J. (2001). The facilitation of the transfer of credit between early childhood education/child development departments in 2- and 4-year institutions of higher education in North Carolina. Journal of Early Childhood Teacher Education, 22, 29–38.

Fenske, R. H., Geranios, C. A., Keller J. E., & Moore, D. E. (1997). Early intervention programs: Opening the door to higher education. Association for the Study of Higher Education-ERIC Clearinghouse on Higher Education Report (Vol. 25, No. 6). Washington, D.C.: The George Washington University, Graduate School of Education and Human Development.

Furr, S. R., & Elling, T. W. (2000). The Influence of Work on College Student Development. NASPA Journal: Student Affairs Administrators in Higher Education, 37(2), 454–470.

Garcia, E. E. (2001). Hispanic education in the United States: Raíces y alas. NY: Rowman & Littlefield Publishers, Inc.

Goldenberg, C., Gallimore, R., Reese L., & Garnier, H. (2001). Cause or Effect? A Longitudinal Study of Immigrant Latino Parents' Aspirations and Expectations, and Their Children's School Performance. American Educational Research Journal, 38(3), 547–582.

Guzman, A. (1996). *Our nation on the Fault line: Hispanic American education.* (A report to the President of the United States, the Nation, and the Secretary of Education, United States Department of Education.) Washington, D.C.: President's Advisory Commission on Educational Excellence for Hispanic Americans.

House, D. J. (1994). College grade outcomes and attrition: An exploratory study of noncognitive variables and academic background as predictors. Paper presented at the Illinois Association for Institutional Research Annual Meeting, Lake Shelbyville, IL (November). (ERIC) Document Reproduction Service No. ED 390 319.

Hughes, S. K. (2001). S. Side districts tackle growth: Trend puts rural schools on the spot. *San Antonio Express News*, (October 28).

Kent, N. G. (1997). Community colleges today – bringing you into the future. *ERIC Review, 5*(3), 17–18.

King, J. E. (2000). *Gender equity in higher education: Are male students at a disadvantage?* Washington, D.C.: American Council on Education, Center for Policy Analysis.

Lee, V. E., & Bryk, T. (1988). Curriculum tracking as mediating the social distribution of high school achievement. *Sociology of Education, 61*, 78–94.

Measuring Up 2000: The state by state report card for higher education. A report by the National Center for Public Policy and Higher Education [www.http//measuringup2000.higher education.org].

Mexican American Legal Defense and Educational Fund Litigation Docket (May 1991–April 1992). Antonia Hernández, President and General Council. San Francisco, CA: MALDEF.

National Center for Education Statistics (2001). *Mini-Digest of Education Statistics 2000.* Charlene Hoffman, Production Manager. Washington, D.C.: U.S. Department of Education, Office of Educational Research and Improvement. NCES 2001-046.

National Center for Education Statistics (1998). *The Condition of Education* (Vols. 1 & 2). Washington, D.C.: U.S. Department of Education.

National Center for Education Statistics (1996). *Enrollment in Public Elementary and Secondary Schools by Race or Ethnicity and State.* Table 44: Digest of Education Statistics 1996. Washington, D.C.: U.S. Department of Education, 1996.

Nora, A., Rendon, L. I., & Cuadraz, G. (1999). Access, choice and outcomes: A profile of Hispanic students in higher education. In: A. Tashakkori & S. H. Ochoa (Eds), *Education for Hispanics in the United States* (pp. 261–283). New York: AMS Press.

Nevarez-la Torre, A. A., & Hidalgo, N. M. (1997). Introduction. *Education and Urban Society, 30*(1). Sage Publications.

Oakes, J. (1985). *Keeping track: How schools structure inequality.* New haven, Conn.: Yale University Press.

Oakes, J., Ormseth, T., Bell, R., & Camp, P. (1990). Multiplying Inequalities: The Effects of Race, Social Class, and Tracking on opportunities to learn Mathematics and Science. Santa Monica: RAND, ERIC document Reproduction Service No. ED 329 615.

Pascarella, E. T., & Terenzini, P. T. (1991). *How college affects students: Findings and insights from twenty years of research.* San Francisco: Jossey-Bass.

Peltier G. L., Laden, R., & Matranga, M. (1999). Student Persistence in College: A review of research. *Journal of College Student Retention, 1*(4), 357–375.

Richards et al. vs. League of United Latin American Citizens (LULAC) et al., 863 S. W. 2nd 449 (Tex. 1993).

Rist, R. C. (1979). Student Social Class and Teacher Expectations: The Self-Fulfilling Prophecy in Ghetto Education. In: J. H. Strouse (Ed.), *Exploring Socio-Cultural Themes in Education: Reading in Social Foundations.* (2nd ed., pp. 176–202, 2001).

Romo, H., & Falbo, T. (1996). *Latino high school graduation*. Austin, TX: The University of Texas Press.

Salas, J. (2000). Mexican American students' perspectives: School success as a function of family support, caring teachers, rigorous curricula and self-efficacy. Doctoral Dissertation, The University of Texas at Austin.

Sedlacek, W. E. (1996). Employing noncognitive variables in admitting students of color. New Directions for Student Services (No. 74, pp. 79–84), cited in: *Leveling the Playing Field: Promoting Academic Success for Students of Color*. San Francisco: Jossey-Bass.

Steinberg, L. D., Brown, B. B., & Dornbusch, S. M. (1996). *Beyond the Classroom: Why School Reform Has Failed and What Parents Need to Do*. NY: Simon and Schuster.

Tracey, T. J., & Sedlacek, W. E. (1987). Prediction of college graduation using noncognitive variables by race. *Measurement and Evaluation in Counseling and Development, 19*, 177–184.

University of California. (1997). *Latino Student Eligibility and Participation in the University of California. YA BASTA!* Latino Eligibility Task Force Report No. 5 (July). Berkeley: University California and the Chicano/Latino Policy Project.

Useem, E. (1992). Middle Schools and Math Groups: Parents involvement in children's placement. *Sociology of Education, 65*(4), 263–279.

West, J., Miller, W., & Diodato, L. (1985). *High school and beyond: A national longitudinal study for patterns in secondary schools as related to student characteristics*. Washington, D.C.: U.S. Department of Education.

RISING IN ACADEMIA

DISTANCE SITE PROGRAMS –
A NEW WAY FOR HISPANICS
TO ENTER THE GRADUATE
PROGRAM PIPELINE

Jose D. Colchado

INTRODUCTION

The Hispanic Association of Colleges and Universities in its August 2000 report, *The Increasing Presence of Hispanics and Hispanic-Serving Institutions*, states that while there has been a 44% increase in the Hispanic population between 1990 and 2000, and a coinciding growth in the number of Hispanics attending college, the percentage of Hispanics has only increased slightly. They report that Hispanic college enrollments grew from 16% in 1980 to 22% in 1997. Colleges and universities continue to write institutional objectives and make public statements about their commitment to increasing the enrollment of Hispanics and still these institutions and the Hispanic community remain dissatisfied with enrollment figures and the enrollment strategies that have been implemented.

Enrolling more Hispanic students in graduate programs has been recognized by universities as a high priority. Not only is this goal important in and of itself, it also has great implication for undergraduate enrollments and graduation. Padilla et al. (1997) identified four classes of barriers that Hispanic students must overcome in order to successfully complete their undergraduate degree. Of the four, two "barriers that are experienced as lack of nurturing" and "barriers

Latinos in Higher Education, Volume 3, pages 133–145.
© **2003 Published by Elsevier Science Ltd.**
ISBN: 0-7623-0980-6

related to lack of presence on campus" are partly defined as "lack of minority role models and mentors." Increasing the number of Hispanics who earn graduate degrees can increase the presence of Hispanic faculty role models and mentors for Hispanic undergraduates. The importance of increasing the number of Hispanics earning graduate degrees has received attention through national programs like Goal 2000 and recruitment programs particular to individual universities. While there has been some success it is clear that continued efforts and a variety of approaches must be developed and implemented if the rate of Hispanic graduate educational success is going to match the growing number of Hispanics eligible to enter higher education programs.

Northern Arizona University (NAU), located in Flagstaff, Arizona, is a comprehensive university offering undergraduate and graduate programs. It offers forty-four master's degrees and nine doctoral degrees. It defines its mission as, among other things: "offering graduate programs and supporting research in areas that are important to the development of our state and region, providing an educational environment that offers a global perspective and values diversity of the human experience, and offering instruction through educational partnerships throughout the state that employ a variety of strategies to support distance learning." Its graduate catalog states, "Because we recognize the reciprocal value of a diverse student population, we have designed specific recruitment, transition, and retention programs to increase the enrollment and graduation rates of students from underrepresented and ethnic groups, particularly Native Americans."

NAU has been charged by the Arizona Board of Regents with "providing university courses and programs in the state's non-metropolitan areas, which includes most of Arizona." Through its Statewide Campus, NAU provides a large number of Arizona citizens the opportunity to enroll in undergraduate and graduate programs without having to attend classes at its Flagstaff campus.

The role of NAU as an institution providing educational courses and programs throughout the state can be traced back to its origin as the Northern Arizona Normal School in 1899. The focus on teacher preparation was further emphasized when in 1925 the legislature changed the status of the institution from a normal school to a four-year college that could grant the bachelor of education degree. Its name was changed to Northern Arizona State Teachers College. This early history is important to the subsequent role NAU would play in statewide education because it would help create an extensive network of connections to many communities throughout the state, especially rural communities, through their schools and school administrators. In 1937 the college received permission to offer a graduate program leading to the master of arts in education. This degree was to become the core of the future statewide program because of the need and desire of many teachers and school administrators to advance their education beyond the bachelor's degree without having to leave their jobs and community. By this time the name changed again to Arizona State College at Flagstaff. The college was granted university status in 1966 and its named changed again to Northern Arizona University. The first doctoral students were graduated in 1973.

When the institution became a university the Arizona Board of Regents included as part of its mission teacher preparation programs that could be offered throughout the state except for the metropolitan areas of Phoenix and Tucson. This aspect of NAU's mission and the support of the regents for statewide outreach was crucial to the development of NAU's statewide program.

In 1984 in a move that would further solidify NAU's role as the statewide program provider, President Eugene Hughes created the Center for Excellence in Education (CEE). The Center was created partly in response to the U.S. Department of Education report, "A Nation at Risk" and the report of the Arizona Governor's Committee on Quality Education, "Education in Arizona, Popular Concerns, Unpopular Choices" both of which criticized public education. Hughes maintained that in order to improve education, teacher preparation would need to be improved. Through CEE the teacher preparation program at NAU became a team effort involving the Arizona Department of Education, the University, and many Arizona school districts. The cooperation and innovation demonstrated by this team not only led to major changes in the teacher preparation program but also led to increased demand by school districts for graduate programs for their teachers and for school administrators. The stage was now set for what was to become a major graduate program in educational leadership that allowed students to work on graduate degrees in their own communities.

Initially NAU's statewide program involved sending faculty from CEE and the Flagstaff campus to distant locations to provide instruction. The demand for courses was such that faculty were flying on a weekly basis to places like Yuma in southern Arizona to offer courses. The response to NAU's statewide program was hailed by both rural residents as well as the legislature. In 1989 the Arizona Board of Regents published a report that forecast an increase of 50,000 more university students by the year 2000. Searching for ways to accommodate the projected student increase, legislators welcomed the option of offering courses to people outside Flagstaff, Phoenix, and Tucson without having to build new campuses.

As the program grew the logistics of sending faculty to teach at distant sites proved impractical.

President Hughes took the demand for courses and the need to develop alternative delivery methods as the basis to propose and implement a statewide network of interactive television classrooms. At these classrooms, scattered throughout Arizona, NAU was able to offer more courses without having faculty travel throughout the state. Faculty based in Flagstaff could originate instruction from the Flagstaff campus and transmit it simultaneously to many sites throughout the state. This network further increased enrollments at statewide sites. It soon became apparent that the students enrolling at distant sites needed support services. Someone needed to assist students with advising and enrollment. In addition, administrative support was needed at the local level to identify courses to be offered, create schedules, enroll students, maintain student records, and other necessary administrative tasks.

Statewide offices were established. The increased student support facilitated even more enrollments. The demand for graduate programs in education was so great that NAU's interactive television network and the few faculty teaching at distant sites were not able to accommodate the demand.

The decision was made to increase the opportunity for statewide students to have face-to-face faculty-student contact by assigning full time faculty to teach at the distant sites on a permanent basis. The number of part-time faculty teaching statewide was also increased. Classrooms were rented from schools and other organizations and instruction became available to students in a more traditional classroom setting.

Many of the part-time faculty teaching in the NAU statewide graduate programs in Educational Leadership were recruited from the ranks of school and community college administrators living and working in the communities where they were to teach for NAU. These individuals had years of experience working in their communities and very often recruited students for the programs from among their fellow employees. These local educational leaders recognized the opportunity to recruit minority members of their organizations to the graduate programs in educational leadership and thus prepare them to fulfilling their organizations' goals to diversify their administrative and teaching ranks.

As the program grew and more individuals from throughout the state participated in the educational leadership program people from fields other than education began to look at the program as a possible way for them to advance their education. People from diverse fields such as law enforcement, health professions, and social services became interested in the program, less for its focus on education and more for its preparation in leadership.

The master's program is a 36-unit program that requires an application for admission that includes writing samples, goals statement, a personal statement of philosophy, and transcripts. No GRE scores are required. Students may choose to write a thesis but it is not required.

The doctoral program is a 90-unit program that requires an application for admission that includes writing samples, a goals statement, a personal statement of philosophy, transcripts, letters of support, and GRE scores. Students are required to write and defend a dissertation. Students may apply up to 36 units of master's work in education and leadership toward the requirements of the doctorate.

Both degrees are practitioner oriented. Readings, research, assignments, projects, and discussions are meant to relate to the issues being faced by students in their place of employment. Whether in the school system, community college or other fields these students grapple with issues of program planning, curriculum planning and assessment, hiring and evaluation of performance, budgets, laws, and facilities. The skills which both programs have identified as essential in the preparation of leaders; problem solving, judgment, organizational ability, decisiveness, leadership, sensitivity, stress tolerance, oral and written communication, range of interest, personal motivation, and educational values are clearly applicable to leadership in any field and students with backgrounds and aspirations in fields other than education have recognized this.

Courses in both degree programs are scheduled in eight-week cycles. There are two cycles every semester. Thus a student enrolled in one course per cycle is able to enroll in two courses per semester. Most but not all students enroll in one course per cycle. Classes meet once a week from 5 p.m. to 10:30 p.m. Courses are also scheduled during the summer. Students can enroll in up to two courses during the summer.

Classes are scheduled in facilities throughout the community. These include public school classrooms, city government and law enforcement facilities, and other facilities as available and needed.

Most support services available to campus students are also available to statewide students. Statewide students are eligible for some financial aid; however, there are no graduate assistantships. Statewide offices are available throughout the state. Office staff operate these offices five days a week from 8 a.m. to 5 p.m. Advising is available during normal working hours. Through agreements with local community colleges students have access to computer labs and other equipment. Students have access to all NAU library services through the Internet. Students can download most materials immediately or they can request books and articles which can be delivered to the nearest statewide office within three days. Through agreements with Arizona State University and the University of Arizona statewide students can access their library holdings.

Enrollments in NAU's statewide programs have been steadily growing since the inception of the program. Data collected by the Office of Institutional Research of Northern Arizona University on the growth of campus and statewide academic programs for fall semesters from 1981 to 2000 is presented in Tables 1 to 3.

Table 1. Flagstaff Campus and Statewide Academic Program Student Enrollment, Fall Semesters 1981 to 2000.

Semester	Flagstaff Campus Students	Statewide Academic Students
2000	14,495	5,469
1999	14,597	5,384
1998	14,675	5,265
1997	14,920	4,698
1996	15,255	4,350
1995	15,413	4,718
1994	15,187	4,055
1993	14,900	3,917
1992	15,219	3,272
1991	14,639	3,059
1990	14,241	2,753
1989	13,698	2,397
1988	12,667	2,392
1987	11,417	2,028
1986	11,301	1,907
1985	10,781	1,834
1984	10,458	1,368
1983	10,423	1,078
1982	10,423	1,242
1981	10,888	1,202

Table 2. Statewide Academic Program Graduate Enrollment, Fall Semesters from 1989 to 2000.

Semester	Graduate Students	% Increase Previous Year
2000	4,155	1.12%
1999	4,109	−1.08%
1998	4,154	12.67%
1997	3,687	7.21%
1996	3,439	−10.51%
1995	3,843	15.89%
1994	3,316	7.21%
1993	3,093	31.90%
1992	2,345	−3.89%
1991	2,440	11.42%
1990	2,190	17.87%
1989	1,858	−3.13%

Table 3. Statewide Academic Program Students by Ethnic Group and Fall Semesters from 1992 to 2000.

Year	White		Hispanic		Asian-American		Native-American		African-American	
	Headcount	Percent	Headcount	Percent	Headcount	Percent	Headcount	Percent	Headcount	Percent
2000	3,925	71.77	883	16.15	69	1.26	420	7.68	109	1.99
1999	3,900	72.44	846	15.71	61	1.13	389	7.23	127	2.36
1998	3,924	74.53	809	15.37	60	1.14	282	5.36	133	2.53
1997	3,574	76.07	716	15.24	46	0.98	222	4.73	115	2.45
1996	3,399	78.14	636	14.62	38	0.87	165	3.79	93	2.14
1995	3,831	81.20	624	13.23	35	0.74	135	2.86	72	1.53
1994	3,300	81.38	529	13.05	21	0.52	115	2.84	69	1.70
1993	3,224	82.31	422	10.77	30	0.77	158	4.03	57	1.46
1992	2,823	86.28	334	10.21	24	0.73	32	0.98	41	1.25

Enrollment figures for 1981 show that there were 10,888 students enrolled at the Flagstaff campus and that there were 1,202 students enrolled in the statewide program. Enrollment figures for the Flagstaff campus show a consistent increase up until 1993 when there was a drop in enrollment on the Flagstaff campus. Enrollments then regained their positive trend beginning in 1994 and continued until 1997. They declined from 1997 to 2000. Enrollment figures for the statewide program show a consistent pattern of growth beginning in 1982 and continuing through 2000 with a slight drop in 1996. Statewide program enrollments have grown even when there was a decline in students enrolling at the Flagstaff campus (1997 to 2000). These figures show that in 1981 statewide students made up 11% of all NAU enrolled students. In 2000 statewide students made up 38% of all NAU enrolled students.

The figures in Table 2 demonstrate a general positive growth trend in enrollment of graduate students in the statewide program. There are years when enrollment declined when compared to enrollment in the previous years; 1992, 1996, 1999, however, the overall figures show a significant growth from 1,858 graduate students enrolled in 1989 to 4,155 graduate students enrolled in 2000. This is a gain of 224% in 11 years.

The information on the historical development of the statewide program, its structure, and its growth provide the foundation upon which to build the case for distant site graduate programs as a viable means for Hispanics to enter the graduate program pipeline.

Table 3 documents the number of statewide students enrolled broken down by ethnicity. Between 1992 and 2000 there is an increase in the headcount number of white students enrolled, however, the percentage of white students declined from 86.28% to 71.77%. During this same period Hispanic student headcount grew from 334 in 1992 to 883 in 2000. And, the percentage of Hispanic students increased from 10.21% to 16.15%. It is worth noting that enrollments for Asian Americans, Native Americans, and African Americans all rose between 1992 and 2000.

In the spring of 2001 the campus enrollment of Hispanic students, both graduate and undergraduate, was 1,059. The enrollment of Hispanics in statewide programs was 920. Approximately 80% of all statewide students are graduate students. Of the total 1,979 Hispanic students enrolled at NAU in spring 2001, 46% were enrolled in statewide programs.

During the year 2001 a survey was conducted of students enrolled in graduate programs in the southern region of NAU's statewide program. The purpose of the survey was to gather demographic data on students enrolled in the program and to gather specific information on Hispanic students enrolled in the program.

The survey was limited by the need to obtain permission from program instructors to conduct the survey during class time. Students in ten different sections of courses being offered during fall 2001 were surveyed. The ten courses provided a good cross section of courses required at different stages of progress through the programs. This provided some assurance that students at different stages of the program were represented in the survey.

Eighty-four students completed the survey. Sixty-six were females and eighteen were males. These numbers reflect closely the percentage of females and males enrolled in the program. The age of respondents ranged from 20 to 62. There have been an increasing number of females over age 40 enrolling in the program. Males enrolling in the program tend to fall within the 20-35 age range. Of those completing the survey 48 identified themselves as teachers in the public schools, 11 as administrators in public schools or community college, seven as teachers in a community college, 12 in some form of law enforcement, and six in other fields not in education.

Seventy-one are working on their master's degree, seven on principal certification, four on doctorates, and two undecided. Of the 84, 47 are the first in their family to be admitted and enrolled in a graduate program.

Of the 84 respondents, 50 are White, 25 are Hispanic, five are Native American, three are African American, and one is Asian. Of the 47 who stated they are the first in their family to enroll in a graduate program, 18 are Hispanic.

Responses from the Hispanic students were examined to gain some insight as to how Hispanic students perceived their access to, participation in, and success in the statewide program in educational leadership.

When asked why they had enrolled in NAU's statewide program the most frequent responses were:

(1) *Time that classes were offered.*
    Since classes are offered in the evening students are able to continue their employment. The eight-week cycle makes students feel that they are making progress toward their degree and keeps them motivated even though they may be taking only one class per cycle.
(2) *Location.*
    The majority of students are able to attend classes at locations that are less than 30 minutes driving distance. When there are enough students in one area of a city to offer a class the statewide office attempts to find a classroom near the majority of students.
(3) *Class size.*
    The average class size is 12 students. The faculty to student ratio is such that students are able to receive a great deal of personal attention.

(4) *Cost.*

The cost to enroll in a three-unit course is $315.00. Generally students believe this is a good value when they consider all the benefits of being able to attend in their hometown. When they compare the cost to what they would pay for a course at a local private, for profit university the cost is very reasonable.

(5) *Accelerated pace.*

Students are able to enroll in at least two classes per semester and two in the summer. At this pace they can complete 18 units in one year.

(6) *Characteristics of classmates.*

Students state that they learn a great deal from the variety of students they meet in their classes. They gain from the diversity of experience students have and bring to the learning in the classes.

(7) *Characteristics of the institution.*

Students respect NAU's reputation as an institution that cares about students and works to make the learning experience applicable to their work. They are more comfortable with the Ed.D. that NAU offers than they would be with a Ph.D. program.

When students were asked to identify the greatest challenges they face in participating in the graduate program there were three areas under which the most frequent responses could be categorized: academic preparation, work related, and personal. The most frequent responses were:

(1) *Academic preparation.*

(a) *Graduate program expectations.*

Most feel that their high school and undergraduate experiences did not prepare them for the kind of expectations there are for graduate students. The emphasis on critical thinking, original ideas from students, and the general knowledge students are expected to have as the foundation for the content of courses are examples of the areas identified in academic preparation.

(b) *Time.*

The eight-week cycle is very fast paced and a great deal of material is covered in a short time. The five hour length of once a week classes leads to decreased learning as students and instructors tire.

(c) *Availability of faculty.*

Most faculty are part-time and are not expected to advise or meet with students outside of class. Most full time faculty have office hours during the day when students work.

(d) *Remembering student skills.*
Students recognize they have forgotten how to be effective students in areas such as critical reading and writing, effective speaking and listening, and research.

(2) *Work related.*
  (a) *Unexpected conflicts that cause absence from class.*
  Missing one class meeting means missing one eighth of the course. Making up what happens during the class is practically impossible.
  (b) *Conflicting priorities.*
  A work project's demands will conflict with a major assignment for the course.
  (c) *Fatigue.*
  Students find themselves tired from attending class or working on assignments and are less effective at work.
  (d) *Lack of support.*
  People at their work site do not understand why they are putting such pressures on themselves or why they are even working on a graduate degree.

(3) *Personal.*
  (a) *Financial.*
  Money spent for education is money taken away from family needs.
  (b) *Child care.*
  It is often difficult to find childcare for the evening classes and during time to do homework and projects.
  (c) *Family emergencies.*
  Missing class causes many problems.

When asked how the statewide program can be improved to assist Hispanic students enroll in and graduate the responses included:

(1) Offer more and a greater variety of courses at more times to make enrollment and progress in the program easier.
(2) Provide more Internet courses.
(3) Open offices on weeknights and weekends.
(4) Reduce the number of courses cancelled or changed.
(5) More financial assistance.
(6) Have faculty more available to students.
(7) Do away with residency requirement in the doctoral program.

(8) Employ more minority faculty.
(9) Improve advising.
(10) Provide more support to students in becoming students again.
(11) Relate course material to the populations we are serving, one that is increasingly Hispanic.

When faculty were interviewed and asked how the statewide program could be more effective in enrolling and graduating Hispanic students their most frequent responses were:

(1) Identify prospective students while they are still in undergraduate programs.
(2) Provide better financial assistance and make it easier to obtain.
(3) Create cohort groups of Hispanic students that can progress through the programs together and take some of the program courses together.
(4) Provide pre-enrollment assessment of skills and knowledge so that they can be advised to take courses at the community college that might help them succeed in the program (e.g. public speaking, advanced writing).
(5) Provide continuous counseling and advising.
(6) Individualize instruction more so students can work on appropriate projects or assignments that relate to their interests and concerns.
(7) Facilitate the creation of Hispanic student support groups.

CONCLUSION

Even though the development of the Northern Arizona University statewide program was focused on providing access to higher education to all Arizona residents the result of its development and implementation is that the number of Hispanic students enrolling in graduate programs has increased dramatically. Without intentionally creating a program to increase Hispanic graduate enrollments the statewide program has clearly demonstrated that there is a Hispanic population demand for graduate study and that when the conditions that have kept Hispanics from enrolling in graduate programs are addressed they will enroll and complete graduate programs.

ACKNOWLEDGMENT

Research assistance provided by Rafaela DeLoera.

REFERENCES

Hispanic Association of Colleges and Universities (2000). *The Increasing Presence of Hispanics and Hispanic-Serving Institutions* (August).

Padilla, R. V. (1999). Chicana/o College Students: Focus on Success. *Journal of College Student Retention, Research, Theory and Practice, 1*(2), 131–145.

FACULTY MENTORING PROGRAMS: PASS THE TORCH PLEASE!

David J. León

INTRODUCTION

Some 20 years ago, when I was an Assistant Professor at UC Berkeley I read an article that detailed the academic difficulties of a minority professor much like myself. Our situations seemed so similar: both Hispanics, hired at the height of affirmative action, and we were both denied tenure. Davidson summed up Hernandez's academic derailment in these terms: "[the department] treated Hernandez as the Iks treat their young, permitting her to succeed or fail on her own. If such institutional behavior is not commendable, neither is it unusual: Large departments often deal with junior members in just this fashion" (Davidson, 1979, p. 45). Large, research universities, do routinely deny tenure to assistant professors because they know it is fairly easy to find replacements. However, is this the model that other colleges and universities should follow?

Although my career suffered a momentary setback, as I quickly found another academic position, my memory of those events continued to trouble me: What did I do wrong? How could I have changed the situation?

Many years later, my directorship of a student-faculty mentor program at a public state university helped me to put my Berkeley experience into perspective (León, 1997). As program director I saw the activities we engaged in benefiting both minority freshmen and their faculty mentors. We scheduled a yearlong series of meetings, lectures, and activities. Year-end evaluations indicated that although students enjoyed the small and large group activities, they preferred the individual contact with their faculty mentor most of all. Faculty mentors

Latinos in Higher Education, Volume 3, pages 147–153.
© 2003 Published by Elsevier Science Ltd.
ISBN: 0-7623-0980-6

also stated that they enjoyed most the interaction with students on a one-to-one basis. This fact should come as no surprise. In a large public university, students rarely come to know their professors, and most professors know their students even less. I wondered if a program like this could be beneficial to assist newly hired faculty gain tenure.

Professor Milton Cox of Miami University answers in the affirmative by providing a rich description of a mentoring program for junior faculty that has been in place for over 22 years (see next section). He states, "[a]fter a brief flurry of attention during faculty orientation, junior faculty may be overlooked by faculty developers and central administrators. What can be done to encourage colleagues and administrators to pay attention to the welfare of these faculty and to help them move from first year to tenure?" (Cox, 1997, p. 225). This is a vital issue for higher education today, especially as it faces the increased retirement of its senior faculty, while trying to promote diversity among its faculty.

METHODOLOGY

In the fall, 1997, the National Education Association (NEA) asked me to comply a list of faculty mentoring programs in higher education, similar to the NEA monograph I authored which focused on student-faculty mentoring (Leon, 1997). I felt confident that this would be an easy task. After all, I recently completed a monograph that described 36 student-faculty mentor programs in colleges and universities across the country. The results of my research proved to be very disappointing.

Most replied to my initial inquiries stating their institutions unfortunately did not offer new faculty mentoring. After many months and countless letters of inquiry, I have received only 12 written responses. This included contacts I made at a recent NEA critical issues seminar, and letters to selected college presidents identified in a book on faculty mentoring (Luna & Cullen, 1996).

I found an interesting contradiction with the responses culled from a NEA publication (León, 1997): institutions found mentoring students important but lacked a program for their faculty. Boice (1992) concurs by stating, "A survey of the literature on [faculty] mentoring indicates that few campuses conduct mentoring in any systematic and demonstrably effective way" (p. 108). It is well known that higher education offers no programs such as those required for educators in the K-12 grades. Why does a Ph.D. in chemistry, sociology, etc., automatically presume the ability to teach *effectively* in the post-secondary classroom? Recently, one of my students complained to me that her roommate and classmates were having an extremely difficult time with a new professor because he was unable to clearly answer student questions referring them to the text and lectured by only reading prepared notes. Most college students have found themselves in a similar situation at some point. While I am not advocating a "student teaching" program for new faculty, some of the faculty mentoring programs (described below) could certainly aid new faculty if made available. These programs not only focus on teaching but the development of a research and publication agenda as well.

CHARACTERISTICS OF FACULTY MENTORING PROGRAMS

Since the 1997 survey I have updated the program descriptions below and added one new program representing a wide range of program models across the country:

Los Rios Community College District, Sacramento, CA: The Los Rios Community College District is composed of three colleges, soon to be four in 2003: American River College, Cosumnes River College, Sacramento City College, and Folsom Lake College. The purpose of the program is to recruit qualified and diverse potential instructors to the District with paid internships. Interns are matched with Los Rios instructors for one class in the spring semester, and together they develop working plans that may include classroom observation, lecturing, writing exams, and grading. Interns meet for monthly workshops on teaching related topics, such as technology in the classroom, learning styles, and diversity issues in the classroom. Interested persons should complete an application form and return it by the October 12 deadline:

Contact: Faculty Diversity Internship Program (916) 568–3106
E-mail: moorer@do.losrios.cc.ca.us

Southern Illinois University, Carbondale: A mentoring program was begun in about 1990 through the office of University Women's Professional Advancement (UWPA). It was directed at women tenure-track faculty in their second year of employment and was meant to give them a structured close relationship with a senior faculty member (female or male) to help them through the probationary period to tenure. Mentors were nominated by deans and by the Associate Vice-Chancellor for Academic Affairs (Personnel and Budget) to be paired with protégées from different departments based on their expressed interests and needs. In addition to the pairings, the program provided workshops on matters such as preparing for tenure, time management, grantsmanship, and

other questions of scholarship and teaching. There was also some funding for
the protegees for travel and equipment. After a short time the Deans of Library
Affairs and the Applied Sciences and Arts both started college-level programs
for men and women tenure-track faculty. These programs did not replace the
UWPA program, and participants were welcome to attend workshops and social
events. Two years ago the then-Associate Vice-Chancellor (now Provost)
managed the extension of these programs to all other academic colleges at
SIUC, of which there are 10. They are more or less successful depending on
the amount of attention being given to them by the deans. Among the issues
to be dealt with is the role of a senior collaborator in research who is not interested in and may not contribute to development in teaching although this person
is the official mentor assigned by the dean. This is a problem in Science,
Engineering, and Agriculture, areas where a somewhat different tradition of
mentoring, although only on the research side, is strong. We are also trying to
work out the sharing of responsibility centrally (workshops, even training of
mentors) with the dispersion of the program to the colleges.

Contact: Margaret E. Winters (618) 453–5744
E-mail: MEW1@SIU.EDU

University of Georgia, Athens, GA: The Peer Consultation Team is an innovative
program designed to provide individual, confidential consultations on issues of
teaching and learning for faculty members. Outstanding university faculty serve
as peer consultants to provide feedback and advice about the scholarship of
teaching for faculty members at any career stage. A peer consultant assesses a
requesting faculty member's goals and objectives for the consultation process,
and then gathers and assesses data (such as student ratings, course materials,
classroom observations, student interviews, videotapes of classes, teaching
portfolios, and classroom assessment data). As a result of this process, the
requesting faculty member develops an action plan to enhance teaching and
learning in his/her courses. For more information, contact the office of
Instructional Support and Development.

Contact: Dr. Tricia Kalivoda (706) 542–1355
E-mail: tlk@uga.edu

Miami University, Oxford, OH: The Teaching Scholars Faculty Learning
Community was developed in 1978, and it has changed the teaching culture at
Miami over the past 22 years. It is a yearlong program offering junior faculty
in their second through fifth years the opportunity to pursue and enhance their

teaching abilities through a wide variety of planned activities. Each year, eight to 14 junior faculty participants, representing a variety of disciplines and needs, are chosen by an advisory committee. Participants receive one-course release time during the year and modest funding for their teaching project. Mentoring is a very important part of the program. Participants select their mentors in consultation with the program director, department chair and colleagues. Regularly scheduled meetings are emphasized. Mentors are invited to tri-weekly, two-hour seminars, where topics include qualities of an effective mentor, interventions to improve teaching and student learning, etc. Mentoring pairs meet to discuss the protégé's teaching project, attend each other's classes, etc. The mentoring aspect of the program is flexible and encourages activities selected from a menu of options. The effectiveness of the program's mentoring component has been rated by the protégés as 7.9 over the years on the scale from 1 (very weak) to 10 (very strong impact). Junior faculty participants are tenured at a rate significantly higher than that of junior faculty who have not participated. For 2000–2001 the Ohio Board of Regents funded Miami to adapt this program to other state-assisted institutions in Ohio, and similar programs are now established at five colleges and universities. Miami has just received a three-year FIPSE grant to extend this faculty learning community approach to more institutions.

Contact: Dr. Milton D. Cox (513) 529–6648
E-mail: coxmd@muohio.edu

RECOMMENDATIONS

After reviewing the relevant literature, I have developed a set of recommendations that closely parallel the recommendations proposed in a NEA publication on student-faculty mentoring programs in higher education (Leon, 1997):

(1) APPOINT AN ADVISORY COMMITTEE – This group should have representatives from the Academic Senate, academic schools, President's Office, etc. It can help to set the course of the program and provide political muscle to overcome potential snares. Committee members may also help locate financial resources and, in general, contribute valuable insights.
(2) FOCUS ON THE TARGET POPULATION – The program should begin with modest goals, those it can accomplish. For instance, it may wish to select only newly hired faculty in their first year of employment.
(3) DEFINE THE TYPE OF PROGRAM – Faculty mentor programs can be

formal or informal. I favor the former rather than the latter. A formal program has regular faculty mentor and mentee contact, intensive faculty training with follow-up meetings, detailed handbook/materials for participants, detailed budget, faculty release time, and on-going evaluations. An informal program has irregular mentor and mentee contact, minimum faculty training, few materials, no budget and no release time.

(4) ACQUIRE OFFICE SPACE – The program must have an office to conduct its business. A formal program may need space for a secretary and director, with the appropriate resources. An informal program could operate out of a faculty member's office.

(5) EXPAND THE RESPONSIBILITIES OF AN EXISTING PROGRAM – Colleges and universities often support Centers for Teaching and Learning, which could include faculty mentoring programs as well.

(6) DEVELOP RESOURCE MATERIALS AND FACULTY TRAINING – The program should have a handbook containing: its objectives, appropriate forms, names of faculty mentors, a calendar of activities and events, and a directory outlining campus resources vital for newly-hired faculty. In addition, the program should train faculty mentors, since few will arrive with perfect skills and knowledge for the job. An informal program may offer only minimal training, such as a one-day workshop, for the entire academic year. A formal one should provide intensive training, at least a two-or-three day workshop, followed by regularly scheduled meetings where mentors and mentees can discuss progress and plans.

(7) CONDUCT EVALUATIONS – The program must poll its mentors and mentees. The results can be very valuable. Results may indicate what works and what doesn't, thereby making programmatic changes in next year's activities.

(8) DRAFT A REPORT – The program should draft an annual report with recommendations for the following year. This document can not only summarize the activities and accomplishments of the program, clearly displaying its worth, but also constitute a solid argument for further resources.

(9) THE ROLE OF FACULTY UNIONS – A perusal of union contracts indicate that mentoring of faculty is included, but how well these activities are carried out is anyone's guess. This provision should be carefully implemented and monitored by the union itself. In fact, faculty unions might spearhead an effort on campus to mentor newly hired faculty. This can be combined with its efforts to enlarge its membership base.

CONCLUSIONS

These descriptions attest to the fact that few institutions have established programs to assist newly hired faculty. Much of higher education still clings to the outmoded "sink or swim" model, even as we enter the new millennium. This is a perfect opportunity to break from the past. Research at Miami University indicates that both junior and senior faculty benefit from a well-organized program designed to increase junior faculty tenure. Also, as faculty across higher education retire in increasing numbers, the promotion and success of a new generation rests squarely on the shoulders of senior faculty. Are we prepared to meet this challenge?

Although these programs do not address the unique needs of newly hired *minority* faculty, the purpose of this paper is to examine what programs exist to help faculty make the transition from graduate school to assistant professor. Obviously, we need to look at these programs closely and glean those activities that can assist minority faculty to attain tenure, especially given the rapid demographic changes occurring in the U.S.

REFERENCES

Boice, R. (1992). Lessons learned about mentoring. In: M. D. Sorcinelli & A. E. Austin (Eds), *Developing New and Junior Faculty* (pp. 51–61). San Francisco, CA: Jossey-Bass.

Cox, M. (1997). Long-term patterns in a mentoring program for junior faculty: recommendations for practice. In: D. DeZure (Ed.), *To Improve the Academy* (pp. 225–267). Stillwater, OK: New Forums Press and the Professional and Organizational Development Network in Higher Education.

Davidson, M. (1979). Affirmative action's second generation: in the matter of Vilma Hernandez. *Change*, (November–December), 42–46.

Leon, D. (1997). *Mentoring minorities in higher education: passing the torch.* Washington, D.C.: National Education Association, Office of Higher Education.

Luna, G., & Cullen, D. L. (1996). *Empowering the faculty: mentoring redirected and renewed.* ASHE-ERIC Higher Education Report No. 3. Washington, D.C.: The George Washington University, Graduate School of Education and Human Development.

Smith, D., Wolf L., & Busenberg, B. (1996). *Achieving faculty diversity: debunking the myths.* Washington, D.C.: Association of American Colleges and Universities.

LATINOS AND ACADEMIC LEADERSHIP IN AMERICAN HIGHER EDUCATION

Roberto Haro

INTRODUCTION

Since the piece on Latino executive selection in higher education appeared in *The Leaning Ivory Tower* (1995), very little has been published regarding the progress of Latinas and Latinos in becoming presidents and academic vice presidents at two- and four-year colleges and universities in the United States. Few of the major national organizations, such as the American Association of State Colleges and Universities (AASCU), the American Council on Education (ACE), the Association of Governing Boards of Universities and Colleges (AGB), the National Association of State Universities and Land-Grant Colleges (NASULGC), and surprisingly Latino groups such as the National Council of La Raza (NCLR) and the Hispanic Association of Colleges and Universities (HACU), to name but a few, have done much to encourage or support research about the progress, or lack of it, by Latinos in becoming college and university presidents. Moreover, the lack of a long term, systematic approach to investigating what conditions and factors are responsible for the appointment or rejection of Latinas and Latinos for top leadership roles in American colleges and universities is puzzling. ACE, to its credit, does publish statistics and information regarding the appointment of women and minorities to presidencies on a fairly regular basis (*The American College President: 2000 Edition,* 2000). The data and information ACE

Latinos in Higher Education, Volume 3, pages 155–191.
Copyright © 2003 by Elsevier Science Ltd.
All rights of reproduction in any form reserved.
ISBN: 0-7623-0980-6

reported pertaining to community college leadership were challenged by the American Association of Community Colleges (AACC) in an article by Jamilah Evelyn in *The Chronicle of Higher Education* (2000, April 6). However, AACC, ACE and other similar organizations have yet to identify access to leadership roles by Latinos as a priority for future investigation. And finally, learning about the challenges and experience of Latinos who were appointed presidents at two- and four-year colleges had to wait for the outcomes of this modest, follow-up study.

Because of my interest in leadership roles in higher education, and the need for Latinos, and others, to better understand the challenges in becoming presidents, a follow-up study to the one done in the early 1990s was undertaken. Preparations for the study were initiated in 1997, and data gathering commenced in late 1998 and through most of 1999. Follow-up interviews and visits to different sites took place in 2000, with the completion of the analysis and writing in early 2001. To encourage cooperation from the subjects involved, strict confidentiality was required. For the first time, sitting Latina and Latino presidents and academic vice presidents (AVP) at two- and four-year campuses were interviewed to gather their thoughts on what challenges they had to overcome in becoming a campus leader. In a few cases, a sitting Latino president or AVP had to step out of such a role. It was necessary, therefore, to pay particular attention to these situations and learn whether the departure was voluntary or involuntary.

While the data available from the American Council on Education on presidential attainment indicate an increasing number and percentage of women, particularly White females, becoming presidents the same is not the case for African Americans and Latinos. The situation for Latinos, in fact, is troublesome even if the number of new presidents within the period 1995 to 2000 increased slightly. Most of the increase in the number of Latino (men and women) presidents during this five-year period occurred at two-year colleges. When the data are disaggregated, some disturbing developments surface. No Latinos were hired as presidents at private, selective four-year liberal arts colleges, and with one exception, no Latinos were hired as presidents or AVPs at major research universities. The appointment of three Latino presidents at publicly supported regional universities was, with one exception, at institutions which offered only the last two years of instruction leading to the Bachelors, and with teacher certification and a few Masters programs. In the meantime, several of the sitting Latino presidents at four-year colleges and universities are reaching retirement age.

The aging, and proximity to retirement, of Latinos in AVP and presidencies encourage a close examination of this situation. With few exceptions, most first time presidents are selected from the ranks of AVPs. Increasingly, governing boards are discussing the merits of selecting vice presidents for development for presidencies because of their experience and value in fund raising. On a few occasions, mainly at two-year colleges and at smaller, four-year liberal arts campuses, boards of trustees have selected a vice president for student affairs to serve as a president. So far, no Latino men or women from the student services ranks have been selected to lead a four-year college or university. Consequently, the traditional path to a first time presidency involves service as an academic dean and then as an AVP (Padilla & Chavez, 1995). Unfortunately for Latinos, very few of them are within the AVP ranks at four-year colleges and universities. The situation for Latinas is even more distressing, as less than a handful is represented within this rank at four-year colleges, while only one was found at the major research and doctoral granting universities.

Before continuing, it is important to consider two important demographic changes. First, Latinos in the United States (U.S.) are the largest ethnic minority in our country (U.S. Bureau of the Census, 2001). In some states like California, New Mexico and Texas they reached that status quite some time ago (Sanchez, L., 2001). Second, Latinos are, from a demographic perspective, a youthful population with a very high percentage of them at peak fertility ages (U.S. Census, 2001). Attracting more Latino youth to higher education is becoming a top priority for many states and educational organizations (Carnevale, 1999; HACU, 2000). However, there has been very little progress in attracting additional Latinos for faculty roles at American colleges and universities. And it is mainly from the faculty ranks that academic administrators are selected. The limited representation of Latino men and women in senior faculty ranks at four-year colleges and universities is one reason that so few of them move into the roles of department chair, or academic deanships. Without these experiences within their portfolios, Latino faculty (men and women) are not competitive candidates for AVP or president jobs, particularly at selective college and university campuses (Haro, 1995). In a recent conversation with two heads of faculty assemblies at major research universities, they indicated that the wave of anti-affirmative laws and legal decisions had seriously curtailed their abilities to recruit talented minority men and women for teaching faculty roles, especially Latinos.

TOPICS FOR REVIEW

To better understand and appreciate the conditions that Latino men and women who aspire to academic leadership roles in American colleges and universities would encounter it was decided to do a follow-up to a previous study of the

selection process for presidents. However, in the current study it was decided
to add information from those who had achieved AVP and president roles.
Thirty (30), two- and four-year, colleges and universities were contacted and
asked to participate in this project. Five (5) of the target institutions/individuals
declined to participate. The other 25 campuses and individuals contacted agreed
to cooperate, but insisted on strict confidentiality. Questionnaires were sent to
the target institutions and subjects in 1998. The breakdown of institutions is as
follows:

- Eight community colleges (two-year institutions).
- Six four-year private liberal arts colleges-three with small graduate profes-
  sional programs in business administration, health services, and social service
  areas.
- Seven publicly supported regional universities with graduate programs at the
  Masters level only.
- Four research universities (public and private) that offer the doctorate.

The enrollment categories for the institutions ranged from a low of 720
full-time-equivalent students (FTES) to more than 25,000 FTES. Subjects
interviewed included Latino men and women in senior leadership roles at five
community colleges, one four-year liberal arts college, three at publicly
supported regional universities, and one at a major research university. Two
Latino academic leaders could not be accommodated in this study because any
discussion of their situation, even a very general one, might have identified
them. However, in the conclusion, some important factors that surrounded their
circumstances and was part of what appeared to be a pattern, are included.

DATA COLLECTION METHODOLOGY

Two structured questionnaires were developed to solicit information from key
people at the target institutions. One questionnaire was designed to gather
information about the search for either an AVP, or a president at target
campuses. The other questionnaire was designed to secure information from
Latino men and women in academic leadership roles at two- and four-year
campuses (Yin, 1984). Two investigators, a male and a female, conducted all
of the interviews and follow-up on the questionnaires. An interview strategy
was developed to control the investigator's intervention into the observational
setting (Webb et al., 1966). Human subject guidelines were strictly adhered to
at this writer's home institution and at the target sites. The questions were
designed to capture specific data about the subject's role and status on the

campus. Where the search for a senior academic leader on a campus was involved, interviews were requested with representatives from any firm that had been engaged to assist in the identification of candidates for the opening. Contact with the interviewees occurred after the search process was completed and a candidate had been selected, or a new search was initiated. People interviewed in this category included faculty, staff, students, administrative personnel, trustees, and, where appropriate, influential alumni. Several of the candidates for the top academic leadership roles at target campuses were contacted and interviewed. Their input was carefully filtered to provide a measured, objective perspective in the conclusion of this piece.

The ten sitting academic leaders were sent a brief questionnaire, and asked to participate in a confidential interview with one of the investigators. Four of these interviews were conducted over the telephone. The others were conducted in person.

A hundred and fifty people were asked to participate in the study. One hundred and seventeen people (78%) agreed to be interviewed. Among the 117 people interviewed, ten were Latino men and women presidents or AVPs. These ten were located at five community colleges, one liberal arts college, three regional universities, and one major research university. Most of the interviews were conducted over the telephone. However, some of the subjects preferred to talk in person with one of the interviewers. Of the 107 interviews that involved selecting a new campus leader, 58 were devoted to presidential searches, and 49 with AVP searches.

STRATEGIES INVOLVING THE SEARCH PROCESS

Both interviewers visited each campus or system office. In a few cases, the search process involved hiring a person to head a multi-campus system, such as a two-campus community college district, or a sitting president identified as the chief executive officer (CEO) of a multi-campus system. Two strategies were involved in visits to target sites. The first were structured one-on-one interviews with persons involved with either the search or selection of a senior campus leader. The other was an informal process of walking around and randomly talking with student leaders, faculty, staff, and in several cases, alumni. The latter strategy was used to gain a sense of the institution's culture, and some of the prevailing attitudes about the search. This was particularly useful in situations involving presidential selection or a sitting president. This technique was mentioned by David Riesman in his study on choosing a college president (McLaughlin & Riesman, 1990). Ephemeral materials that include newspaper articles, letters to the editor of campus and off-campus newspapers, and flyers-where available-were also gathered. In three cases, private correspondence and memoranda that were highly critical about a sitting president or a presidential finalist were reviewed as part of the overall process of learning about the local attitudes toward a Latino leader. In two out of the 15 institutions that were involved in a search (13%), there was a failure to make an appointment, resulting in a new search that concluded in the appointment of a new campus leader. Both of these cases were carefully reviewed to determine why the original search had failed. In both cases it was learned that in the first search the leading finalist was a Latino. The rejected Latino finalists were contacted and asked to be interviewed. Both agreed. Their information has been incorporated into the conclusion only.

In cases involving the selection of a campus leader, data secured from the interviews with members of the search or screening committees, and other sources, were compiled and structured into six categories to allow for computer manipulation:

Academic preparation;
Experiential background, especially fund raising;
Scholarly accomplishments;
Matters of style;
Recommendations;
Interview impressions.

The following discussion will focus on the above categories and provide information about outcomes in the search process. Later in this piece, the strategy used to review the status and circumstances surrounding a sitting Latino academic leaders will be discussed.

AVP AND PRESIDENTIAL SEARCHES

The reader should realize that the sample size for new appointments in this investigation is very small. This is because out of the 25 institutions included in the study, ten involved sitting presidents or AVPs. Consequently, only 15 colleges and universities comprised the pool of campuses involved in searches for top academic leaders. And in two out of these 15 cases, the initial search did not result in an appointment. However, in the follow-up searches there were two appointments, a White male at one institution, and a White female at the other campus. While the overall number of presidents and AVPs at the target institutions may reflect a slight increase in Latino CEOs, it is important to underscore that the selection of the target institutions was skewed in order to include Latino sitting presidents and AVPs. Moreover, the majority of new Latino presidents are mainly at the two-year colleges, and publicly supported regional universities. One important development, as expressed in Table 1, is the percentage of White women appointed to leadership roles. The number of White women campus leaders increased from the level reported in the 1995 study (Haro, 1995).

GENERAL OUTCOMES

Among the 15 candidates appointed as new presidents or academic vice presidents, six were White males (40 percent), six were White females (40%), two were Latinos (13%) and one was a non-Latino minority (7%). There was a dramatic increase in the percentage of White women appointed as senior campus leaders between the 1995 study and this one (from 24 to 40% of the totals). While the absolute number of Latino appointments remained at two, in percentages there was an increase from the 10% of the previous survey to 13% in the current one. Consequently, just looking at the percentage of new Latino senior executives on college and university campuses would not provide a real-istic assessment of their limited progress in attaining these leadership roles, particularly at four-year universities and research campuses. In the category of presidential appointments, four White females were 45% of the total, three White males were 33% of the total, and one Latino and one non-Latino minority appointments were each 11% of the total. In the AVP appointments, three were White males (50%), two were White females (34%), and one was a Latina (16%). In the current sample, no non-Latino minorities were selected to serve as academic vice presidents. One of the White males appointed as a president

Table 1.   Appointments by Ethnicity and Gender.

Category	Number	(W) Males	(W) Females	Latinos	Non-Latino Minority
President	9	3	4	1	1
AVPs	6	3	2	1	0
Totals	15	6	6	2	1

Table 2.   Finalist Pool ($n = 83$).[1]

White Females	White Males	Latinos	Non-Latino Minorities
28	33	9	13

in this survey was a sitting president at another institution. Out of the remaining two White males, one was a vice president for development.

There were 83 finalists within the 15 cases reviewed (Table 2). All of the target institutions had a finalist pool that included one or more women. Among the 15, two had finalist pools that did not include any Latinos. Overall, White women outnumbered Latino candidates by slightly more than a three to one margin in the applicant pool of finalists for campus leadership jobs. Three Latinas were represented in the finalist pool for presidents, but only in searches at two-year colleges. No Latinas were in the finalist pools for presidents at four-year liberal arts colleges, regional universities and major research universities. White females made impressive gains in the search for presidencies among the target institutions. Four White females were appointed presidents, while only three White males were offered presidencies at the target campuses. In the quest for AVP jobs, White women were selected at the same rate as White males. However, White females were appointed to AVP jobs by a margin of three to one over Latinos. The same was the case for White males. In the searches for academic vice presidencies, there were only two Latinas in the finalist pool. None were in the major research university, and in the four-year liberal arts campus searches.

SPECIFIC OUTCOMES

Academic Preparation

The academic preparation of the candidates for leadership roles and the caliber of the institution where their doctorates were earned was solicited in two questions that were asked of those involved in the selection process. One question asked, "was it important to you in ranking the candidates where she or he earned the Bachelors' degree?" The other question asked, "how important is the academic reputation of the institution where a candidate earned the doctorate?" Three responses were possible: not important, important, and very important. Among the 107 persons interviewed, 55 (51%) were White Males, 34 (32%) were White females, and 18 (17%) were minorities. The 107 responded in the following manner. For 29 White males (or 53% of this category), the reputation of the institution granting the B.A. or B.S. was very important. For 19 of the White females (or 56% of this category), the caliber of the institution granting the B.A. or B.S. was very important. When asked about the caliber of the institution granting the doctorate, 46 White males (or 84% of this group), and 30 White females (or 88% of this category) indicated it was very important. Among the minorities, 16 (or 90% of this group) thought

Table 3. Pool of People Interviewed.

Category	Number	(W) Males	(W) Females	Minorities
President	49	25	16	8
AVPs	58	30	18	10
Totals	107	55	34	18

it was very important. The caliber of the institution awarding the baccalaureate and doctoral degrees was not as significant in the case of a sitting president. All of the applicants for presidencies who were already CEOs at a college or university were White.

The academic subject background or area of concentration of the candidates was part of another set of questions asked of the interviewees. The broad areas used were: visual and performing arts, education, engineering, humanities, science (biological and physical), social sciences, the professions (law medicine, etc.), and other. The two most frequently cited academic areas mentioned by respondents as the ideal background for AVP candidates were the sciences, and the social sciences. Engineering was a very close third, and quite popular at the major research institutions. Had the first and third priorities been determinative, all but five of the White female and minority candidates would have been eliminated from serious consideration for appointment. Females and minorities stood a better chance of appointment to a campus leadership role if they were in the social sciences rather than in the arts, education or humanities. Almost 40% of the minority candidates had degrees in education.

Experiential Background

In the selection process for the AVP positions, respondents ($n = 58$) were asked to indicate how important it was for a candidate to have been the chair of a teaching department and an academic dean. Of the 30 White males, 20 (or 68%) believed that it was very important. Thirteen out of the 18 (73%) White females thought it was very important. For minorities, six out of ten (almost 61%) thought it was very important.

For those involved in CEO searches ($n = 49$), a similar question was asked about the experiential background of candidates for presidencies. People were asked to rank the importance of having served as an academic vice president or an academic dean. Nineteen White males (76%) thought it was very important. Among White females, 11 (69%) thought it was very important. Among the minorities interviewed, five (63%) thought it was very important. The White males were more inclined to consider a presidential candidate with service as a vice president for development in place of service as an academic vice president than either the White females or the minority interviewees. However, among the White males interviewed, 23 (92%) indicated that any candidate for president, regardless of his/her service as a vice president for development, had to be a faculty member and undergone a successful tenure review. When the White males and females were asked how important service as an AVP and academic dean might be for a minority candidate, collectively 38 (93%) said it was very important. This represents a substantial difference between the response of the minority interviewees and the Whites.

Scholarly Accomplishments

It was decided in this study, not to include information on the teaching accomplishments of prospective candidates for either presidencies or AVP jobs. After the 1995 study, a follow-up with people who had been interviewed and read the final report, recommended that teaching experience not be a factor in the present investigation. There were sound reasons for this position. As a result, it was decided to consider scholarly accomplishment in the broadest sense possible.

For presidential candidates, 29 (59%) of the respondents believed that it was very important for a presidential candidate to have demonstrated some form of scholarly activity. However, when White male and female responses were aggregated, 29 (71%) said it was very important for minorities to have demonstrated scholarly activity. Among the 16 White females, 12 (75%) thought it was very important for minority candidates to have achieved some scholarly accomplishment, while 17 White males (68%) thought it was very important. Among the minority respondents to this question, five (63%) thought it was very important. Again, there was a considerable difference between the responses of Whites and minorities on the importance of one of the categories reviewed. It was not possible to attain a useful level of specificity regarding the perceptions and standards to which Latino candidates were held regarding this factor. The numbers were just too small to be meaningful.

In the AVP searches, the results were fascinating. Among the 58 respondents, 39 (67%) believed that a record of scholarly achievement was very important. Nineteen (19 or 63%) of the White males and 13 (72%) of the White females responded that this factor was very important. Six (60%) of the minorities interviewed responded that it was very important. However, when asked about the importance of scholarly accomplishments by White women, 21 (70%) of the White males responded that it was very important. When asked about minority candidates, 23 (77%) of the White males thought it was very important. Fourteen White females (78%) thought it was very important for minority candidates to demonstrate a record of scholarly achievement. Among the minority respondents, six (60%) thought it was very important for White women to have a record of scholarly accomplishment, the same as for the total grouping of men, women and minorities. While this sample is a limited one, the results dramatize a higher level of concern for the scholarly accomplishment of women, and especially minority candidates for AVP positions. Moreover, White females in numbers and percentages seemed to believe that minority candidates should have a track record of greater scholarship than expected for White males, and females.

Matters of Style

The topic of a candidate's style, was dealt within two parts. The first involved the management behavior of the candidates, and the second the personal characteristics or qualities of the leaders. Every attempt was made to avoid an overlap between these two areas. However, in the interviews, the two would often be mixed, requiring the interviewers to return to the original question and make the distinction between them. Regarding management behavior/style, the following themes were pursued:

Consensus building
Communication skills (written and oral)
Diplomacy/tact
Shared governance
Decision making

The above themes were explored through questions asked of the persons involved in the search process for a new president or AVP (Loftland, 1995).

The respondents considered *consensus building* as involving team building and coalition development on and off the campus. This was especially true for presidential candidates. Several respondents indicated that minorities had not yet reached a point in academia where they understood and could work successfully at building coalitions on and off the campus, especially with groups such as alumni and wealthy potential benefactors. This was most often mentioned at the four-year private liberal arts colleges, and at the major research universities. Several female respondents (White women for all practical purposes) indicated that White females because of their growing national networks and alliances, and having been in the academy in more numbers and for a longer time than minorities better understood how to forge coalitions and get people on a campus to reach common ground. A few White males indicated that "recent attention" focused on the limited representation of White women in leadership roles in the academy was helpful to female candidates for leadership roles, particularly where they were able to identify experiences that demonstrated successful consensus building on a campus, or elsewhere. At publicly supported two-and four-year colleges and universities, respondents also mentioned the need to work closely with elected officials. In this area, several of the respondents indicated that White males and females had an advantage because the majority of elected officials were White.

In the area of *communication skills* the responses revealed two intriguing perspectives. One grouping stressed the need for a campus leader to be articulate and a polished speaker, adept at talking to large groups, as well as in smaller setting that might even include one-on-one conversations. These respondents indicated that oral communication skills involved excellent vocabularies, and strong organization qualities that would make their messages explicit and persuasive. When asked if women and Latinos, specifically, demonstrated these qualities, most of the respondents said "they showed promise, but not the type of success enjoyed by male leaders." When pressed on this topic, two members of governing boards and three White faculty indicated that White females they had interviewed for leadership roles had this talent and just needed to be put into the right job to actualize on their potential. The same confidence was not accorded to minority candidates, especially Latinos, by these persons. Responses on written communication skills also revealed important differences in the way candidates were perceived. Desirable skills as a writer were almost taken for granted in the case of White males. One respondent tersely said, "White male leaders got to where they are because they learned to write well, and have been successful in demonstrating this talent." When asked about Latinos, he replied, "I guess they are a little behind in this area, perhaps because English is not their native tongue." This perspective that Latino candidates still had to improve their writing abilities, seemed to fly in the face of candidates with strong publication records that demonstrated considerable facility with the English language. However, a senior faculty member at a major research university dismissed this by saying, "all of us know that scholarly journals tend to have a strong editorial process that will recast marginally prepared material." With this he dismissed the written communication skills of a Latino candidate. As an aside, this Latino candidate for a presidency had several years before been identified by *The New York Times* as one of the top researchers and writers in his discipline. How interesting that there was such a discrepancy between the perspectives of this senior faculty member and a major newspaper known for its high standards.

Diplomacy was often mentioned as a very significant quality required of a campus leader, especially at the presidential level. The ability to serve and act as the senior spokesperson for a campus, particularly where sensitive issues were involved was stressed by many of the respondents. One female trustee at a liberal arts college stressed that the rapport between the campus and the local community depended on the sustained tact and personal relationships between the president and the upper-middle class groups that lived close to the college. She doubted that a minority person would be as successful in maintaining this rapport as someone "more like the leaders" in the geographical area surrounding the campus. When asked if this would be the case for a White woman, she indicated that perhaps it would be possible if the female was outstanding. A vice president at a four-year college, with responsibility for campus security, was candid in stating that his college had been the target of recent newspaper articles accusing it of being a "party school." For him, a strong moral leader was essential to diplomatically cope with the negative publicity. When pressed on this issue, he went on to say that a female president might not make a sufficiently strong "statement" in upholding the campus values. Asked about the possible appointment of a minority male, he guardedly said that the "disadvantages outweighed the potential benefits." One can only surmise that in the mind of this vice-president, and others like him, minorities were perceived to lack the moral fiber and character to deal as effective diplomats in situations that questioned the reputation and image of a campus.

At the AVP level, the term "linking-pin" was frequently mentioned along with tact and diplomacy. An academic dean at a regional university put it succinctly when she said, "faculty need to know that the academic vice president will be their ambassador to the president and the board of trustees." She went on to say there were very few minorities capable of doing so at her institution. Others on that same campus were not as glib as the dean. However, in their actions, the message was quite clear. They hired a White male for the AVP job at this campus. One question that was asked of people involved in the AVP searches was if the opportunity for hiring a woman or a minority was affected if the CEO was a White male, a White female, or a minority. Most of the respondents said that if a White male was the president, and enjoyed the confidence of the board of trustees and the faculty, then a White female might be looked upon favorably, provided she had the requisite academic background, skills and experience. The same level of confidence in the appointment of a minority for an AVP job was not expressed by the respondents. When asked about the appointment of a White male or female internal candidate for an AVP job, the level of confidence was much higher for them than for a minority candidate. In one case, an internal minority candidate for an AVP job at a university was not selected because some members of the search committee indicated that he was "just going to use this job as a stepping stone to a presidency elsewhere."

Shared Governance was a very important quality that preoccupied the conversation of faculty in the selection of a campus leader. In this category, there was a very distinct difference between those institutions where faculty had either a union, or regularly engaged in a formal type of collective bargaining with the campus administration, and those that did not. At a college where there was no union or collective bargaining by the faculty, the emphasis on the selection of a new campus leader, whether a president or an AVP, revolved around an often used term, "collegial process." This was used to surface a form of cooperation between a president and the faculty, staff and students that involved regular informational meetings and conversations. The term most often used by faculty on campuses where a "collegial process" operated was regular "consultation." When asked about the expected performance of a White male, a White female, or a minority under this type of shared governance structure, the majority of respondents indicated that a White male might have an advantage, especially if he had worked within such a form of collaboration. There was less confidence in the ability of a White woman to operate well under such a system of shared governance. And when respondents were asked about Latinos, specifically, several of the respondents indicated a lack of confidence in Latinos because they might not have worked at institutions where this type of relationship and campus governance was the norm. The expectation, particularly for presidential candidates at private liberal arts colleges, was that without experience at a comparable campus with a collegial process selection for a senior level leadership position was not feasible. The very small number of Latina and Latino faculty in department chair and academic dean roles at these colleges effectively eliminates all but one or two of them from qualifying as viable candidates for AVP jobs and, especially, presidencies.

Where collective bargaining agreements were formalized and bound by contractual relationships, having experience working with unions was far more important than being involved in the "collegial process." This was the one area in which public supported two-and four-year colleges and universities tended to rank the three categories of applicants practically the same. The difference in confidence level between White males and White females was about 2% in favor of White men. Minorities were just slightly behind White males and females at 3.5%. The determining factor in shared governance at campuses with formal collective bargaining was experience working with unions. Without that management experience and style of shared governance, any candidate, regardless of ethnicity/race or gender, would not be successful in getting a senior leadership job.

The area of *decision making* proved to be difficult to quantify. The term was initially defined for being able to make well-informed decisions, without delay and equivocation. Also factored into the definition was soliciting timely input from groups on and off the campus. And finally, the willingness to revisit a difficult decision and perhaps modifying or overturning it was very important. For the AVP jobs, the most critical aspect of decision making was the need to be "tough minded." By this, faculty underscored the need to reduce and reallocate resources based on realistic measures, such as enrollment pattern changes. However, they also wanted an AVP to protect core disciplines in the sciences, mathematics and humanities. Most of the respondents indicated that White males seemed to have the "right qualities" to make hard choices. Several respondents indicated that unless a White female had come through the school of "academic hard knocks," she would not be effective in "playing hard ball" with groups on the campus. When asked about Latinos, one prominent botanists and a search consultant at a major executive search firm indicated that "too many Hispanic candidates were 'soft option' managers." By this, they meant that most Latinos did not have a successful track record of handling confrontation well and making tough decisions. When they were asked to cite an example of this, one stated that a Latina acting vice president for student services would almost completely capitulate to the demands of the people in the office of campus safety and security within her portfolio. Following up on this situation, the researchers discovered that the president and the head of campus security at this particular institution were close friends and played golf together at least once a week. In another example from a regional university the search consultant indicated that she knew of a Latino academic dean who could not control several of the teaching departments within his area of responsibility. After visiting this campus and speaking with several people it was learned that the president and academic vice president were not supportive of the Latino academic dean, and had overturned his decisions on several occasions when influential faculty members came to complain and threatened to file grievances. It seemed that in both situations, the Latino administrators had an unearned reputation as weak and indecisive decision makers.

With respect to presidents, two areas for concern in decision making surfaced: athletics, and fund raising. More than 50% of the respondents involved in presidential searches indicated that most women and Latinos were not "sufficiently familiar or experienced" in dealing with intercollegiate athletics. One emphatic president of an alumni association stated that a White female would never be able to understand the importance of intercollegiate athletics at his institution. He said, "she would be a pushover for those fuzzy headed professors who want to abandon football at this campus." In the area of fund raising, the chair of a selection committee indicated that Latinos did not seem to have the experience when it came to decisions about cultivating organizations that might have ties to tobacco or liquor producing firms. He went on to say that "money has no memory." A final note with respect to this category is important. The majority of respondents were willing to cite positive examples of decision- making that almost exclusively represented the behavior and actions of White males. In only three instances were positive decision-making examples of White females mentioned. Within the screening of presidential candidates, no examples of positive decision-making by a Latino were offered. The reader should remember that the number of people interviewed in presidential searches was 49.

RECOMMENDATIONS

In the previous study on executive selection in higher education (Haro, 1995), no category was available to deal with matters involving the source and influence of recommendations for candidates. The topic was mentioned often by members of the search and screening committees, and particularly by consultants and representatives from executive search firms. As a result, it was decided to craft three questions that would try to solicit information on sources of recommen-dation, to include letters of nomination, for candidates applying for senior leadership roles on a campus. Some intriguing things were uncovered. While it was not possible to read any letters of nomination or recommendation, a question was asked about the significance of the person or organization doing so. Another question dealt with telephone follow-up by a member of the search or screening committee, and by a search consultant if assigned this task, with the nominator/recommender. A third question attempted to solicit information regarding networks or the use of a political process to try to influence the decision making of a group or individual in the appointment of a senior level campus executive.

It was learned that the *source* of a nomination or recommendation for a candidate was very significant in 13 of the searches (87%). The two types of institutions that uniformly considered the source of a nomination or recommendation as very significant were private four-year liberal arts colleges, and major research universities. At these two types of institutions, there was a strong correlation between the source of the communication and input from *informal*, but highly regarded, *networks*. For example, at several private liberal arts colleges, where a president of a comparable, or highly selective institution nominated or recommended a candidate for an open presidency, a very high value was given to it. If there was a follow-up conversation or input from a network to which the original nominator/recommender belonged, an attempt was made to determine the importance of this contact in determining whether the candidate became a finalist stage. An example to demonstrate this is provided. In the search for a president at a four-year liberal arts college, the president of a highly regarded midwestern campus sent a strong letter of nomination. When the candidate became one of the top three finalists for the presidency, a *telephone* call from the head of an informal group of college presidents underscored the original nomination, reinforced a letter of recommendation provided by a member of the group, and followed-up with an oral discussion of why the preferred finalist would be ideal for the presidency at the college. The informal group was composed almost exclusively of White males, many of whom had attended one or more of the following: a Harvard program for education leaders; a summer seminar for new college presidents; and participation in either the Woodrow Wilson, or American Council on Education fellowship program. It is important to note that the finalist supported by this network was offered the job.

Women have started to use different strategies in helping female candidates become appointed senior level executives on college and university campuses. At five of the campuses reviewed, an *informal network* of prominent White women administrators played a significant role in the candidacy of several White females. At a two-year college, and at a four-year university, White female leaders in higher education associations and in women's groups sent strong letters of support, followed by *telephone* calls to friends of theirs on the campus. In both of these cases, influential state legislators were contacted by female leaders and "briefed" on the "outstanding qualities" of the two women finalists. Both female finalists supported by such efforts were offered the jobs.

When asked whether the sources of letters of nomination or recommendation for minority candidates were significant, the responses were mixed. Several respondents expressed a favorable disposition where an African American woman was a candidate. Again, there was a combination of factors that added value to the candidacy of this woman. A local council of African American ministers had demonstrated strong support for the African American female, and encouraged several local politicians to call the campus and express their enthusiasm for this female finalist. She got the job. In one of the university level searches, a Latino candidate was successful because of a strong coalition between minority members of the state legislature, influential Latino alumni in the business sector of the community where the campus was located, and three minority members of the university's governing board. However, this was the only case where nominations and recommendations, and follow-up by informal groups and networks helped a Latino become a senior level campus executive.

Consequently, the use of highly respected college and university leaders to serve as sponsors and allies, particularly at liberal arts colleges and major research universities, and the use of external networks and political influence was significant in *several* of the searches. However, in only *two* searches were an African American and a Latino able to use this strategy successfully.

INTERVIEW IMPRESSIONS

The interviews with members of the selection or screening committees for top executive leadership roles on a campus resulted in the accumulation of highly impressionistic attitudes and images of what a successful senior manager should be. It was decided to focus attention on the nine presidential searches to determine the influence of interviews in ranking finalists. It was in these nine cases that it was possible to aggregate and generalize the information volunteered by the respondents. In the searches for AVPs, especially where the candidates were from within the target institution, the interviews were not given a high priority by the members of the search or selection committees. But in presidential searches, there was a definite "image" for an "ideal candidate" to have that was vocalized by many of the respondents. In his early study on Chicano administrators in the Southwest, Esquibel mentions some of these characteristics (Esquibel, 1992). Consider the following elements in the development of a typology that played an important role in evaluating the finalists:

Presidents should be tall and "distinguished."
They should be polished speakers.
They should be at ease in any setting.
Their personal grooming should be of the highest order.
They should be attentive and good listeners.
They should be measured in their responses, and calm under stress.

The subjective nature of the responses solicited from the interviewees made it very difficult to quantify the level of importance that should be ascribed to the interview of a finalist for a presidential role. Nevertheless, 44 out of the 49 persons (90%) involved in the search process believed the interview was a very significant factor in the selection of a president. In fact, many of the respondents indicated that most of the elements listed above were important to them as they evaluated a finalist during an interview.

The term *distinguished* was mentioned by 41 of the 49 respondents (84%) in describing the desirable "image" of a college or university president. Height was important. In four searches, among the male finalists only two were under 5′10″. In one case, two members of the governing board said they thought the minority finalist was short and not very impressive (he is 5′6″ and with developing patterned male baldness). In another search, a Latina was identified as "pudgy and tired looking." The two successful finalists in the above searches were an attractive, slender White female in her late forties, and a tall, White male with a full head of gray hair and a smile that reveals beautiful, white teeth.

During the scheduled interviews, each finalist was given the opportunity to make an oral presentation. The *speaking* ability of the finalists was important for 38 (78%) of the respondents. One vice-president at a two-year campus thought a Latina candidate appeared reserved and timid in her presentation. A senior faculty member at the institution thought that her presentation was "uninspired and lacking a dynamic quality." Needless to say, she was not offered the position at this college. Another unsuccessful minority candidate was given low marks because in his presentation, "most of the words he used were monosyllabic." The successful candidate for this particular presidency is a chatty and gregarious individual with a slightly Southern accent and an initial impression of charm and openness. However, since he has been the president of this campus, his removals of three popular administrators and several grievances that were filed have resulted in a growing movement among the faculty for a vote of no confidence in him. In three separate cases, minority candidates were ranked lower than other finalists because respondents said "they had an accent" or used terminology and pronunciation in their vernacular that "did not sound like good English." Regarding the former, one of the Latino candidates did have a slight inflection in his voice. However, it is a soft Southern drawl, and to the trained ear not as conspicuous as President George W. Bush's Texas manner of speaking. It was finally possible to determine what a respondent meant by something that did not sound like good English. The finalist in question was a Black male who was raised in the Caribbean and spoke with what sounds like an English accent. In both of these cases, the speaking style of a finalist was used as a negative factor in their interview evaluation by respondents who felt these candidates did not measure up to "a desirable speaking style," however subjective that might be.

It was difficult to try to quantify what it meant for a candidate to *be at ease* in any setting. Questions were asked to determine how the finalists presented themselves to different individuals and groups with which they met on the campus during their interviews. It was decided to ask three different groups of interviewees about this: faculty; members of the governing boards; and senior administrators on the campus. Students were not included in this grouping because they were difficulty to contact, evidenced quite different perspectives resulting from their undergraduate or graduate status, and the nature of their campus participation – part-time, full time, commuters, residential, etc. White males were considered most at ease in any setting, with White women and minorities a distant second and third. Almost 80% of the respondents thought that the White male candidates for presidencies looked relaxed and "comfortable" during the interview process at the target campuses. However, the same was not the case with women and minorities. Less than 70% of the respondents indicated that women and minorities looked at ease, or seemed to be "comfortable" during the interview process. A senior level administrator at a liberal arts college stated that a White female candidate "had not done her homework and made a few faux paus regarding the role of religious groups on the campus." An influential faculty member at a major research university indicated he ranked a minority finalist low because "he seemed young, unsure of himself, and nervous during the faculty meeting where the topic of university support for research funding was discussed." By the end of the intensive interviews presidential candidates had endured, ranging from one and a half to three days, the respondents had definite impressions about which ones seemed better prepared and able to handle questions and comments from various people at the scheduled meetings. After talking with a few representatives from the executive search firms, it was learned that several of the White male finalists had used consultants who prepared them for interviews and video taped them to work on "tips and techniques" to enhance their performance. Only two of the White women finalists had done so, while none of the Latinos had. Consequently, it may be possible to say that some finalists where much better prepared to project a calm and relaxed image during the interview process.

Personal grooming included attire and what were really "cosmetic" factors that respondents noted and remembered. Clothing seemed to make an important first impression. At a two-year college, one of the members of the governing board indicated that she was distressed by the appearance of a Latina candidate. When asked what it was that caused this reaction, she said the woman was overweight, and that her blouse was too tight and was straining two of the buttons. Another respondent in the same two-year college indicated that it appeared the Latina finalist in question was "using too much make up!" Both respondents were White. At a research university, a minority candidate was criticized for casual attire. It seems that this finalist presented himself on the second day of the interview wearing a blazer and tan slacks. Although he wore a shirt and tie, the respondent was quick to note that among the finalists for this presidency, he was the only one who did not wear a suit during the entire interview process. A woman finalist was given low marks by two respondents at a private liberal arts college because she wore "loud jewelry." When asked about this, the respondent indicated that "flashy oversized earrings and a necklace deliberately made visible by a revealing blouse" was not in good taste. As a result, this candidate did not get the job.

Among the candidates who earned top marks for their attire, it became evident that dark suits for the men and conservative attire for women finalists were well received. Several respondents indicated that they wanted their president to look "professional" because he or she would be dealing with wealthy people and corporate heads to attract resources for the campus. Three of the members of governing boards at private liberal arts colleges indicated that the president was the single most important person in communicating the type of successful impression they wanted to project about their institution. Although none were explicit when responding to questions about whether a minority person, and in particular a Latino, measured up to the image, they had in mind for a campus leader, their remarks about why they selected a White male or female left little doubt regarding what type of person they wanted in that role. And, a minority did not seem to fit their typology.

The group most concerned with how *good a listener and attentive* finalists were, was faculty. They more than any other group of respondents measured a presidential finalist by how well she or he listened to what they had to say. Moreover, several faculty indicated that they tried early in their interactions with the finalists to "develop some kind of rapport along academic lines." By this, faculty meant that it was important for them to probe a finalist to find intellectual interests or subjects that could serve as the basis for important discourse. One minority finalist was summarily dismissed as "not intellectually disposed" by faculty at a research university because he had never published a scholarly book. One of the respondents rejected this finalist with the following comment, "obviously he is nothing but an administrative functionary." This same respondent was enthusiastic about the conversation he had with the interim president at this institution because it dealt with themes in his area of teaching. Several of the respondents sent mixed messages regarding the listening skills of the finalists. The chair of a screening committee indicated that the female presidential candidates did not seem interested in the role that athletics played on her campus. When asked if she had questioned the female candidates about this, she replied, "no, their indifference was apparent from their behavior." Perceptions, unfortunately, are misleading and should not be taken as fact!

The last thing that respondents stressed in the interview process was how well a finalist responded *under stress*. One member of a governing board stated that she did not care for a minority finalist because after an intense question and answer meeting, before he left to attend another interview session, he shook hands with her. "He had sweaty palms," said the respondent, and that made her uncomfortable with his candidacy. The White male selected for the job had been noticed by students on the campus as wiping his upper lip with a handkerchief. Following-up on this, it was learned that the new president did have a problem with perspiring heavily, especially around the face, during tense situations.

At a liberal arts college, the faculty prepared questions for the candidates that dealt with diversity and whether the curriculum should be modified to accommodate this. The minority finalist was cautious but optimistic about what needed to be done. However, several follow-up questions were asked about specific goals that might be needed. A female finalist was selected because she took a very cautious approach, stating that it was important to "follow the law even if it meant postponing plans or programs to promote affirmative action." The minority finalist for this position had seemed animated and enthusiastic about finding ways to pursue diversity at this campus. The respondents felt that his "zealousness" on this matter was not well conceived, or realistic. In other words, his response was not measured! At a two-year campus, a member of the elected board for the district directly challenged a female finalist in a "gruff and confrontational manner." The female finalist was initially unsettled by this type of behavior. However, this was a ploy by the board member to "test the reaction" of the candidates with a confrontational attitude. Two of the White male candidates, one of them a sitting president, remained passive and did not respond to this attempt at intimidation. The board member said that he thought the "female candidate would 'crack' under that kind of pressure." As a result of her behavior, he voted against her. The strategy employed by the board member to test how well a finalists performed when stressed might not be an effective way to determine how well a person might perform as a president, even under stress.

A few remarks are important regarding the importance of the interview process in the selection of a president. The respondents were asked how important the interviews they observed were in ranking the finalists. Almost 90% of the respondents in the nine presidential searches answered that these were "very significant." Several respondents stated that their decision to vote for a particular candidate was determined by how well the finalists performed during the interviews. It was during this highly subjective process of evaluation that predilection suggesting discomfort with female, and especially minority finalists, surfaced.

LATINA AND LATINO CAMPUS LEADERS

It was decided to interview ten Latina and Latino campus leaders who were in presidencies or AVP positions at two-year colleges, and four-year universities.

Unfortunately, there were no Latino presidents at four-year private liberal arts colleges, and major research universities [at that time]. There was one AVP at a research university. Five of the Latino men and women leaders were at two-year colleges, one was at a major research university, and four were at four-year regional universities. Two of the regional universities were upper division campuses only. The persons interviewed must have been appointed to these roles within the last four years. Three critical topics were explored with these leaders: what factors or strategies were most significant in their appointment; what major challenges had they faced during the first two years; and what groups or individuals were most critical of their leadership.

THE APPOINTMENT PROCESS

The selection of a campus leader, especially a president, at a two-year college presents intriguing opportunities for the researcher. Governing boards for two-year colleges are, for the most part, elected. The increasing election and participation of minority board members in the decision making of community colleges have resulted in some fascinating decisions regarding leadership roles. However, an important distinction needs to be made that explains why in some districts with high concentrations of minorities, White males and females continue to be selected as presidents or superintendents. If board members for a community college are elected at larger, rather than representing districts within the geographical area covered by the system, some important patterns develop. In California, at two community college systems that are adjacent to each other, one elects their board at large from within the general area, and the other by districts within the jurisdiction. Both community college systems have minority populations that combined are more than 51% of the total population in their respective geographical areas. The system that elects its board members at large has never had a minority president, or academic vice president. The system that elects it board members from districts within the jurisdiction has had three different minority men and women presidents in the last ten years. Two of the presidents from the latter system have gone on to become the Superintendents of multi-campus systems in California and elsewhere.

To test a hypothesis regarding district verses at large elections in community college systems and the possible effect on leadership selection, a quick and limited survey was done to review several community colleges in different states to determine if there was a correlation between the way board members were elected within a geographical area with a high percentage of minorities and the selection of minorities as campus leaders. While this was a very limited survey and captured information for a short time span, 1995 to 1999, the results are intriguing. Among the 17 community colleges reviewed in six states, in all but one geographical area where board members were elected at large there had been only two minority leaders selected in the last five years. In those geographical areas where board members were elected by district, better than 72% of the campus leaders appointed in the years between 1995 and 1999 were minorities. The reader should realize that this sample size is small, and that other factors influenced the selection of minority campus leaders. However, there are enough data and anecdotal information to warrant an investigation of this hypothesis.

Factors and Strategies

A few examples may shed light on why Latino females and males may have been selected for leadership roles at two- and four-year colleges and universities. The selection of a Latina AVP at a four-year university involved some fascinating factors. First, the target institution was having difficulties with the faculty and in particular with minority faculty. Second, the president of the campus is not particularly well liked by either the faculty or the staff. The president is a much better "off campus" person with very good contacts with "friends" of the campus in neighboring areas. And third, there is a mixed minority community adjacent to the campus, and a much larger minority population that is comprised mostly of Latinos in an urban area within the university's service area. Two major grievances, and a law suit were pending against the president and the campus. When interviewed, the Latina AVP indicated that she had been given the opportunity to serve in this leadership capacity because of what she considered being a "high risk" situation. When asked if she was selected for this role if the president was on better terms with the faculty and staff, and the campus operating without major challenges, she indicated "probably not." She volunteered information that perhaps the governing board and the president may have agreed that selecting a minority AVP in a very difficult situation was a strategy that did not pose a major risk. If the minority woman failed, then "her lack of preparation and experience" could be used to rationalize the outcome. If she was able to prevail, then the president and the governing board would be able to take credit for making a wise decision.

   At a two-year college, a talented Latina was selected as the president. When she was asked about factors that may have contributed to her appointment, she cited two important things. First, she indicated that an elected female board member had called several sitting Latino and Latina presidents at community colleges and asked for the names of suitable candidates for the position of president at her college. Her name surfaced as one of the top potential candidates on the list of names given to the board member by five community college leaders. Second, Latino faculty, staff and particularly students at the college encouraged the community to take an active interest in the search for a new president. She was called by several people and groups and asked to apply. During her campus visits this very talented Latina easily conveyed her intellect, outstanding experiential background, and leadership skills. There was, however, one stubborn group of faculty who opposed her appointment because they said she had never held a presidency before. The student body president for the campus, a Latino and an Army veteran, rallied the campus and off campus community, and spoke to the local newspapers in favor of this Latina. The Latina was eventually selected to become the president. She is extremely talented and earning high marks for her leadership at this campus.

One final example of the strategy used to help a Latino become the president of a four-year campus is informative. The four-year campus in question is in a region with a very large population of Latinos. However, the institution had a "history" of unfortunate experiences with the appointment of senior level Latinos. The root of the problem seemed to be a suspicious and intimidating core of White faculty who had mounted several campaigns against a Latino academic dean – who had resigned and returned to a teaching role – and a Latino vice president who left after a two-year running battle with White faculty. A fascinating campaign was devised by a prominent Latino businessman in the immediate area. He brought together three of the most influential members of the governing board, and five of the elected member of the legislature who were either from the geographical area where the campus was located or were on the budget allocation committees in the legislature. This businessman forged a strong coalition that asked for the support of influential African American leaders in the community, and also the assistance of several White women's groups in the area and in the state. Without a doubt, this was a well crafted political effort designed to condition the decision by the governing board. When the Latino president was asked about this process, the answer given was simple. "As a way to influence the governing board, and send a strong message to the faculty about what they would need to contend with, the [coalition] was invaluable." Was the president's appointment directly related to the work of this group? The answer is probably yes.

Major Challenges

The Latino superintendent of a community college system indicated that the major challenge he faced in his first two years involved a hostile elected board member for the district. This particular board member had supported a White candidate for the job of superintendent and had relied heavily on the advice of a White search consultant. The White search consultant was an older man who had been the president of two community colleges, and was very active in an "old White boys' " network within a national community college organization. After his appointment, the White board member became quite contentious about the planning and priorities developed by the new Latino superintendent. The superintendent indicated that on several occasions the antagonistic board member had made snide remarks about his decisions, and tried to lobby other board members against him. During the second year of his tenure, the Latino superintendent learned that the White board member had held three meetings with White instructors to "learn about their concerns with the performance of the new superintendent." Fortunately, the woman who chaired the elected board for the district had never been informed by the antagonistic board member of his decision to meet with White instructors. She then publicly reprimanded the board member for holding meetings with college instructional staff without notifying her, and the superintendent. When asked about the long term effects of this challenge, the Latino superintendent said that he fully expected the antagonistic board member to "hound" him at every step and try to find ways to "embarrass" him.

At a regional university, a Latino president revealed that the major challenge he faced was the intention of members of the governing board to offer him an "interim appointment" as president. He went on to explain that several governing board members had been lobbied by older faculty and senior administrative staff at the campus to make an interim appointment. The rationale for their position was twofold. A White woman finalist, popular with the faculty/senior administrators had withdrawn from an earlier search for the presidency of the campus to accept a major political appointment at the federal level. Her appointment was for two years only, after which she indicated an interest in being considered for a university presidency. Second, the Latino president had been a strong proponent of diversity in his previous job. He had been accused by some of the White faculty at his home campus of "being too pro-Hispanic," in his hiring practices. After reviewing his direct and indirect appointments, it was discovered that out of the nine people he hired, or encouraged to be hired, over a four-year period, three had been White females, three had been White males, and three had been minorities. Two of the minorities were new faculty hires, and one was a senior level appointment in business services. One of the White females had been appointed as an academic dean. Two of the White males had been appointed to executive level academic positions. However, this information had been couched in a manner that made it appear as if six (by including the White females with the three minority appointments) had been affirmative action hires. Several members of the governing board when presented with this information were sympathetic to an "interim appointment." When asked about taking the position on an interim basis, the president said it was a risk, but one he was willing to take. After the governing board had received an objective account of the Latino leader's performance in his previous role, and received letters and calls of support on his behalf from groups on the new campus and elsewhere, the chair of the governing board shared this with the other members and moved to make his appointment permanent. When asked if he would endure such an ordeal again, the Latino president said "maybe!"

Antagonistic Individuals and Groups

It was surprising to learn from a Latina president of a two-year college that her most outspoken critics were a group of Latino student activists. As far as these students were concerned, she had not done anything to move forward a "Chicano Agenda" for the college. Such an agenda had not been discussed during her campus interviewed, and had not been mentioned to her until two days before the students held a press conference to complain about her. In addition, the students, almost all of them part-timers, had wanted the president to remove a senior level officer in student services responsible for community liaison and appoint a Latino community activist in that role. The students also criticized the president for not attending their off campus meetings, and for not being active in "the community." A major skirmish took place over the release of a part-time instructor teaching a course on minority literature. The enrollment of the course had, over the past three years continued to decline and was enrolling less than six students each term. Campus policy was clear that enrollment had to be at least 12 for a course to be taught. The students blamed the president for this decision. Reviewing the dynamic at this campus and in the surrounding community, it was learned that the antagonistic Latino students were not part of a campus recognized organization. The community that they continued to refer to was vague in both its identity and location. The person the students wanted to serve in a community liaison capacity was a worker in a community-based organization who lacked the necessary credentials or experience to qualify for a staff hire at the college. The Latino instructor the students wanted retained, even though the enrollment in that class had declined well below the cut off level, was working on a Masters at a regional university nearby, and was popular with these students because he "never gave less than a 'B' to a Latino in his classes." Nevertheless, these strident student voices did manage to make their way to the attention of the elected board members for the college. Fortunately, the Latina president was able to prevail by providing objective information to counter the sometimes "wild accusations" that were leveled against her by this splinter group of Latino student agitators.

At a regional university, a senior Latino leader shared his disappointment and conflict with a group of older science faculty. These faculty, almost exclusive White males, were annoyed because their concerns were not being "adequately" addressed. The science faculty were upset because they were required to teach four courses each year, one of which could be a graduate seminar or directed study class. The faculty wanted the campus to allow them to teach three courses a year, and allow them to team teach a research method's class that would qualify for the fourth course. They also wanted one of the three courses they would be required to teach to be a graduate seminar. In response to their request, the campus administration demonstrated that the state provided a formulaic amount of money for faculty that was based on four courses each year, and that graduate seminars and directed study did not carry the same level of weight from the state as undergraduate classes. Moreover, by team teaching a course, with two or more instructors, only partial compensation for the percent of time given to the course would be allowed. The science faculty were furious when their proposal was rejected. They accused the Latino leader of being "anti-science, and anti-research." The chairman of one of the leading science departments took it upon himself to try to rally support among the campus faculty for a vote of no confidence in the Latino leader. He claimed that the Latino leader was not a scientist and had a doctorate in a "soft discipline," perhaps explaining why he could not understand the need for the science faculty to have more time to do research. It should be understood that at this particular institution, the major criterion by which faculty are measured is their teaching, followed in a lesser order of importance by service to the university, and then scholarly productivity.

"No one ever told me that being a campus leader would be so difficult," said a Latino former AVP, "or that because I was of Mexican blood my accomplishments and activities as an administrator would always be suspect." This talented Mexican American academic leader, forced to resign from his role as an AVP at a four-year university was remarkably calm and philosophical about the shabby treatment he had received by irate faculty and a member of the governing board of the university. A talented scholar, this Latino leader had been the victim of a "house cleaning" move by a coalition of faculty, alumni and governing board members that targeted the president and two of his senior aides. "As the appointee of an unpopular president, I was the victim of guilt by association," he said. When asked to comment on what influence, if any, his being a Mexican American might have had in the decision to seek his ouster, he calmly said, "it did not help that I was of Mexican heritage." After pressing him to follow-up on this theme, he said, "my last words on this topic are that as a minority, I was always suspect in the eyes of many campus people who wanted to believe I reached the level of vice president because of preferential treatment, and to satisfy some flimsy and unwritten diversity policy." His words are haunting.

CONCLUSIONS

It is difficult to generalize about the conditions that were examined in this study on Latinos and the selection process for senior campus leadership roles because of the small number of target sites and subjects interviewed. Moreover, for many exacting scholars and researchers, the mix between survey and case study methodologies used in this study may not be as standardized and precise so as to allow acceptable generalizations and conclusions. Mindful of this, the reader is encouraged to consider the following as strong personal comments that stem from long term reviews of these phenomena.

Patterns of Behavior. The almost total exclusion of Latino men and women in presidencies at highly selective private four-year liberal arts colleges is troublesome and disappointing. Interviews and conversations with governing board members at several highly regarded liberal arts colleges indicated that Latinos had not yet established a successful "track record" of work as tenured faculty and academic administrators at this type of institution. As a follow-up, interviews with five presidents of these institutions in different parts of the country revealed some fascinating perceptions. First, they indicated that the pool of successful Latino teaching faculty at private liberal arts colleges was very small, and non existent in some disciplines. Second, they were not privy to any "reliable" networks that might provide them with dependable information on Latino teachers and scholars "suitable" for their campus. Third, geography was often mentioned as a factor that inhibited the recruitment of Latinos for faculty roles at their colleges. The impression given by these White presidents was that Latinos would not move out of the Southwest or California to other areas of the country where their colleges were located. And finally, the presidents indicated that it would be "most helpful" in reviewing a Latino candidate for a faculty opening at their campus if they had attended a private liberal arts college. The above indicators provide a few inklings of the challenges Latinos need to consider if they are interested in securing faculty positions at selective liberal arts colleges. Consequently, the limited number of Latino faculty at liberal arts campuses may partially explain why opportunities for them to be promoted to the chair of a department or eventually an academic dean is remote.

Successful experience in these roles determines whether a Latino candidate will ever qualify for an AVP or presidency at these selective institutions.

A similar situation exists at the major research universities. There are simply too few Latinas and Latinos with the scholarly accomplishments who are eligible to be department heads and academic deans at these universities. Moreover, the standards by which Latinos are gauged at these research institutions tend to be quite subjective, often constituted in ways that impede rather than aid their evaluations as viable candidates. Latino candidates for faculty positions at top research universities, even if they have earned their Ph.D. at one of the top 20 research campuses in the country, are often passed over for appointment because they may "lack evidence of a successful post-doc." And where some of the Latinos had done post doctoral study, White faculty were critical of them because the postdoc was not done at "the right" institutions, or with an "appropriate mentor." It is a long and difficult road that a faculty member must negotiate if she or he wants to become a senior level academic leader at a major research university. The level of attainment required of Latino faculty for advancement as a department head, or academic dean tends to be different and more demanding than for non-Latinos. The regent of a major university was candid in commenting to me about this process. He said that Latinos [men and women] were newcomers to the world of higher education. They did not have the "kinds" of training and experience in the academy that would make him comfortable with them in a leadership role. "I will not vote for a person to lead my institution unless he has the qualities, the temperament and style that reflect the performance of previous presidents," he said. As I looked at the pictures of the previous presidents of this university, they were all White males. The image he had of a successful president did not seem to accommodate Latino candidates, or White women!

The role of White faculty in the selection and retention of Latino senior level leaders on a campus is not as well researched as it could be. As a result, the way some White faculty can negatively influence the candidacy of a Latino or a Latina applicant needs to be better understood and shared. There continues to be a lack of confidence among too many older White faculty, including men and women, about Latinos in leadership roles. Words like "good, but not exceptional credentials," "a need for more seasoned experience," and "limited maturity as a leader" were mentioned frequently by faculty in the interviews. They had an image of whom they preferred to occupy a leadership role, and it was almost a mirror image of current campus leaders. The data and the follow-up conversations were consonant in this regard. On the campuses where Latino leaders were under suspicion or scrutiny, terms like "emotional," "isolated," "indecisive," and "playing favorites" were used by the faculty in open forums. It appeared that many Latinos at selective institutions were still perceived by White faculty as unprepared, or even unsuitable, for leadership roles. A few respondents indicated that for them, too many minorities did not yet have the makings of a desirable president and referred to literature about what makes a successful president (Shaw, 1999).

Role of Executive Search Consultants. While the number of search consultants and representatives from executive search firms was low – a total of six – they did play an impressive role in the selection process for presidencies. A few of the firms were retained because of their size and prestige. In two instances, search consultants were hired because presidents from similar institutions had recommended them. After lengthy conversations with these search consultants, some important factors surfaced. First, all but one of the consultants were unaware of networks or experts that provided reliable information on Latinos suitable for senior leadership roles in higher education. The one consultant retained to assist with searches at two-year colleges had very close working relationships with Latino community college presidents, and knew about and regularly contacted Latino networks. This was not the case with the other five. Second, several of the consultants used perfunctory measures to identify Latina or Latino candidates. In one case, the search consultant had contacted several campuses that had recently hired a president to inquire if any Latinos had been in the pool. When asked about this strategy, the respondent said all she needed was "one good Hispanic" candidate in the pool. She had not bothered determining whether or not the Latino finalist had been a "viable" candidate. If the Latino candidate's background or qualities had not been sufficient at another campus, search committee members would call that campus and the home institution of the Latino to gather opinions on him or her. If negative information was transmitted about a Latino from her or his home campus, this would be tantamount to programming them for failure. Third, several of the consultants appeared to have favorite candidates for presidencies. They viewed their task as "highlighting" these top candidates. Their secondary concern was to present "a balanced list" of candidates for the search committee and the campus to consider. The balance they referred to was an ethnic/racial and gender mix. The prevailing undercurrent in the search process for presidents, however, was the reliance by several consultants on informal networks of sitting presidents, mostly White males but with a growing number of White women, that continue to influence the appointment of members from either their network, or who could be adopted into it.

There was one condition regarding the use of "Hispanic" resource persons in presidential searches that proved difficult to flesh out fully. I refer to this process as "overreach" by Hispanics who profess to be experts in finding suitable

Latino candidates for senior level leadership jobs. By overreach is meant that behavior on the part of some Latinos who attempt to extend their knowledge or expertise about the qualifications and suitability of favorite candidates for presidencies beyond the range of institutions with which they are familiar. For example, a Latino whose professional career and experiences were exclusively at two-year colleges and attempts to parlay that knowledge and experiential background as applicable to four-year major research universities should be suspect. In one instance, a "Hispanic" expert used by a major search firm was known for participation on numerous national committees and groups. This person was selected as a consultant because service on these committees and national groups appeared to represent the "kind of knowledge" required to identify suitable Latino men and women candidates for leadership roles in higher education. After looking briefly at some of the Latino candidates this individual recommended for presidential openings at four-year liberal arts colleges and universities, it was found that none of them had been hired. It is difficult to determine, therefore, whether the recommendations of this "Hispanic" expert were judiciously arrived at, or if groups on campuses searching for presidents-especially those that might include members suspicious of Latinos-would use this input against these minority candidates.

While the negative aspect of the secondary part of the above comment may appear to be an unsubstantiated suspicion, conversations with several Latino and non-Latino academic leaders and administrators at major research universities continue to reinforce this as a "hidden agenda" by groups who influence presidential selection at selective colleges and universities. This begs the question of why more research is not underway to better understand what critical factors will surface in presidential selection that may work against Latino finalists. Even though well intentioned, the efforts of the "Hispanic" expert mentioned above may have worked a disservice for Latino finalists.

Latino Leadership Aspirations-Unrealistic Expectations. As the data were reviewed and the names of Latino candidates for senior level leadership roles on two- and four-year campuses were compiled, several individuals were identified as unsuccessful finalists in more than two searches. An effort was made to meet and interview this small number of Latinos (approximately seven). Four were willing to be interviewed. The other three refused to return calls. Of the four, one had been searching for a two-year college presidency for three years, and had finally been selected as the president of a two-year campus in the Western U.S. She had not yet completed her Ph.D. when she was a candidate for the first two community college presidencies. In her third try for a presidency, she had been passed over for superintendent of a multi-campus community college system. On her fourth try, she was successful in gaining appointment at a small community college with the support of two Latino elected Board members. When asked why she had applied for presidencies before earning her Ph.D. she stated she was encouraged to do so by the search consultants-one an older White male, and the other a White female. In retrospect, she believed it was premature for her to have applied for the first three positions. When asked if she felt the search consultants had not been realistic about her chances to actually secure the first three positions for which she applied, she answered in the affirmative. Her suspicions were that she had been used to provide a "diverse group of candidates" for the two presidencies, and for the superintendent job.

Another case involved the applications for other senior level jobs by a sitting president. In speaking to this person it was learned that a Latino (X) had become a finalist for four presidencies at major universities. Always a top finalist in four presidential searches at selective four-year campuses, X wanted to move from a regional university to a major research or doctoral granting institution. X was lobbied extensively by representatives from search firms and selection committees to become a candidate for different presidencies. The results each time were the same: a bridesmaid, but never a bride! Applicant X is now about 59 years of age. Visiting the campus where X is the president, reveals a subtle form of contempt for this person's leadership and behavior, mainly by older White faculty. These same faculty have consistently spread unfavorable comments about X's "leadership," or lack of it. Moreover, news of X's failure to gain another presidency, especially at a larger university campus, has resulted in some overt forms of antagonism toward this leader. Part of X's campus White faculty have brought grievances against the administration, while others recently began to question the propriety of X's applying for other presidencies, and attempted to influence the members of the board of governors for the university to remove X as the president.

A third situation involves a very talented Latino administrator (Y) eager to become a president. An excellent writer, tall and attractive, and gifted with a keen intellect, this Latino has been sabotaged by older faculty on two campuses where Y was first a dean and later a provost. Direct, and some-times outspoken, Y has worked tirelessly to identify and encourage the appointment of young Latino men and women faculty at these two campuses. However, Y's detractors have been relentless and on one occasion managed to get a majority, by one person, of the faculty to vote "no confidence" in Y's performance as the provost. Although the president at this campus protected the Latino provost, this individual has agreed to take a sabbatical for a year. In an interview with this person, Y shared a perspective about deserving to be a president because of previous accomplishments and desirable leadership qualities. The operant phrase here is "deserved to be a president." There are many people who deserve to be presidents, but the persons-mainly members of the governing board – making the selection must be convinced that applicants not only have the requisite personal/professional qualities and experience, but also can meet their objective and subjective criteria for leadership. In this case, wanting to be a president, or believing that somehow Y was special and should be given a presidency because of previous accomplishments was not enough.

Latino Z is a talented, hard working, but quiet type of person. Z was recently promoted to the position of provost at a regional university. Z's career advancement does not reflect solid scholarship. A review of Z's publication record finds five items, none of them a solid monograph. Z is someone who has been labeled an "affirmative action opportunist." This Latino has also not been recognized for exemplary management activities or programmatic development at Z's home institution. However, this Latino continues to believe that another campus should make a decision in Z's favor for an open presidency because of Z's ethnic background and time as an administrator. Z said in an interview, "I've paid my dues, done the networking stuff, and put in my time as a provost. Now it's time for the 'system' to reward me with a presidency." It is doubtful if Z will ever be appointed a president, especially with such an attitude and comments like these.

The above unrealistic expectations by a handful of Latino leaders who want very much to become presidents cannot be used to generalize. However, such expectations, even by a small number of minority leaders, are never well defined or adequately discussed at major national meetings. Moreover, the factors and conditions that foster such unrealistic expectations are not understood or considered during meetings of the American Council on Education, the American Association of Higher Education, the Association of Governing Boards, and NASULGC to name but a few. It is essential that such expectations be identified and discussed by Latinos as well as non-Latinos responsible for selecting provosts and presidents. Regents and trustees at colleges and universities need to be better informed and responsible about leadership diversity at their institutions (Haro, 1995). Unless such perceptions are understood and strategies developed to deal with them, particularly by people responsible for making senior level campus appointments, Latinos will continue to find themselves frustrated by rejection, and bitter because of the disappointment of reaching a "glass ceiling."

To their credit, the American Association of State Colleges and Universities (AASCU) with its Millennium Leadership Initiative (MLI) and the American Council on Education (ACE) Fellows Program attempt to provide selected individuals in higher education with leadership training that will prepare them for executive level roles in American colleges and universities. The ACE Fellows program is broadly based and does not focus on one type of institution or specific leadership job. This program provides for a year-long experience that includes relocation and work with a mentor, seminar type meetings during the year, and the opportunity to participate in a network of professional colleagues, many of whom have achieved senior level leadership roles in higher education. The AASCU MLI project is an intensive four-day experience followed by a form of professional development through a year-long mentoring program. The MLI program is designed to strengthen the preparation and eligibility of traditionally underrepresented persons for roles as chancellors or presidents. Both programs try to identify and prepare underrepresented persons for executive level jobs at colleges and universities. From a programmatic perspective, these efforts are worthwhile, along with others like the Harvard University Institute for Educational Management (IEM). The reality, however, is that on a practical level, no matter how well prepared or trained a person may be, there is no guarantee of an AVP or presidency following the completion of one or more of these programs. Often, the preparation and experience of participants in these training activities provides them with strong motivation to achieve a top-level job at a college or university. They do offer tangible skills that can improve the ability of some participants to better present themselves as effective candidates for leadership roles. However, there are factors identified in this discussion that become determinative in the selection process for executive level leadership roles which override the experiential background or participation in leadership training programs of Latinos and some other minorities in American higher education, and recommend steps that should be taken in the future to move from challenges to opportunities. The simplicity of such a strategy makes me wonder why it has not been supported by the foundations previously. Perhaps now, "its time has come."

NOTE

1. This total includes finalists interviewed in the two follow-up searches where the original ones had been cancelled.

ACKNOWLEDGMENTS

The author wishes to thank the following persons for their willingness to review this project and provide feedback on its design and implementation: Dr. Eugene

Cota-Robles, Professor Emeritus, University of California, Santa Cruz; Dr. Betty Duvall, Professor, Oregon State University; Ms. Cheryl Fields, NASULGC; Dr. Patricia Gandara, Professor, University of California at Davis; and F. Chris Garcia, Professor of Political Science, University of New Mexico.

REFERENCES

Birnbaum, R. (1988). Presidential searches and the discovery of organizational goals. *Journal of Higher Education, 59*(5), 489–509.

Bolman, F. (1965). *How college presidents are chosen.* Washington, D.C.: American Council on Education.

Carnevale, A. P., & Fry, R. A. (2000). *Crossing the great divide: Can we achieve equity when generation Y goes to college?* Princeton, NJ: Educational Testing Service.

Carnevale, A. P. (1999). *Education = Success: Empowering Hispanic Youth and Adults.* Princeton, NJ: Educational Testing Service/Hispanic Association of Colleges and Universities.

Cohen, M. D., & March, J. G. (1974). *Leadership and ambiguity: The American college president.* New York: McGraw-Hill.

Denzig, N. K., & Lincoln, Y. S. (Eds) (1994). *Handbook of qualitative research.* Thousand Oaks, CA: Sage.

Esquibel, A. (1993). *The career mobility of Chicano administrators in higher education.* Boulder, CO: Western Interstate Commission for Higher Education.

Evelyn, J. (2001). Community colleges face a crisis of leadership. *The Chronicle of Higher Education,* (April 6), A36, A37.

Haro, R. (1995). Choosing trustees who care about things that matter. *The Chronicle of Higher Education,* (December 8), B1–B2.

Haro, R. (1995). Held to a higher standard: Latino executive selection in higher education. In: R. V. Padilla & R. C. Chavez (Eds), *The Leaning Ivory Tower: Latino Professors in American Universities.* Albany, NY: State University of New York Press.

Hispanic Association of Colleges and Universities (1999). *Hispanic voter registration and Hispanic-serving institutions: Emerging trends.* San Antonio, TX: HACU.

Hispanic Association of Colleges and Universities HACU (2000). *The increasing presence of Hispanics and Hispanic-serving institutions.* San Antonio, TX: HACU.

Haddock, V., & Heredia, C. (2001). State's kids even more diverse than its adults. *The San Francisco Chronicle,* (April 3), A13, A16.

Hecht, I. W. D., Higgerson, M. L., Gmelch, W. H., & Tucker, A. (1998). *The department chair as academic leader.* Washington, D.C.: American Council on Education/Oryx Press.

Kaplowitz, R. A. (1973). *Selecting academic administrators: The search committee.* Washington, D.C.: American Council on Education.

Leatherman,C. (1991). Colleges hire more female presidents, but questions linger about their clout. *The Chronicle of Higher Education,* (November 6), A19–A21.

Lively, K. (2000). Diversity increased among presidents. *The Chronicle of Higher Education,* (September 15), A31.

Loftland, J. (1995). *Analyzing social settings: A guide to qualitative observation and analysis* (3rd ed.). Belmont, CA: Wadsworth Publishing Company.

Marchese, T. J. (1987). *The search committee handbook: A guide for recruiting administrators.* Washington, D.C.: American Association for Higher Education.

McLaughlin, J. B. (1985). From secrecy to sunshine: an overview of presidential search practice. *Research in Higher Education*, 22(2), 195–208.

McLaughlin, J. B., & Riesman, D. (1990). *Choosing a college president: Opportunites and constraints*. Princeton: Carnegie Foundation for the Advancement of Teaching.

Moses, Y. T. (1993). The roadblocks confronting minority administrations. *The Chronicle of Higher Education*, (January 13), B1.

Ross, M., & Green, M. F. (2000). *The American College President*. Washington, D.C.: American Council on Education.

Sanchez, L. (2001). State sees new Latino revolution take hold as population booms. *San Diego Union*, (January 7), 1.

Shaw, K. A. (1999). *The successful president*. Washington, D.C.: American Council on Education/Oryx Press.

Stern, P. C. (1996). *Evaluating social science research* (2nd ed.). New York: Oxford University Press.

Sturnick, J. A., Milley, J. E., & Tisinger, C. A. (Eds) (1991). *Women at the helm: Path finding presidents at state colleges and universities*. Washington, D.C.: American Association of State Colleges and Universities.

U.S. Census Bureau (2001). *The Hispanic population in the United States* (March). (Current Population Reports, P20-535). Washington, D.C.

Webb, E. T., Campbell, D. T., Schwartz, R. D. D., Sechrest, L., & Grove, J. B. (Eds) (1981). *Nonreactive measures in the social sciences* (2nd ed.). Boston: Houghton, Mifflin.

Yin, R. (1984). *Case study research: Design methods*. Beverly Hills, CA: Sage.

BUILDING A LEAP FOR LATINOS IN HIGHER EDUCATION

David J. León

INTRODUCTION

Latinos are rare in the upper echelons of higher education, even in states like California and Texas. At the same time, their numbers are growing in the population – there are now some 30 million Latinos in the U.S. – so the problem becomes more acute every day. What can we do about it?

In the summer of 2001 I attended the Leadership Development Program for Higher Education sponsored by the Leadership and Education for Asian Pacifics (LEAP). This intense four-day program aims at increasing the percentage of Asian-Pacific-Americans (APAs) in top positions in higher education. Participants went through a series of workshops and lectures, and, finally, mock interviews for aspirants to administrative positions.

Although the program focused on Asian-Pacific-Americans, this model could also help Latinos. As LEAP instructors said repeatedly, leadership can be learned and its lessons apply to every ethnic group. Hence I propose creating a LEAP-based program for Latinos.

CURRENT LEADERSHIP PROGRAMS

Latinos are drastically underrepresented as students, faculty, and administrators in higher education (Aguirre & Martinez, 2001; Carnevale, 2001; Haro, 2001), and find it very difficult to secure leadership positions there. This is a serious

Latinos in Higher Education, Volume 3, pages 193–205.
Copyright © 2003 by Elsevier Science Ltd.
All rights of reproduction in any form reserved.
ISBN: 0-7623-0980-6

problem, since Latinos constitute the largest minority population in the nation, according to the 2000 census, and will overtake the white population in key political states by the mid-century.

Leadership programs may offer one solution. Aside from LEAP, there are four major ones in higher education: (1) the Fellows Program, supported by the American Council on Education; (2) the Harvard Institutes for Higher Education (HIHE); (3) the Millennium Leadership Initiative (MLI), sponsored by the American Association of State Colleges and Universities; and (4) the Summer Institute for Women in Higher Education Administration, co-sponsored by HERS, Mid-American, and Bryn Mawr College.

The year-long Fellows Program chooses 35 Fellows annually, and the "nominating institution pays the salary and benefits of the Fellow for the Fellowship year and covers all interview and placement process expenses, regardless of the placement option selected" (http://www.acenet.edu/programs /fellows/selection.cfm). These are major expenses, and most participants can enter this program only if their universities are willing to pay them. Only two are part Hispanic out of this year's class of 34 (Marlene Ross in conversation).

The Harvard Institutes for Higher Education offers four main summer programs: the Management Development Program (MDP), the Institute for Management & Leadership In Education (MLE), the Institute for Educational Management (IEM) and the Seminar for New Presidents (a six-day program). Each of these programs addresses campus leaders at a different tier of experience. The MDP seeks administrators early in their careers, while the MLE focuses on seasoned administrators, and the IEM and the Seminar for new President attracts most senior-level individuals. Though much more economical than the Fellows program, these are still relatively expensive. The MDP and MLE cost $4,296, the IEM costs $5,595, and the Seminar for New Presidents costs $3,200. These fees cover tuition, room, most meals, and program materials (http://www.gse.harvard.edu/~ppe). About 320 to 350 people take part in these summer courses annually (Joseph Zolner, in conversation). The programs admit about three-quarters of applicants, and they accept individuals from academic affairs, student affairs, and business affairs backgrounds, since HIHE believes this mixture fosters a rich learning environment. Two foundations have provided financial support to encourage minority attendance. Even so, the total number of Latinos in all four programs in 2001 was 12, or less than 4% of the 340 participants.

The Millennium Leadership Initiative (MLI) is somewhat different. It focuses directly on persons "traditionally underrepresented" in the upper echelons of higher education, training high-level administrators to become presidents. It costs just $1,500 per session. Of all current programs, it appears that only the

MLI offers an outreach strategy to increase Latino representation, by teaming up with the Hispanic Association of Colleges and Universities (HACU). Yet its effectiveness remains unclear. Of the 100 participants in its three-year existence, seven were Latinos. Five enrolled in 1999, two in 2000, and none in 2001 (Rosemary Lauth, in conversation).

The Summer Institute for Women In Higher Education Administration, co-sponsored by HERS, Mid-America and Bryn Mawr College, also has a special focus. It aims to "improve the status of women in the middle and executive levels of higher education administration, areas in which women traditionally have been under represented" (http://www.brynmawr.edu/summerinstitute). In existence for 27 years, the 4-week residential program costs $6,100, which covers tuition, room and board, and educational materials. The Institute encourages participants "to request sponsorship for the whole or part of the cost from their institutions" (http://www,brynmawr.edu/summerinstitute). In 2001 it admitted 79 women out of 102 applicants, and only one was a Latina. In 1999 there were three Latinas, and in 2000 there were also three (Betsy Metzger, memorandum).

LEAP resembles these efforts on some scores. Like all of them, it occurs just once a year. Like the Fellows program and the MLI, it trains relatively few individuals, and last year's class of 25 was its largest.

However, LEAP also stands out in significant ways. First, it is the least expensive program, costing only $1,000 for about four days. Of this total, $595 covers educational materials and tuition, and $405 room and board (http://www.leap.org/programs/programs-ldphe.html). It is non-selective, since it accepts virtually everyone who applies. Finally, APAs developed LEAP to serve APAs, so it directly addresses the experience of a specific minority. As will become clear, this is a crucial benefit. Overall, LEAP is inexpensive, accessible, and minority-focused.

Since these features offer major benefits to APAs, the LEAP program attracts them. Its enrollment of 25 in 2001 almost certainly exceeds the total enrollment of Latinos in all other programs combined, and Latinos are a much larger ethnic group.

THE LEAP MODEL

To illuminate the program I will describe my experience at the LEAP Institute over the four day program. The guest lecturers change from year to year, so each course is different, yet I will recapitulate the messages I heard, since they both convey the tone of the talks and bear on the larger issue of leadership itself.

The First Day. On the morning we arrived, we received a three-ring binder containing a schedule of events and articles relating to leadership, organizational dynamics, and topics specific to APA students, staff, faculty and administrators. Participants had no chance to review the binder beforehand, and speakers rarely referred to its contents.

Two APA consultants who hold high administrative positions in California community colleges welcomed the participants. They noted that this class was the largest in the five years LEAP has sponsored this program, with 25 individuals from community colleges as well as the California State University and University of California systems. Roughly half were student affairs officers and half were faculty members. They said LEAP aims to expand both the minds of the participants and their career possibilities. The consultants asked participants to think about their future career options as the program progressed.

The mix of student affairs and academic personnel poses some problems for LEAP. The student affairs officers have no chance of becoming college presidents, unless they are at community colleges. The faculty can become college and university presidents, though only if they advance administratively through the ranks, from department chair to dean of a college to provost/academic vice president. Of course, there are exceptions to this path.

Next, the executive director of LEAP explained that its mission is to enhance the status of APAs through training leaders, holding empowerment workshops, and sponsoring policy reports. The Leadership Development Program aims to increase the number of APAs in higher education administration.

He defined a leader as a person who accomplishes tasks through other people by persuasion or example. A leader must be passionate, persistent, and people-oriented, he said, and listed five characteristics of a 21st century leader:

(1) Being comfortable with oneself.
(2) Understanding the relationship between perceptions, behaviors, and values.
(3) Being a visible and positive community representative and a multicultural bridge to other people and communities.
(4) Developing and using a wider range of leadership skills and qualities beyond ones comfort zone.
(5) Dealing effectively with ambiguity and change.

How does one acquire leadership skills? "Practice, practice, practice," he said. One should also attend workshops, training sessions, and classes, and find a mentor. Since leadership skills are transferable from one organization to another, he suggested that participants assume positions of responsibility in the community, at work, in professional associations. He also noted that people need not change their values to succeed.

To practice these skills, he requested that participants pair off and answer the following questions: Who are you? What do you want? What are you afraid of? He asked them to provide ten short responses to each question and make a short presentation to the group.

In the afternoon, an ethnic studies professor showed slides of women from Asia and asked participants to identify them. All the women held high political positions in their countries, so she asked, "Why don't we see Asian American women in comparable positions in our nation?" The professor drew concentric circles to illustrate power distribution in the university. At the center, white males are largely represented. Next are white women, then men of color, and finally women of color. The professor argued that minorities view power as negative because it so often affects them negatively. She urged participants to seek power to improve the status of minorities in the universities.

In the afternoon, one of the consultants asked participants to reflect on APA cultural values by answering the following questions: How are Asian Americans viewed on campus? What were you taught growing up? The participants were asked to compare the traits listed for each question in the context of morning speaker's presentation.

That evening, the speaker was an APA president of a state university in California. He sketched the history of his campus, then recounted his academic career, which culminated in his accepting his current position. He emphasized that APAs are severely underrepresented in higher education leadership, despite their educational achievements. He offered the following advice to individuals interested in administrative careers:

(1) Apply for several positions and if you make the final pool, realize that it then becomes a dice throw. Don't take it personally if you don't get the job.
(2) Become active in civil rights and community organizations. Work with volunteers to develop your leadership skills. Gain as much experience as you can.
(3) Strive to empower people at the individual level. Don't overmanage staff because the freedom to make mistakes may actually empower people.
(4) Spend a lot of time conveying your vision to the campus. The basic challenge of an administrator is to implement his or her vision through the various levels of the university.

He noted that, as an administrator, one can have an enormous impact on thousands of young people, and this fact makes all the challenges worthwhile. He urged participants to take risks and become campus leaders.

The Second Day. A consultant asked participants to list the characteristics of a leader. Among their responses were: vision, experience, inclusiveness, team-orientation, passion, boldness, organization, risk-taking, political sense. Participants discussed the previous day's activities, identifying pros and cons as a group.

The morning speaker gave a workshop on presentation skills. She listed three approaches of effective speakers:

(1) Be no one but yourself at your confident best.
(2) Present your own uniqueness.
(3) Practice, practice, practice.

The expert began her own speech with this quote: "Communication is not what you say, or thought you said. It's what THEY hear and what THEY think you meant. Therefore, communication is not intent, it is PERCEPTION. And perception equals reality."

She then addressed first impressions. Psychologists say that whenever people meet APAs, they make instant judgments primarily on a subconscious level. That first impression is most often visual and occurs before individuals utter a single word. The audience will form similar judgments of a speaker, and these assessments continue through the first 30 seconds of the presentation. Within the first 10 seconds alone, the audience is capable of making as many as 10 judgments, on such variables as social position, education, economic level, social heritage (race/ethnicity), educational heritage, economic heritage, trustworthiness, sophistication, successfulness, and moral character. The audience gauges the speaker's traits in the following order: color, gender, age, appearance, facial expression, eye contact, movement.

Since nonverbal cues are critical for effective communication, the expert suggested the following:

(1) Start and end the presentation in the power stance position, with your feet directly beneath your shoulders.
(2) Keep your hands at waist level, and separate your hands and arms from your body.
(3) Your hands must be expressive. To be inclusive, hold your palms up and extend them to the audience. To be emphatic, gesture in the air or strike something.
(4) Make eye contact with individual audience members. It will make them feel as if you're talking to them.

The expert stressed the importance of eye contact and body movements. She stated it was very important to make eye contact with as many individuals as possible, and recommended selecting an individual at random and holding eye contact for three seconds. Turning toward that individual will make you aware of your body language, she said. If you wish to make an important point, take one-and-one-half steps toward that person.

To become a persuasive speaker, the expert suggested following Monroe's Motivation Sequence:

(1) Arouse curiosity. This is the attention step.
(2) Create a need. Provide factual statements wherever possible.
(3) Tell them what you want them to do. This is the action step.
(4) Use real life examples. This is the visualization step. If you use a negative example, conclude with a positive example.
(5) Identify key benefits. This is the satisfaction step.

In the afternoon, the mentor panel assembled. Members included administrators and faculty from the community colleges and state universities. Each panelist addressed the following three questions:

(1) What path did you take to arrive at your present position?
(2) What obstacles did you face?
(3) What are the benefits and rewards of being a leader?

After the panel discussion, participants divided into groups, and the panelists moved from group to group engaging in informal discussions. Later, participants were matched with mentors, who had an opportunity to chat with the participants informally.

The evening featured a guest speaker who discussed his involvement with the Asian American community.

The Third Day. As on the second morning, a consultant asked participants what they liked and disliked about the previous day's activities. She urged participants to write a report about their LEAP experiences and share it with their campus presidents. She also asked them to identify people on their campus who might want to attend next year's conference or serve as mentors. Finally participants identified the position they wished to seek in the mock interviews slated for the afternoon.

The morning speaker addressed the issues of power and leadership in organizations. He said California is at a critical stage because its minority population is now the majority population. Yet there is a severe lack of diversity in our institutions, especially in higher education. Minorities cannot become leaders unless they understand power in organizations. However, a grasp of it can accelerate the acquisition of power for people of color.

After providing diversity training to America's top corporations for over thirty years, he has come to the conclusion that minorities perceive power differently from whites. People of color see power as earned. Minorities say, "If I work hard enough, I will be promoted." Whites see power as a prerequisite for a promotion. They say, "If I gain enough power, I'll get promoted." He urged participants to change their mindset. Minorities must acquire power first before advancing within the organization. Power and the competition for power are the key dynamics in any organization. Every group in a university competes for power, and some group will eventually win.

What is power? The speaker defined power as the ability to impose personal preferences on the behavior of others. To help analyze it, he raised these questions concerning the values, mindset, emotions, and orientation of individuals:

> Values: Do you see a conflict between your personal values and those of the institution where you work?
> Mindset: What are your operating values?
> Emotions: How do you feel about acquiring power?
> Mastery Orientation: Do you have a mastery orientation? Leaders are people who feel comfortable imposing. To become a leader, you must be comfortable imposing and inspiring people. At this point, he provided anecdotal accounts of how he imposes on people without risking his career, by asking for an upgrade hotel room, rental car, and first-class airline seating.

The expert outlined six sources of power:

(1) Rewards, such as positive comments, a better office, or more money.
(2) Coercion, the ability to provide a negative, unpleasant response.
(3) Traditional power, exercised by holding a powerful position.
(4) Associative power, stemming from the perception of one's close ties to a powerful leader.
(5) Expertise, the ability to impose by superior knowledge.
(6) Charisma, power arising from a compelling personality.

The expert argued that four key skills are necessary to gain power: politics, loyalty, socialization, and subordination.

> Politics: Politics involves relationships, whom you know and who knows you. Since teams of people align into power interests in any organization, you must be able to identify the key players and know who is on what team. Collect data, go to lunch, play golf, attend specific functions, he advised. He also suggested that each participant be on someone's team.

Loyalty: "Wrap yourself in the flag of the university," he said. Individuals must convey loyalty for the institution to gain power. "You must be able to say that you love your institution," he asserted, "since the more you love it, the more you can criticize it. You must practice saying, 'I love my university.'" The phrase must sound natural; it must roll off the tongue. People of color must dispel the myth that they are not loyal. Whites don't see minorities as loyal and patriotic. Displaying loyalty is a skill, he said, and can be learned.

Socialization: Power-seekers must be able to do business in social settings. View these settings as opportunities to develop relationships, he said. Find out who will attend and target at least two or three individuals who can enhance your power base.

Subordination: "Brown-nosing" and "kissing up" is a skill, he said, and advised against being obvious about it.

In the afternoon, a community college APA president discussed his strategies for a successful interview:

(1) Do a pre-visit.
(2) Be on time. In fact, arrive early and chat with the secretary.
(3) Learn the names of the committee members, their areas of expertise, positions, and other useful information about them.
(4) Don't be afraid to ask for clarification or to have the question repeated.
(5) Express what you have accomplished.
(6) Balance between "I" and "we" statements because you want to convey a team-leader approach.
(7) After the interview, write a personal note to each committee member.

In the afternoon, participants divided into small groups of four people each. Members of the mentor panel became the interview committees. They interviewed participants for 15 minutes, with a five-minute evaluation.

In the evening, an APA administrator was the featured speaker. She described three difficult situations involving an evaluation for tenure, unfounded professional criticism, and a stressful administrative assignment. She advised future administrators to build a support base with people they trust avoid an extreme ego, be consistent in word and deed, and be resilient.

The Fourth Day. Again, one of the consultants began with a review of the previous day's activities, outlining pros and cons.

In the morning, participants listened to a panel of administrators and faculty who discussed APA issues in higher education. One professor noted the "very nasty" environment for APAs in higher education. Faculty enjoy the shield of academic freedom, and it creates an environment where they can make many irresponsible statements. The principles of confidentiality also protect faculty members, letting them say one thing and vote differently. Faculty can continue to abuse their power once the case leaves the department.

On his campus, he noted that departments typically reject APAs before they reach the interview stage, and sometimes use their accents against them. APAs are underrepresented on his faculty even though they comprise over 40% of the student population.

After hiring, the next barrier is tenure and promotion. He observed that even though APAs are more productive than their counterparts, they are not retained and promoted. He noted that he is the only non-white member of the Academic Senate's Executive Committee, and the only one to raise issues of race in the University. He felt he couldn't count on his white colleagues to bring up these matters. To effect change in the university, the professor urged participants to develop relationships with state and national politicians.

The next panelist discussed her areas of concern in higher education: access, equality, inclusion, hate crimes on campus, assaults, civil rights violations, and racial discrimination in hiring. These undercut the self-confidence and safety of Asian Americans. Through her professional association, she continues to stress the importance of access through affirmative action. The academic pipeline concerns her as it relates to APAs. Some 20 APAs are college presidents across the country, but only three are at research institutions and the rest are at community colleges. She advised participants to: (1) join local, state, and national associations; (2) maintain and support their perspective; and (3) find a mentor.

The last panelist offered another view from a faculty member. He stated that he is committed to the education of immigrants using the activism of the 1960s combined with the best practices of the 1990s. His stressed three main topics: demographic trends, exclusion of APAs in national higher education reports, and the future of Asian American Studies.

He presented a quick demographic sketch of APAs. They live all across the country, although they are concentrated in key states like Hawaii, California, and New York. Generational issues can also be important. For instance, Chinese have been in California since 1849, while most Southeast Asians arrived in America soon after the fall of South Vietnam.

Second, he observed that the annual ACE report on minorities in higher education has again excluded APAs. This report targets the educational gaps of Latinos, Blacks, and Native Americans, and neglects the diversity of groups within the APA population.

Finally, he questioned the current state of Asian American Studies in higher education. These programs were supposed to transform the university, but over time the university transformed them. Since the high schools rarely teach Asian American Studies, he noted, we should not be surprised that APA college students know little about their history.

After lunch, each participant had five minutes to present his or her personal career goals/plans.

Both consultants moderated the closing segment of the conference. They emphasized four points:

(1) Urge colleagues to attend next year's conference.
(2) Mentor someone in the organization.
(3) Practice, practice, practice your leadership skills.
(4) Keep working on your own professional plan.

Then each participant received a plaque, along with a few photographs taken of him or her throughout the program.

SUMMARY AND RECOMMENDATIONS

LEAP is a reasonable approach to providing leadership training to people of color. In general, it urged participants to explore their cultural values, compare them to the everyday reality of their institutions, and become change agents. This program has the signal advantage of being designed and run by Asian Americans who wish to serve their community. It is a sensible model for Latinos, and the Latino higher education community can learn much from it.

Below are five recommendations for strengthening the LEAP model:

(1) Hand out materials earlier. Mail the three-ring binder to participants several weeks before the program begins. To insure that everyone reads the materials beforehand, have participants answer questions at the end of each section. Facilitators can incorporate the answers into the sessions themselves.
(2) Hold two kinds of sessions, one for student affairs officers and one for faculty members. The groups have different needs and opportunities.
(3) Develop more hands-on exercises. The lectures are often illuminating, but they are not practice. Thus, for example, after the lecture on presentation skills, participants should have a chance to try out nonverbal cues under the eye of the presenter.

(4) Devote more attention to participants' career goals and plans. The Institute held mock interviews, but otherwise set aside little time for the participants to develop their professional plans in consultation with mentors or LEAP consultants.

(5) Strengthen post-workshop contact with mentors. LEAP expects participants to stay in touch with their mentors after training concludes. It should formalize this relationship by urging attendees to meet regularly with their mentors to update their professional development plans.

Nonetheless, LEAP provides a unique and important service to APAs. First, it is non-selective, so it lets anyone learn about leadership. Second, its orientation toward APAs may encourage some to take the training who otherwise might not have. Finally, the instruction focuses directly on APAs and the challenges they face. LEAP also offers valuable contact with role models, APAs who have succeeded in higher education administration. Likewise, a Latino LEAP would be non-selective, deal specifically with Latino issues, and offer contact with role models. The program would provide benefits available nowhere else.

The absence of a Latino LEAP hurts Latinos in two ways. First, they miss the training in leadership that could help them. Second, people in other ethnic groups do receive such training, and hence likely outperform them in the competition for administrative positions. As long as current programs train a lower proportion of Latinos than other ethnic groups, relative to their percentage in the population, they will give an advantage to others and constitute an obstacle, in some degree, to equity for Latinos.

Clearly, the colleges and universities must do a better job of preparing Latinos for high-level administrative positions. Our nation's changing demography demands it. A Latino LEAP would deliver invaluable services to Latinos, and ultimately to our pluralistic society as a whole. It is an apparently small step that could have large consequences.

REFERENCES

Aguirre, A., & Martinez, A. (2002). Resource shares and educational attainment: the U.S. Latino population in the twenty-first century. In: D. León (Ed.), *Latinos in Higher Education*. Greenwich, Connecticut: JAI/Ablex Press.

American Council on Education (2001). The Fellows Program. Retrieved December 28, 2001 from the World Wide Web: http://www.acenet.edu/programs/fellows/selection.cfm

American Association of State Colleges and Universities (2001). Millennium Leadership Initiative. Retrieved December 28, 2001 from the World Wide Web: http://www.aascu.org/mli/default.htm

Anonymous (2001). *Handbook: leadership development program for higher education*. Los Angeles, California: Leadership education for Asian Pacifics, Inc.

Carnevale, A. (2002). Seize the movement: a unique window of opportunity. In: D. León (Ed.), *Latinos in Higher Education*. Greenwich, Connecticut: JAI/Ablex Press.

Haro, R. (2002). Latinos and academic leadership in American higher education. In: D. León (Ed.), *Latinos in Higher Education*. Greenwich, Connecticut: JAI/Ablex Press.

Harvard University (2001). Institutes for Higher Education. Retrieved December 28, 2001 from the World Wide Web: http://www.gse.harvard.edu/~ppe

HERS Institute (2002). Retrieved January 7, 2002 from the World Wide Web: http://brynmawr.edu/summerinstitute

Leadership Education for Asian Pacifics, Inc. (2001). Leadership Development Program in Higher Education. Retrieved January 3, 2001 from the World Wide Web: http://www.leap.org/programs/programs-ldphe.html